George W. Hunt, S.J.

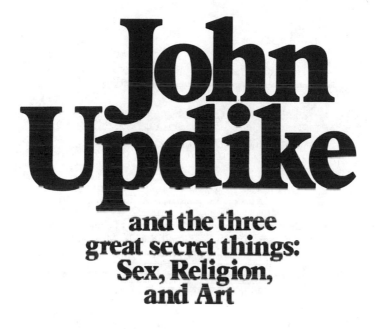

John Updike

and the three great secret things: Sex, Religion, and Art

Grand Rapids
WILLIAM B. EERDMANS PUBLISHING COMPANY

Copyright © 1980 by Wm. B. Eerdmans Publishing Co.
255 Jefferson Ave. S.E., Grand Rapids, Mich. 49503

Printed in the United States of America

Library of Congress Cataloging in Publication Data

Hunt, George W.   1937-
John Updike and the three great secret things.

Includes index.
1. Updike, John—Criticism and interpretation.
I. Title.
PS3571.P4Z72   813'.54   80-23796
ISBN 0-8028-3539-2

Grateful acknowledgment is made to Alfred A.
Knopf, Inc. for permission to quote from the
copyrighted works of John Updike.

For My Parents,
  the Late George and the Lovely Grace

Contents

Acknowledgments   ix

Chronology   xi

Introduction   1

1. *The Poorhouse Fair* and *Rabbit, Run*   13
2. *The Centaur*   49
3. *Of the Farm*   81
4. *The Music School*   103
5. *Couples* and *Marry Me*   117
6. *Bech: A Book*   153
7. *Rabbit Redux*   165
8. *A Month of Sundays*   181
9. *The Coup*   195
   Epilogue   207

Notes   215

Index   229

Acknowledgments

John Updike in his poem "Midpoint" observes that "the Book of Life is margin more than text." That is also true of less important books such as this one. In the wide margin of this text there are the following to whom I am most grateful: to John Updike himself, who could not have been kinder and more helpful even in the face of exasperating questions and who continually encouraged me throughout this study's development, and also to his wife Martha, the reader in the family, who would graciously inform me of typos and oversights in the manuscript; to Fr. Robert McCarty, S.J., who read and often amended its various versions, and all of whose criticisms and suggestions I followed and incorporated; to the Jesuit community at Le Moyne College in Syracuse, N.Y., who supported me in literal and more subtle ways so that I could complete it; and, finally, to my typist Mrs. Jean Britt for her consistently excellent work—no mistake here is hers.

Parts of Chapter 1 appeared originally in *Thought* and *Christianity and Literature*; part of Chapter 4 appeared in *Studies in Short Fiction*; part of Chapter 8 appeared in *Critique*. I am grateful to these journals for permission to recycle this material in a larger context.

I would also like to thank Alfred A. Knopf, Inc. for permission to quote from the copyrighted works of John Updike.

Chronology

1932   Born on March 18 in Shillington, Pennsylvania, the only child of Wesley Updike and Linda Grace Hoyer Updike. Lives with them and his mother's parents, John and Katherine Hoyer.

1945   His family moves to the ancestral farm in Plowville, Pa.; he continues his education at Shillington where his father teaches mathematics.

1950   He enters Harvard from which he graduates in 1954 *summa cum laude*. He is editor of the Harvard *Lampoon* and majors in English, choosing the poetry of Robert Herrick for his A.B. thesis.

1953   At the end of his Junior year he marries Mary Pennington, a Radcliffe graduate, on June 26.

1954-55   "Friends from Philadelphia," his first published story, appears in *The New Yorker* magazine. Upon receiving a Knox fellowship, he spends the year 1954-55 at the Ruskin School of Drawing and Fine Arts in Oxford; while there he is visited by Mr. and Mrs. E. B. White and is offered a job at *The New Yorker*. His first daughter Elizabeth is born.

1955-57   He lives in New York City and works as a "Talk of the Town" writer for *The New Yorker*. (Some of these essays will be reprinted in *Assorted Prose*.) He writes a lengthy autobiographical novel, *Home*, but declines to publish it. In April 1957 he moves with his family to Ipswich, Massachusetts, where he will live for 17 years, changing houses twice. His son David is born.

1958   His first book, a verse collection entitled *The Carpentered Hen*, is published.

1959   His first novel, *The Poorhouse Fair*, is published and receives the Rosenthal Award. A short story collection, *The Same Door*, is published; his son Michael is born.

1960   *Rabbit, Run* is published; his youngest child Miranda is born.

1962   *Pigeon Feathers and Other Stories* is published.

1963   *The Centaur* is published and wins the National Book Award; more verse, *Telephone Poles and Other Poems*, is published.

1964   *Olinger Studies: A Selection* (from the previous two collections) is published. He is elected to membership in the National Institute of Arts and Letters, the youngest man ever elected, and is invited to represent the U.S. in a U.S.-U.S.S.R. cultural exchange program. He travels throughout Eastern Europe, and some impressions there are later reflected in *Bech: A Book*.

1965   *Of the Farm* and *Assorted Prose* are published.

1966   *The Music School*, his third story collection, is published; one of its stories, "The Bulgarian Poetess," wins the O. Henry award.

1968   *Couples* is published. Updike is featured in both *Time* and *Life* and other national publications.

1969   The autobiographical long poem "Midpoint" is published in *Midpoint and Other Poems*.

1970   *Bech: A Book* is published.

1971   *Rabbit Redux* is published.

1972   *Museums and Women and Other Stories* is published.

1974   A play, the closet drama *Buchanan Dying*, is published. He and his wife separate and he moves to Boston; subsequently they are granted a no-fault divorce in Massachusetts.

1975   *A Month of Sundays* and his second collection of non-fictional prose, *Picked-Up Pieces*, are published.

1976   *Marry Me* is published; he moves to Georgetown, Massachusetts.

1977   *Tossing and Turning*, another verse collection, is published, as well as a new edition of *The Poorhouse Fair* with his own introduction. On September 30 he marries Martha Ruggles Bernhard.

1978   *The Coup* is published.

1979   *Problems and Other Stories* and his collection of stories about the Maple family, *Too Far to Go*, are published.

Introduction

Since 1958 and the publication of his first novel, *The Poorhouse Fair*, John Updike has written nine novels, four books of verse, five short story collections, the hybrid *Bech: A Book*, and two lengthy collections of prose-pieces, plus innumerable uncollected reviews, formal addresses, and interviews. Such productivity in a little over twenty years would merit praise for a beaver with versatility, much less for a serious writer born in 1932. Without doubt Updike is the most prolific major American writer of his generation. The volume of this writing production is itself an extraordinary achievement, but more extraordinary still is its consistently high quality. Since the publication of *Rabbit, Run* in 1960, no novel of Updike's has appeared without the attention of a serious review in our major magazines or without subsequent closer scrutiny in our academic quarterlies. Not all critics, of course, have been kind to Updike, and yet one could cite a chain of encomia uttered by our ablest critics about his work that might itself be book length.

To offer an exacting critical study of such a prolific author who is still so relatively young is, I admit, a risky enterprise. By doing so I am not presumptuous enough to assume that Updike will not mature further as a writer or that his fiction will not possibly move forward in a different direction. The recent publication of *The Coup* is evidence of this possibility and ought to generate such critical caution. Nonetheless, I am convinced that Updike's work is already sufficiently large, and at once diverse and unified enough, to warrant critical reading of it as a *corpus*. No doubt in the future certain interpretative emphases might need alteration or addition in the light of subsequent work, and yet this realization ought not inhibit a serious scholarly investigation at this time. After all, Updike's *corpus* will be closed only when he himself is but *corpus* only. At that time a truly definitive study can be offered that makes use of biographical material so central to the inspiration of much of his fiction, of literary notebooks, letters, and diaries if there are any. A Leon Edel or Joseph Blotner, perhaps yet unborn, will take on a more thorough, though no less enjoyable, task than mine.

Consequently, a critical study done in this present spirit is not intended to be a gesture of closing but one of opening. Let us call it a modest attempt to fulfill four of the six functions assigned to critics by W. H. Auden in *The Dyer's Hand*:

> 1) Convince me that I have undervalued an author or a work because I had not read them carefully enough.
>
> 2) Give a "reading" of a work which increases my understanding of it.
>
> 3) Throw light upon artistic "Making."
>
> 4) Throw light upon the relation of art to life, to science, economics, religion, ethics, etc.

The organizing thematic principle that shapes this study is inspired by Updike's remarks made in his 1962 memoir entitled "The Dogwood Tree: A Boyhood." In that memoir Updike discussed his boyhood fascination with what he called the "Three Great Secret Things: Sex, Religion, and Art." My contention is that these three secret things also characterize the predominant subject matter, thematic concerns, and central questions found throughout his adult fiction. In his earlier novels Religion is the secret that enjoys emphasis; beginning with *The Music School* collection (1966) Sex does; and with *A Month of Sundays* (1975) Art and the problems relating to fictional creation come to the fore. However, this is a matter of emphasis only; this study will take pains to demonstrate that at every stage the Three Great Secrets interweave, complement, and illuminate each other in each of his works. Like a musical composition with themes and variations, these are his motives or tonic centers that, even when muted or wedded with subordinate themes, still resonate for the attentive listener. In addition to their significance as themes, there is often an intermutuality among symbols and images whereby, for example, a sexual (or artistic) image will have, in subtle fashion, a religious referent, or an explicit religious image will disclose, besides, a sexual (or artistic) referent, and so on. An investigation of these symbol or image clusters as they interact with each other will point up, I hope, the extraordinarily complex texture and multi-referential quality of his fiction. Furthermore, it is Updike's often subtle employment of the techniques of irony, humor, and myth that enables him to maintain both an ambiguous tone and an artistic tension amid this interaction.

In "The Dogwood Tree: A Boyhood" Updike described his fascination with art and concluded with this reflection, a reflection so characteristic of his adult fiction that it is worth quoting in full.

> He saw art—between drawing and writing he ignorantly made no distinction—as a method of riding a thin pencil line out of Shillington, out of time altogether, into an infinity of unseen and even unborn hearts. He pictured this infinity as radiant. How innocent! But his assumption here, like his assumptions on religion and politics, is one for which I have found no certain substitute. He loved blank paper and obedience to this love led me to a difficult artistic attempt. I reasoned thus: just as the paper is the basis for the marks upon it, might not events be contingent upon a never-expressed (because featureless) ground? Is the true marvel of the Sunday skaters the pattern of their pirouettes or the fact that they are silently upheld? Blankness is not emptiness; we may skate upon an intense radiance we do not see because we see nothing else. And in fact there is a color, a quiet but tireless goodness that things at rest, like a brick wall or a small stone, seem to affirm. A wordless reassurance that these things are pressing to give. An hallucination? To transcribe middleness with all its grits, bumps, and anonymities, in its fullness of satisfaction and mystery: is it possible or, in view of the suffering that violently colors the periphery and that at all moments threatens to move into the center, worth doing? Possibly not; but the horse-chestnut trees, the telephone poles, the porches, the hedges recede to a calm point that in my subjective geography is still the center of the world.

These remarks on the artistic vocation and on the magic of artistic creation strongly suggest an additional religious dimension to that fascination, the sense of enchantment with an even more primal creation. Updike's conviction that "blankness is not emptiness," that "we may skate upon a radiance we do not see because we see nothing else," that "a tireless goodness" is sensed in reality is repeated with variations throughout his writings. At root it is a religious conviction that buttresses his conviction about Art.

My efforts, especially in considering his earlier novels, are intended to demonstrate that this attitude is more than a merely spontaneous one, but is in fact a most sophisticated religio-artistic vision, informed and often shaped by a very complex and subtle theology. My rather lengthy expositions of the theologies proper to Kierkegaard and Kark Barth are, I believe, an indispensable aid for understanding the spiritual depth and range of Updike's fiction. If a reader remains unaware of the reasons for

Updike's interest in their theologies and of their influence upon his intelligence and imagination, I think he remains blind to Updike's fictional vision, at least blind to a Great Secret Thing that animates it.

I am well aware, however, that religio-critical readings of any writer's work are fraught with interpretative hazards. Here the temptations and pitfalls are many: a covert baptism of many unregenerate elements, a simplistic reduction of art to the theologically stateable, an overly precious attention to one tree at the expense of the forest. No one can deny that in the past some critics of Updike's work have fallen prey to such temptations. Still, temptations and pitfalls aside, neither can one deny that there exists in his fiction a religious dimension that both invites and rewards sophisticated theological analysis. To use the word "vision" in describing a writer can mean many things, but, being an optical metaphor, it does imply a consistent angle of insight, a distinctive perspective of concern that distinguishes his point of view from that of another. A Marxist, Freudian, nihilistic, or Christian perspective will differ from each other since the concerns and convictions of each adherent inevitably influence what each one expects to see, hopes to see, and invariably does see in reality. The kinds of questions one asks assume something about the meaning one hopes to find in reality; from the questions asked and the tentative answers proffered, a reader begins to discern a structure or order of meaning and import in an author's work. This is an artist's "Vision." As such it necessarily embraces his convictions about Nature, Man, and what, if anything, transcends both, the structural order and meaning of the world, and the significance of ultimate questions about goodness and evil, something and nothing. It is unwise, generally speaking, to prescind from an author's vision since so very often this is precisely the source of his distinctiveness.

This critical study will argue that Updike's is a religiously informed vision of a special kind and, although it does not explicate all his work, it does point up several Ur-questions that pervade it. Critical claims about a religious vision must be modest perhaps, but such modesty need not minimize its importance. Flannery O'Connor, another writer with a religiously informed vision, once observed in *Mystery and Manners:*

> It makes a great difference to the look of a novel whether its
> author believes that the world came late into being and continues to
> come by a creative act of God, or whether he believes that the world
> and ourselves are a product of a cosmic accident. It makes a great
> difference to his novel whether he believes that we are created in God's

image or whether he believes that we create God in our own. It makes a great difference whether he believes that our wills are free, or bound like those of the animals.

In short, I shall argue likewise: that for Updike and his characters such considerations do make a difference. Furthermore, they make a difference with regard to the artistic structure of his novels, a structure and shaping that reflects his views on our moral universe and on the dramatic contrarieties experienced by those who inhabit it. Updike's employment of the Adam and Eve myth and his willing acknowledgment of its outcome, that is, the mixed blessing granted by man's knowledge of good and evil, highlight his conviction that the human condition is intrinsically a "mixed" condition, an on-going struggle between our impulses toward goodness and toward its opposite. As the citation from his boyhood memoir expressed it, he further perceives within reality itself both "a tireless goodness that things at rest seem to affirm" and also "the suffering that violently colors the periphery"; thus he sees his task as artist as an effort to "transcribe middleness with all its grits, bumps, and anonymities, in its fullness of satisfaction and mystery."

This effort to "transcribe middleness" will issue in fiction that is characterized by ontological and moral tension, by dialectical oppositions, by the exploration of dramatic contrarieties. In his essay on Poetic Tension in *Hateful Contraries* W. K. Wimsatt describes the artistic tension that a "Christian" author seeks because he necessarily perceives the human condition as such a "mixed" condition, embracing the forces of both good and evil. Wimsatt's words describe the Updikean world well.

> Let us say that we recognize the fact of material concreteness in human experience, and though matter itself be not evil . . . yet it does seem the plausible enough ground for some kind of dualism, division, tension, and conflict, the clash of desires, and evil and pain. Spirit and matter, supernatural and natural, good and evil, these tend to line up as parallel oppositions. . . . We say that art ought to have the concreteness of recognition and inclusion; it ought to have tension, balance, wholeness. . . . Of course we will say that we don't call evil itself, or division, or conflict, desirable things. We only call facing up to them, facing up to the human predicament, a desirable and mature state of soul and the right model and course of a mature poetic art.

Perhaps Updike himself best summarized Wimsatt's words in his own poem "Apple."

Since Time began, such alphabets begin
With Apple, Source of Knowledge and Sin.
My child, take heart: the fruit that undid Man
Brought out as well the best in Paul Cézanne.

Wimsatt further argues that the best instrument for capturing and presenting this "mixed" perception of reality is metaphor. Metaphor is the "holding together of opposites," *not* a reconciliation of opposites, and therefore best reflects the complex nature of our mixed experience. As we shall investigate, in Updike's fiction metaphor (and sometimes its more universalized manifestation as myth) is his vehicle not only for exploring the dialectical complexity of experience but also for extending the imaginative range of the implications of that complexity. This often elaborate employment of metaphor enables Updike to avoid fiction that lapses entirely into the flatly "symbolic" or, on the other hand, into the purely "representational." It is true that Updike's novels will, in the main, be "realistic" in that they refrain from distorting the world and our common-sense perception of it, and yet their metaphoric structure and the metaphoric probing within them allow these novels to transcend the limits of realism and unite the keenly observed detail with the symbolic.

Aligned with this instrument of metaphor is a second, often concomitant, instrument: wit. Several of Updike's novels are funny indeed, and humorous incidents are found even in his most sober fiction. By "wit," however, I mean something else: an artistic attitude of mind that ever reveals itself as an unwillingness to ignore the complexity of human experience. Cleanth Brooks' definition in *The Well-Wrought Urn* captures well what I perceive as Updikean wit; and Brooks enunciates the reasons for it while at the same time differentiating it from metaphor, its most likely instrument.

Wit is not merely an acute perception of analogies; it is a lively awareness of the fact that the obvious attitude toward a given situation is not the only possible attitude. Because wit, for us, is still associated with levity, it may be well to state it in its most serious terms . . . it is possible to describe it as merely [an artist's] refusal to blind himself to the multiplicity which exists.

Wit, in this sense, is not merely some kind of adornment; it is, rather, an indication of a mature, expansive, and adroit mind. As such, wit is, as Wimsatt said in *The Verbal Icon*, a "cognitive principle" that operates by means of metaphor, irony, and paradox and best resonates within dramatic contexts. In Updike's case, his imagination is always oriented toward the multiple; and that "middleness" toward which his intelligence strives will ever issue in wit.

These observations are especially important in any consideration of Updike's treatment of the other Great Secret Thing: Sex. Much will be said on this subject later, but let it be stated honestly here that there is no denying that Updike has become famous or infamous, depending on one's perspective, for his explicit handling of sex. A good number of decidedly un-Puritanical readers have been either disconcerted or perplexed that a writer of such refined sensibility in other areas should be so uncharacteristically obvious and rather indelicate in this one area. Perhaps the greater irony, however, is that the sexual scenes in his novels often constitute those novels' weakest sections, that is, the least artistically integrated, the most dramatically unrealized, the least likely to be tempered by wit. It is possible, then, that these are the unstated reasons for a reader's unsettlement and disappointment. John Cheever said it well in a recent interview when he was asked what, if any, is the difference between himself and Updike. Cheever answered, "Updike writes far more explicitly about sex, for one thing. Explicit sex scenes don't particularly interest me. Everybody knows what's going on. I can't think, in the whole history of literature, of an explicit sex scene that was memorable, can you?"

Updike in his own defense has asserted that he agrees with "Freud's notion about the centrality of sex," and that his efforts are directed toward presenting the "truth about sex." When asked in a 1968 interview about the oral-genital sexual episodes in his fiction, he stated that "it matters among my humans, not only what they're made of, but exactly how they attach to each other." One must stress, however, that Updike's intentions are the exact opposite of pornographic; he takes this Secret Thing seriously and believes that Art, the other Great Secret, imposes standards upon its depiction. An interesting insight into Updike's own feelings as a reader himself is provided in his strongly negative comments on Terry Andrews' *The Story of Harold* (1974) and its coarse emphasis on anal intercourse.

> This trans-anal passage tells me more than I want to know; it has the frightful melancholy of the purely physical; I can hardly bear to read it. . . . Where we draw back varies; but our sexual natures, even in this age of competitive license and Freudian sanction, do ask limits, for their own protection. The angel of disgust guards the seeds of life. Sexual excitement arises from an arcanum; some stimuli must be kept

in safe deposit. Just as moral prohibitions have as their end our own
safety, some boundary to the exploration of the bodies of others, some
economy in knowledge, is asked for, that potency be preserved.

At its best and least explicit, Updike's treatment of sex will participate
in the same dialectical vision of man's "mixed" human condition, a vision
tempered by wit and resonant with metaphor, that his other themes will
reflect. The mystery of sexuality is ever that, a mystery; and yet the sexual
encounter not only involves the mysterious "Other" but is revelatory of
the mystery of the self as well. In his extensive review of De Rougemont's
study of the Tristan and Iseult myth in *Love in the Western World* and *Love
Declared*, Updike summarized one aspect of this mystery, an insight to
which he later subscribed.

> . . . a phrase identifies a man's Iseult as "the woman . . . of his most
> intimate nostalgia." This hint is provocative. While nostalgia does not
> create women, perhaps it does create Iseults. What is it that shines at
> us from Iseult's face but our own past, with its strange innocence and
> its strange need to be redeemed? What is nostalgia but love for that
> part of ourselves which is in Heaven, forever removed from change
> and corruption? A woman, loved, momentarily eases the pain of time
> by localizing nostalgia; the vague and irrecoverable objects of nostalgic
> longing are assimilated, under the pressure of libidinous desire, into
> the details of her person.

This theme of the male's search for his self and his discovery of it in
his simultaneous quest and discovery of the mysterious "Other" will characterize the dialectical nature of sexuality throughout Updike's fiction. As
in his use of the Adam myth, it will also dramatize the tension between
man's "strange innocence" and his "strange need for redemption." This
theme is thus very pertinent for appreciating the narrowness of Updike's
sexual world. His is a resolutely heterosexual world, tightly enclosed by
female emotional parameters. Few contemporary male writers have imaginatively entered so successfully a woman's thought-world and sensibility
as has Updike. And yet his fiction is always a man-centered fiction in
that the controlling voice retains an ultimately masculine perspective.
Even when the female characters' ruminations are expertly entered and
recorded they remain enclosed within that encompassing voice; the focus
might be on them but the view is "his." This is a curious phenomenon,
for one must admit that in Updike's fiction that female characters are
generally the most keenly observed, the most perspicacious, practical, and

mature; they are given the best lines, endowed with the most genuine wit, and privy to the most realistic opinions and sensations about life's mysteries. Yet the overarching sexual theme itself always betrays a masculine viewpoint, a Tristan in search of Iseult—never vice versa.

The narrowness and particularity of Updike's sexual world, however, do generate critical difficulties. One strongly suspects that a good many male critics grow restless with the passivity of his typical male "heroes"—with their irresolution, their overly sensitive wool-gathering, and with their pronounced deficiency in violent impulse. (This reaction is by no means an exclusively male one. Flannery O'Connor said of the early Updike: "I don't like people that are all that sensitive. I just never know if the thing they're being sensitive about is *there* or not.") Updike's world is usually devoid of any responsive males in it, save for the central character and occasionally a father and son. Unlike the world in which most men live, no Updike character seems to have a friend or confidant to whom in pique or beery embarrassment he can blurt out even a tongue-tied truth. In Updike such truths are expressed either in familial or in mistress-sexual contexts, circumstances that are, admittedly, more intimate but not necessarily more generative of sexual honesty or its attempt.

One might argue that such a circumstance is an accurate depiction of the typical American male's situation in contemporary society. For most adult American men today, women are their only true confidantes. But the extreme, one feels, is the Updike character: he has no brother with whom he can purge at least some irredeemable resentments, no memories of special friends from childhood or adolescence that would spur him to seek the nostalgic solace of a masculine environment, no golf or poker companion whom he senses, given the telling emotional vagaries of those games, is a man capable of even the most restrained sympathy and understanding.

That said, it is indeed remarkable that Updike has successfully managed for over twenty years to create his own credible world, a narrow world perhaps but one pulsating with James' "felt life," a world enlivened by the ambiguity and tensions so emblematic of the similarly narrow worlds in which all of us necessarily live. This study will attempt to explore the complex richness of that fictional world by concentrating on each of his novels in the sequence in which they have appeared. An effort has been made to compose each chapter in such a way that the criticism of one novel can be read as a unit without pronounced dependence on previous material. Whenever possible I have tried to avoid repetition; and yet, since I like to think that the argument moves forward, that one chapter complements each of the others, that there is continually present a unified thesis, thematically interwoven, I urge the reader to begin at the beginning rather than read selected chapters. For some, the immediate dive into the chilly waters of Kierkegaard and Barth might seem a formidable prospect, but I believe they present important illustrations of Updike's sophisticated intelligence and are an introduction to one significant aspect of his vision. In brief, what might seem skippable I like to think is not.

I devote close attention to only two of Updike's short stories: "The Astronomer" and "Leaves" (the latter Updike considers his best story). My somewhat lengthy and exacting explication of each of these stories is not the result of an arbitrary impulse on my part, but is meant to be illustrative of a crucial phase in his authorship. Similar consideration of Updike's other stories, I felt, would divert attention from the particular novel under examination. I realize, though, that a book devoted entirely to an analysis of Updike's finest stories would be a most worthwhile project since he is among the best practitioners of this dying genre.

Despite the fact that this study will touch upon the theologies of Kierkegaard and Barth, the psychology of Jung, the literary theory of Northrup Frye, the artistic inspirations of Herrick, Milton, Hawthorne, Stevens, Nabokov, and others, I hope that these intrusions do not become distractions. The emphasis is meant to be on Updike himself, Updike the artist and his artistic ordering. Austin Warren in his *Rage for Order* describes the successful poem and its origin in the poet's sensibility. One can, without distortion, transcribe his words to the successful novel. Warren says that such a work succeeds only when it achieves "an equilibrium where there is also a tension, where there is a rage waiting to be ordered and a rage to find, to make that ordering." He goes on to say that when an artist succeeds, he makes his work "a kind of cosmos; a concretely languaged, synoptically felt world; an ikon or image of the 'real world' . . . [which] cannot be abstracted from the language and mythic structure in which it is incarnated." Warren then offers this important addendum: not only the artist, but the critic too, the ideal reader, must be moved by a rage for order of his own. A critic's rage is

> a passionate desire to discover, by analysis and comparison, the systematic vision of the world which is the poet's construction, his equivalent of a philosophic or conceptual system. He judges it a test of a mode of order that it be imaginable as well as conceivable. He hy-

pothesizes that the cosmos of a serious poet is, intuitively and dramatically, coherent. He seeks to define the spiritual cosmos of each and the specifically literary structure which corresponds to it.

A formidable task always but a fascinating one too, especially if, in his rage for order, the reader-critic is in pursuit of the significance of the Three Great Secret Things.

1: *The Poorhouse Fair and Rabbit, Run*

A. KIERKEGAARD AND BARTH AND THE DIALECTICAL

In a poem published in 1963 called "Die Neuen Heiligen," Updike linked together the teutonic "saints" in his own pantheon: Søren Kierkegaard, Franz Kafka, and Karl Barth. The lines about Kierkegaard and Barth read:

> Kierkegaard, a
> cripple and a Dane,
> disdained to marry;
> the consequent strain
> unsprung the whirling
> gay knives of his wits,
> which slashed the Ideal
> and himself to bits.
>
> . . . .
>
> . . . Karl Barth, more healthy,
> and married, and Swiss,
> lived longer, yet took
> small comfort from this;
> *Nein!* he cried, rooting
> in utter despair
> the Credo that Culture
> left up in the air.[1]

At the conclusion of his autobiographical poem *Midpoint*, five years later, Updike "catalogues his heroes," and the first two singled out for special praise are the Protestant theologians Søren Kierkegaard and Karl Barth:

13

> Praise *Kierkegaard*, who splintered *Hegel's* creed
> Upon the rock of Existential need;
> Praise *Barth*, who told how saving Faith can flow
> From Terror's oscillating Yes and No. . . .[2]

Any reader of John Updike is aware of the recurring allusions made to Kierkegaard throughout his writings. In addition to these poetic paeans, explicit references to Kierkegaard throughout his short story fiction will be employed to reinforce the humorous or serious direction of the narrative. This is especially true of the following stories: "Sunday Teasing" from *The Same Door* (1959); "Lifeguard" and "The Astronomer" from *Pigeon Feathers* (1962); "The Slump" and "God Speaks" from *Museums and Women and Other Stories* (1972). There the "Kierkegaardian connection" is expressed and so central to it; elsewhere it is implied; but the Kierkegaardian allusions are most important.

In a 1970 conversation Updike was asked whether he subscribed to Camus's brand of existentialism or any other brand, and he replied:

> . . . Essentially it was my own upbringing, the kind of family and the Church I was raised in, which disposed me to fall in love with Kierkegaard in my early twenties. I read him quite a lot. I read the works of other existentialists, but mostly of the Christian existentialists, from whom, funnily enough, it's not much of a jump to Camus and Sartre in whom I found the same gravity of moral concern persisting even though they had done away with the theism. . . . I remember reading *The Plague* in college and it didn't seem to me then to solve any problems the way Kierkegaard's approach did. I have quite forgotten Kierkegaard's books or even his sentences, but somehow the whole idea I got from him of existence preceding essence was very liberating for me; it seemed to give me some kind of handle on my own life. As a young person, I felt that thinking of myself as being suspended quite pointlessly in an immense void of indifferent stars and mathematically operating atoms made it difficult to justify action. To act because, if you don't, you'll get hungry—to act simply because of animal reaction to stimuli—was not to act in a way that gave shape to my life.[3]

Updike's intellectual self-estimation is overly modest; so too his remarks about his familiarity with Kierkegaard, perhaps rooted in that modesty, are in fact inaccurate. Updike's interest in Kierkegaard did not end for him in his twenties as is implied here, but has persisted. His play *Buchanan Dying* (1974) has for its first epigraph an apt quotation from Kierkegaard which Updike comments upon at length in the play's Afterword. In *A Month of Sundays* (1975), the narrator, the Rev. Thomas Marshfield, both flippantly and seriously alludes to Kierkegaard and other Christian theologians throughout the novel. Furthermore, in the more scholarly sphere, Updike has written two lengthy essays on Kierkegaard: one was a biography for *Atlantic Brief Lives* in 1971; and another in 1966, which is now anthologized in *Kierkegaardiana*, an exhaustive critical analysis reviewing Kierkegaard's *The Last Years*.[4] Not only are these essays elegantly phrased, but they demonstrate for any doubters Updike's profound grasp of Kierkegaard's theology and his appreciation of its dramatic subtlety.

Updike's interest and expertise in the theology of Karl Barth are equally well documented. As late as 1976 he reiterated that "theologically I favor Karl Barth"[5] and that in 1959, while he was writing *Rabbit, Run*, he suffered a severe spiritual crisis and "got through it by clinging to the stern neo-orthodoxy of Swiss theologian, Karl Barth."[6] In 1963 he wrote a lengthy review article on Barth's most difficult pivotal work *Anselm: Fides Quaerens Intellectum* for *The New Yorker*, a piece he later admitted "was written in acknowledgement of a debt, for Barth's theology, that at one point in my life, seemed alone to be supporting it (my life)."[7] The epigraph to *The Centaur* (1963) is a quote from Barth's *Dogmatics in Outline* and provides a thematic key to that novel. Also central to the thematic structure of *Of the Farm* (1965) is the minister's sermon, which is actually a paraphrase of Barth's exposition of the Creation of Male and Female. Later, in 1972, in an article we shall soon investigate, Updike wrote an introduction to Frank Sheed's collection *Soundings in Satanism*, and in it makes extensive use of Barth's *Church Dogmatics: A Selection*. More recently, in March 1979, he wrote an extensive review of Eberhard Busch's definitive biography of Barth and of the Pauchs' biography of theologian Paul Tillich. Other less obvious examples of his interest in Barth abound in his fiction and occasional prose and it is evident that, early and late, Barth's theology is important for understanding Updike's own world-view and religious attitude.

There are several reasons for Updike's special enthusiasm for these two rather complex and difficult Protestant theologians. The first reason relates to his boyhood and his being raised by devout, churchgoing parents. As a boy he was a Lutheran; later, for the sake of family peace (his first wife was a Unitarian), he compromised and his family joined the Congregational Church. Yet, as he tells it, the Nordic brand of Lutheranism retained its spiritual appeal for him, and his interest in the Lutheran

Kierkegaard and the Reformed Calvinist Barth reflects this. In a 1968 *Time* cover story, Updike indicated why he supported this more rigorous brand of Protestantism by saying:

> I wouldn't want to pose as a religious thinker. I'm more or less a shady type improving his way from book to book and trying to get up in the morning without a toothache. At one time I held strongly to the opinion that Paul Tillich and religious liberals like him were traitors to the theological camp because they were trying to humanize something that is essentially non-human. They were trying to make Christianity less than a scandal, as Kierkegaard called it. Well, it is a scandal; it's obviously a scandal because our life is a scandal.[8]

Both Kierkegaard in the nineteenth century and Barth in the twentieth were suspicious of any attempt to water down the stark mysterious sayings of Christianity. The theological efforts of both were directed against the liberalizing tendencies of the age, i.e. those attempts to translate the Christian message into humanistic terms by making it either a bourgeois ethic or a lofty rationalistic philosophy or an elevation of man's instinctive spiritual sentiments.[9] According to Barth such liberal or humanistic theology ended up domesticating God and substituted for theology itself a concern with man and his piety, with the result that "to think about God meant to think in scarcely veiled fashion about man." One might say that to Barth for the liberal humanist theologian to speak of God meant merely to speak of man in a loud voice.

Though a century apart, both Kierkegaard and Barth counteracted this humanistic tendency by striving to remind Christians that Christianity is grounded in Revelation, that is, it is not grounded either in speculation or in sentiment but in surprise—the surprise of Christ as the God-Man, a revelation that is also simultaneously a paradox because, in the very act of our joyfully hearing this revelation, as Kierkegaard put it, our "reason beats its brow until the blood comes." Although Kierkegaard and Barth are radically different in their approaches for doing theology, both stressed the radical centrality of Revelation and the importance of reasserting the "orthodox" beliefs of Christianity articulated in the early creeds and stressed by the early Protestant Reformers such as Luther and Calvin. In fact, with Kierkegaard as an initial inspiration, Barth is credited with that theological movement called "Neo-Orthodoxy" that came into prominence between World War I and World War II. In this connection, during the post-Barthian era of the late Sixties, Updike commented in a

Life interview upon a lengthy period of existential ennui he had experienced by saying, "I've felt in myself and in those around me a failure of nerve—a sense of doubt as to the worth of any action. At such times one has nothing but the ancient assertions of Christianity to give one the will to act, even if the act is only the bringing in of the milk bottles off the front porch."[10]

In that same interview Updike was asked why he inserted in his autobiographical poem *Midpoint* a quote from Barth that "a drowning man cannot pull himself out by his own hair." He answered that he interpreted this to mean "There is no help from within—without the supernatural, the natural is a pit of horror. I believe that all problems are basically insoluble and that faith is a leap out of despair."

Updike's own personal religious convictions are most explicitly offered in interviews such as these and in his light verse. Among the early poems, "Fever" and "Seven Stanzas for Easter" are joyous assertions of orthodox Christian belief without the rather dour overtones found in the quotations we have seen. This celebratory tone also characterizes the conclusion to *Midpoint*, which Updike has asserted is meant to be a summary of his philosophy of life. The conclusion begins:

> An easy Humanism plagues the land;
> I choose to take an otherworldly stand.
> The Archimedean point, however small,
> Will serve to lift th'entire terrestrial Ball.
> Reality transcends itself within;
> Atomically, all writers must begin.
> The Truth arrives as if by telegraph:
> One dot; two dots; a silence; then a laugh.
> The rules inhere, and will not be imposed
> *Ab alto*, as most Liberals have supposed.
> Praise *Kierkegaard*, who splintered *Hegel's* creed
> Upon the rock of Existential need;
> Praise *Barth*, who told how saving Faith can flow
> From Terror's oscillating Yes and No. . . . (p. 38)

The middle section of the conclusion of *Midpoint* contains several lines that are in many ways a summary of the central theological emphases found in Kierkegaard and Barth. Such as:

> Each passing moment masks a tender face;
> Nothing has had to be, but is by Grace. (p. 40)

and:

> Our Guilt inheres in sheer Existing, so
> Forgive yourself your death, and freely flow.
>   Transcendent Goodness makes elastic claims;
> The merciful Creator hid His Aims. (p. 42)

The autobiographical manifesto then ends with these lines:

> Born laughing, I've believed in the Absurd,
> Which brought me this far; henceforth, if I can,
> I must impersonate a serious man. (p. 44)

It would be erroneous, however, to give the impression through such extensive quotation that Updike's interest in Kierkegaard and Barth is restricted to their therapeutic value during his occasional crises of spirit. Updike is the most intelligent of men, a perceptive and discriminating reader, and it is evident that the appeal of these two theologians is quite clearly an intellectual one, embracing yet also transcending the pious. One of the attractive features of both Kierkegaard and Barth is that each speaks with a distinctively *dramatic* voice—Barth in the preacher's tone, Kierkegaard in the poet's or novelist's tone. Thus their writings address the reader with a sense of personal urgency and ever make use of dramatic techniques such as irony, hyperbole, repetition of phrase, and the allusive aside. No doubt Updike, as a writer himself, was drawn initially to the sound of these compelling voices. What he has said of Kierkegaard is appropriate to Barth as well: "perhaps it is his voice—that extraordinary insinuant voice, imperious and tender, rabid and witty—that excites our devotion."[11]

But more need be said. It is equally true that Updike is attracted to their distinctive mode of theological argument. Updike's own mind delights in ambiguity; he has said that "everything unambiguously expressed seems somehow crass to me,"[12] and that "I like middles. It is in the middles that extremes clash, where ambiguity restlessly rules."[13] In a 1968 comment on *Couples* he stated further that "Unfallen Adam is an ape. Yes, I guess I do feel that. I feel that to be a person is to be in a situation of tension, is to be in a dialectical situation."[14] Ripeness is all, and it is the ambiguous and the dialectical that engender ripeness.

In the history of modern theology Kierkegaard and Barth are credited with founding that "school" of theology called "Dialectical Theology." As in so many so-called schools, further investigation reveals that the differences are often greater among the "scholars" than their agreements (as is true of the later Barth's relation to Kierkegaard); but the term "dialectical" does characterize well a specialized method of argument and theological perspective they share. Kierkegaard was a genius at dialectics, that process of argument whereby the mind moves forward along the avenues of state-ment and counterstatement, of Yes and No followed by another Yes and No, wherein each new answer initiates a further opposite qualification in order to point up and at the same time preserve the complex, contradic-tory nature of reality and thought. The young Karl Barth found Kierke-gaard's dialectical method most congenial and saw in it the method of St. Paul and the theologians of the Reformation. He, like Kierkegaard before him, will exploit this method in order to elucidate the profoundly para-doxical nature of the "truth" of the Christian message and also to remind the Christian that not only his rational intelligence but his very existence is plunged into what Updike refers to as "a dialectical situation."

The dialectical method used by Kierkegaard and the early Barth, however, is quite different in intent from that of Hegelian or Marxist dialectics in that "synthesis" or resolution is not its goal. Quite otherwise. Kierkegaard believed that "truth" is not found in the smooth Hegelian rationalist transition from thesis to antithesis to synthesis, from Yes to No to their union. Rather, he emphasized that truth must ever be existential, i.e. must engage one's most profoundly personal human concerns, con-cerns that affect not only man's intelligence but also his affections and decision-making powers. Kierkegaard was suspicious of rationalism and its non-existential, reductive notion of truth; instead, he stressed that the acquisition of truth is a dynamic, dramatic process. One never enjoys an intellectual purchase on the truth; one can only *become* the truth, i.e. appropriate it in one's mode of living. He further argued that truth is found only in the dialectical tension between competing truths—a tension that precisely because it is existential can never be fully resolved. He wrote: "Every truth is nevertheless truth only to a certain degree; when it goes beyond, the counterpoint appears, and it becomes untruth."[15]

Kierkegaard was never a sophist or relativist, though, despite the boldness of such phrases. He believed in truth, namely the Truth of Chris-tian Revelation (at the center of which is the God-Man), but he stressed that this is a *revelatory* truth and thus is the result of the union of time and eternity, the natural and the supernatural. Since this truth is of such a paradoxical nature, man has no adequate language to express it. Being paradoxical, the truth of Christianity frustrates his reason and his intellectual efforts at synthesis; consequently, on the intellectual level of discourse man is better advised to resort to dialectical expression, paradoxical assertions with emphasis on dramatic polarities, and so on. The dialectical character of Kierkegaard's thought makes his work at once stirring and perplexing, gripping and ever elusive; and the same is true of Karl Barth. Barth eventually went further than Kierkegaard's more subjective concerns and dived into the cold waters of Christian dogma, thus increasing the degree of difficulty for the reader-diver who followed him. And yet, in probing dogmatic questions, he will retain the precarious techniques of the true dialectician. Barth made this important statement in that collection which Updike offers as the best introduction to his theology:

> This way [the dialectical] from the outset undertakes seriously and positively to develop the idea of God on the one hand and the criticism of man and all things on the other; but they are not now considered independently but are referred constantly to their common presupposition, the living truth which . . . lies between them and gives to both their meaning and interpretation. . . . The genuine dialectician knows that the Center cannot be apprehended or beheld, and he will not, if he can help it, allow himself to be drawn into giving information about it.[16]

When one returns to a consideration of Updike's *oeuvre*, the overarching themes of his novels stand revealed as dialectical in character and sympathetic to the Kierkegaard-Barth perspective on the elusiveness of conceptual "truth." Updikean fictional truth, instead, will be existential and will elude any facile reductionist explication, for a realization of human ambiguity will be their inspiration and the dialectical will be their artistic effect. In an interview in 1968, Updike corrected a misunderstanding on the part of his univocally-minded questioner and reviewed his own previous work by saying:

> No, I meant my *work* says "yes, but." Yes, in *Rabbit, Run*, to our inner urgent whispers, but—the social fabric collapses murderously. Yes, in *The Centaur*, to self-sacrifice and duty, but—what of a man's private agony and dwindling? No, in *The Poorhouse Fair*, to social homogenization and loss of faith, but—listen to the voices, the joy of persistent existence. No, in *Couples*, to a religious community founded on physical and psychical interpenetration, but—what else shall we do, as God destroys our churches?[17]

Updike's novels might be dialectical in thematic structure, but he is not a dialectician. He is, above all, an artist, and as such he will always transform the categories and attitudes of Kierkegaard and Barth into dramatic, fictional language. What was theology now becomes in his hands story. What Kierkegaard and Barth discussed, he dramatizes.

B. KIERKEGAARD AND THE DREAD OF NOTHINGNESS: "THE ASTRONOMER"

Updike concluded his appreciative biography of Kierkegaard in *Atlantic Brief Lives* with these words:

> It remained for Karl Barth to build upon the basis of God's otherness
> . . . an inhabitable theology; it remained for Kafka, though the Dane's
> journals abound in miniature fables, to develop Kierkegaardian sen-
> sations into real fiction, into epic symbols.[18]

In the middle and late 1950's, Updike read a number of Kierke-gaard's major works.[19] Many of the short stories from that period, which appeared eventually in the collections *The Same Door* (1959) and *Pigeon Feathers* (1962), reflect both a conscious and unconscious effort to develop "Kierkegaardian sensations" into real fiction. The stories "Dentistry and Doubt," "Toward Evening," "Sunday Teasing," "Intercession," "Wife-Wooing," "Pigeon Feathers," "The Astronomer," "Lifeguard," "The Blessed Man of Boston, My Grandmother's Thimble, and Fanning Island," "Packed Dirt, Churchgoing, A Dying Cart, A Traded Car" all betray to a greater or lesser degree an appropriation of or a grappling with a theme proper to Kierkegaard.

Of course, other non-Kierkegaardian readings of these stories are not only possible but perhaps equally rewarding. Nonetheless, it is surprising that so few critics of Updike's fiction have investigated the implications of this ardor for Kierkegaard. Those who have tend to restrict their attention to the more abstract, ideational "influence" of Kierkegaard upon him, rather than examine more specific connectives that would assist an understanding of particular episodes, imagery, and technique found in his work.[20] Furthermore, even this more abstract or generalized interpretation of Kierkegaard's influence is itself often prescribed because Kierkegaard is himself understood in the light of that shared perception of his thought once popular in the 1950's.[21] This view depicted Kierkegaard as "the father of Existentialism" who inspired writers to portray man as one who seeks authentic selfhood despite his own anxiety and despite the absurdity of the bourgeois world. This narrow, generalized interpretation was appropriate, perhaps, for reading Updike's *Rabbit, Run* in 1960, but not only does it fail to characterize the expansive range of Kierkegaard's thought, it also limits consideration of the extent of his influence on Updike's less obviously "existentialist" fiction.[22]

In the last five years or so, however, excellent studies of Kierkegaard have appeared which demand that he be read afresh. Renewed interest in Kierkegaard's dialectical method,[23] in the importance of his literary techniques,[24] and in his attitudes toward the mental-world of science[25] has uncovered further layers of ambiguity owing to the subtlety of structure and artistic craft found in his work. This fresh rereading of Kierkegaard, then, inspires a fresh rereading of his influence upon Updike beyond the prevailing "existentialist" diagnosis.

Here, of course, the cautions offered by the New Criticism are well taken. Updike is a selective reader and an imaginative writer and will shape any influence, significant or not, to his own design. And yet, though mindful of these cautions, many avenues for tracing this influence, tracking down "Kierkegaardian sensations," seem open for fruitful study.[26] A complete study would demand a book-length investigation of considerable size; for our purposes, it is sufficient to concentrate on one brilliantly designed story entitled "The Astronomer," which was published April 1, 1961, and now appears in the collection *Pigeon Feathers*.[27] This brief story, overlooked by the critics,[28] is perhaps most representa████n ░ Kierkegaard's influence and therefore provides a paradigm for further analyses of Updike and Kierkegaard. Like some of the work of Walker Percy and W. H. Auden,[29] "The Astronomer" is Updike's successful attempt "to develop Kierkegaardian sensations into real fiction." The dramatic action, the characters, the imagery, and even some apparently insignificant details can be understood and appreciated only in terms of these "sensations." Here recent Kierkegaardian scholarship provides invaluable assistance in perceiving these "sensations." The story begins:

> I feared his visit. I was twenty-four, and the religious revival within myself was at its height. Earlier that summer, I had discovered Kierkegaard, and each week I brought back to the apartment one more of the Princeton University Press's elegant and expensive editions of his works. They were beautiful books, sometimes very thick, sometimes very thin . . . and Kierkegaard's own endless footnotes, blanketing pages at a time as, crippled, agonized by distinctions, he scribbled on

and on, heaping irony on irony, curse on curse, gnashing, sneering, praising Jehovah in the privacy of his empty home in Copenhagen. The demons with which he wrestled—Hegel and his avatars—were unknown to me, so Kierkegaard at his desk seemed to me to be writhing in the clutch of phantoms, slapping at silent mosquitoes, twisting furiously to confront presences that were not there. It was a spectacle unlike any I had ever seen in print before, and it brought me much comfort during those August and September evenings. . . . (p. 125)

The story starts with an anticipatory fear, a fear which is unexplained because of the digression about Kierkegaard. Kierkegaard brings the narrator "comfort" although his "demons" were unknown to him, like "phantoms," "silent mosquitoes," "presences that were not there." The narrator describes the setting: the sixth floor of an apartment overlooking the Hudson where "the river would become black before the sky, and the little Jersey towns on the far bank would be pinched between two massive tongs of darkness until only a row of sparks remained." (p. 125) The reflections of these sparks, after a boat passed by, would "tremble, double, fragment, and not until long after the shadow of the boat passed reconstruct themselves." (p. 125) At the story's end, this scenic perception with its imagery will reappear; there it will suggest an emotional "pincher" movement between earth and sky and a quite distinctive "reconstruction" of sparks will take place. The story itself is like the ship's passing.

The narrator, named Walter, fears the visit of the astronomer, an Hungarian named Bela, a man immensely self-assured, brilliant, "like Kierkegaard a bachelor" (ironically, the only tenuous resemblance), who "gave an impression of abnormal density; his anatomical parts seemed set one on top of the other without any loose space between for leeway or accommodation of his innards." (p. 126) Bela's physical, space-less, innards-less solidity has its intellectual counterpoint, for "he had an air of seeing beyond me, of seeing into the interstellar structure of things, of having transcended, except perhaps in the niggling matter of lust, the clouds of human subjectivity—vaporous hopes supported by immaterial rationalizations." (p. 126) No sooner does the astronomer arrive when, after the perfunctory greetings

. . . he spotted the paperback *Meno* that I had been reading, back and forth, on the subway, two pages per stop. It is the dialogue in which Socrates, to demonstrate the existence of indwelling knowledge, elicits some geometrical truths from a small boy. "My Lord, Walter," Bela said, "Why are you reading this? Is this the one where he proves that two and two equals four?" And thus quickly, at a mere wink from this atheist, Platonism and all its attendant cathedrals came tumbling down. (pp. 126-27)

At first glance Walter's shaken reaction to Bela's airy dismissal of Plato's *Meno* seems unfounded—unless we detect "Kierkegaardian sensations." The only answer to Bela's question why an acknowledged Kierkegaard devotee would read the *Meno* is that its problem ("How far does the Truth admit of being learned?") is the central question of Kierkegaard's *Philosophical Fragments*.[30] This book was Kierkegaard's ingenious attempt to re-emphasize the unique character of Christianity as a *revelatory* religion over against every species of humanism or Idealism, whether Platonic or Hegelian. Socrates in the *Meno* had argued that man actually possessed the truth but had forgotten it; hence, the function of the teacher was to stimulate another's recollection of the truth. The teacher was important only in that he provided the occasion for the self-discovery of truth. Kierkegaard argued the contrary, that unlike Socratic recollection the "truths" of Christianity must be brought to the learner, one of the essential truths being that the learner is in sin or "untruth." The learner cannot discover this truth by himself, therefore; at best he can become aware that he lacks the truth. Since they must be brought, the one who brings these truths—the teacher (Christ)—is of utmost importance, unlike Socrates, and *when* He brings them—the "Moment"—designates a crucial transition for the learner between untruth and truth. In *Philosophical Fragments* Kierkegaard called this Christian "Moment" the "Fullness of Time," for it describes the Eternal (Teacher-Christ) entering Time and addressing believers. Not only was the historical Incarnation such a "Moment," but everyone who confronts Christ in faith thereafter confronts such a "Moment."

Consequently, Walter's upset at Bela's remark is double-rooted. First, it unsettles the religious "comfort" Kierkegaard had brought; secondly, it unearths and exposes a lingering Idealism within him, the hope that perhaps memory/recollection might bring truth. Above, he had felt that Kierkegaard's "demons—Hegel and his avatars" were unknown to him; now he himself encounters them. Walter's distress is described first in imagery reminiscent of the opening paragraph—but here the river's blackness represents his emotional and religious condition, recalling an image prominent in Kierkegaard—[31] and thereafter in imagery proper to the vision of an atheist astronomer.

We ate dinner by the window, from which the Hudson appeared a
massive rent opened in a tenuous web of light. . . . I felt the structure
I had painstakingly built up within myself wasting away; my faith (existentialism padded out with Chesterton), my prayers, my churchgoing
. . . all dwindled to the thinnest filaments of illusion, and in one flash,
I knew, they would burn to nothing. I felt behind his eyes immensities
of space and gas, seemed to see with him through my own evanescent
body into gigantic systems of dead but furious matter, suns like match
heads, planets like cinders, galaxies that were swirls of ash, and beyond
them, more galaxies, and more, fleeing with sickening speed beyond
the rim that our most powerful telescopes could reach. (p. 127)

Walter's faith has been shaken by cosmic dread, dread translated into
the vast emptiness and ash of an astronomer's vision, a dread reminiscent
of Pascal. However, after dinner, as he smokes his ash-laden cigar, Bela
decides to describe a funny parody he had seen on the B.B.C. because he
knows that Walter is, "to some extent, a humorist." (p. 127)

The word "humorist" here seems insignificant, but in fact it is replete
with "Kierkegaardian sensations." For Kierkegaard the term "humorist"
was descriptive of a type of person, not unlike Walter at this juncture, who
has reached the final *confinium* or boundary-line which separates the ethical from the religious sphere of personal existence.[32] No doubt the most
famous feature of Kierkegaard's thought is his morphology of the three
spheres of existence (aesthetic, ethical, religious) to delineate the controlling motivation and orientation that typifies human behavior. Aesthetic existence is characterized by pursuit of personal satisfaction, the
ethical by moral commitment and a sense of personal duty, and the religious by an intensely personal relationship to God in faith. Each of these
spheres has a boundary-line which can be crossed only by a "leap," i.e.
a decision to renounce the former sphere and embrace the next; it is the
"leap of faith," the decision to entrust one's life to God in faith, that bridges
the boundary between the ethical and the religious. The "humorist," then,
is one who stands before this final boundary but does not cross it. He is
sympathetic with the follies of the human comedy (Aesthetic) and aware
of the limits of moral effort (Ethical) and, though he is attracted to
religious commitment (Religious), he seeks a way out of it. He is called
a "humorist" because in his situation he is very cognizant of the contra-
dictions of life, the basis of all humor; as a result he retreats to the shared
laughter and acknowledged foibles of common humanity rather than confront the highly individual demands that faith requires.

That "humor" is a boundary for Kierkegaard is important in terms of the story since Bela's recounting of the humorous parody, as the scientific "boundary" images suggest, restores Walter once more to the humorist's boundary-line prior to faith.

> Knowing that . . . I was to some extent a humorist, he told me of a parody he had seen of the B.B.C. Third Programme. It involved Bertrand Russell reading the first five decimal places of π, followed by twenty minutes of silent meditation led by Mr. T. S. Eliot, and then Bertrand Russell reading the *next* five hundred places of π.
>
> If my laughter burst out excessively, it was because his acknowledgment, though minimal and oblique, that Bertrand Russell might by some conception be laughable and that meditation and the author of "Little Gidding" did at least *exist* momentarily relieved me of the strain of maintaining against the pressure of his latent opinions my own superstitious, faint-hearted identity. This small remission of his field of force admitted worlds of white light. . . . (pp. 127-28)[33]

The ensuing after-dinner conversation consists of two "recollections" Bela recounts to the young couple. The first memory is of his first teaching assignment in Michigan where in the bitter cold everyone wore ear muffs. Bela admits that "at first he didn't believe in the ear muffs" and that "it had taken him months to muster the courage to go into a shop to ask for such childish things"; but once he did, he was happy with them, in fact kept them "though in the East they did not seem to be the fashion." (p. 128)

This recollection of Bela hints at the first ironic reversal in the story. Bela's admission that at first he could not "believe" the ear muffs, needed courage, but then found them "sensible" and became "happy" with such childish, unfashionable things is a concrete counterpart to Walter's more abstract problems of faith. This irony is reinforced when Bela, in trying to describe the ear muffs on some girls, uses language containing ash and astronomical imagery—a reverse reminder of Walter's horrific vision.

> "And the girls," Bela said, "the girls in the Midwest wear *immense puffs*, as big around as—" He cupped his hands, fingers spread, over his ears. . . . He had retained, between two fingers, the cigar, so his head seemed to have spouted, rather low, one smoking horn. His hands darted away, his chest expanded and became rigid as he tried to embrace, for us, the sense of those remote pompoms. "White, wooly," he said sharply, giving each adjective a lecturer's force. . . . "They're like the snowballs that girls in your iceshows wear on their breasts." He

pronounced the two s's in "breasts" so distinctly it seemed the radiator had hissed. (p. 128)

The mention of the girls' breasts recalls the description of Bela's "air of having transcended, except perhaps in the niggling matter of lust, the clouds of human subjectivity," (p. 126) and so this marks his brief return to those "white, wooly" clouds. However, Bela's second "recollection" proves more surprising to Walter and his wife, for, a most unlikely sight-seer, they learn the astronomer had "with incongruous piety visited the Grand Canyon, Yosemite, a Sioux reservation." (p. 129)

He described a long stretch of highway in New Mexico. "There are these black hills. Utterly without vegetation. Great, heavy, almost purplish folds, unimaginably ugly. Mile after mile after mile. Not a gas station. Not a sign of green. Nothing." And his face, turning rapidly from one to the other of us, underwent an expression I had never before seen him wear. His black eyebrows shot up in two arches stretch-ing his eyelids smooth, and his upper lip tightened over his lower, which was retracted in a way that indicated it was being delicately pinched between his teeth. This expression, bestowed in silence and swiftly erased, confessed what he could not pronounce. He had been frightened. (p. 129)

Walter, the unsteady believer or humorist, and Bela, the scientific rationalist, share a similar confrontation with nothingness, but each from a different perspective; for one, the nothingness of outer space, for the other, that of the earth itself. Like the apartment's earthly setting where the river's light seemed pinched between tongs of darkness and where, during Walter's upset, the river's light seemed "rent," now Bela's own countenance is "pinched." Furthermore, Walter's description of Bela's expression has a religious ring: "This expression, bestowed in silence and quickly erased, confessed what he could not pronounce." Like the hu-morous parody of Russell and Eliot and the immense puffs of ear muffs, Bela's mute confession unites him with Walter in a most ironic way.

Before we go on to the story's two final paragraphs, let us note that Updike has dramatized in integral fashion several "Kierkegaardian sensa-tions" at once. First of all, both Walter and Bela undergo the experience analyzed by Kierkegaard in The Concept of Dread.[34] For Kierkegaard the experience of dread was not like common instances of fear or emotions of fright, for, unlike them, dread has no object. Rather, dread was pre-cisely fear of the unknown, the unknown possible, that is, fear of what

can be and what *one can* become—in short, fear of literally "nothing" in
the specific sense of the word. Man's basic freedom issues in dread because
he realizes that he confronts "infinite" possibilities for choice, possibilities
that both attract and repel his imagination. This dread-ful situation is
inevitably ambiguous, then, because man becomes simultaneously aware
of his own finitude, especially the limits of time upon him, and of the
infinite range of possibilities open to him. But man is not only temporal
and finite; because of his spiritual nature, he possesses an "eternal" component within him that allows him to transcend time. That experience,
whereby *awareness* of *both* the eternal and the temporal conjoins in a
man, Kierkegaard calls "the Moment" in *The Concept of Dread*. Here in
this story, Bela and Walter both experience such "Moments," but the
Moments are induced by opposite dread-ful visions of no-thing; for Walter,
by cosmic infinity; for Bela, by telluric nothingness.

Recent studies of Kierkegaard have emphasized the deliberate dialectic
structure of his whole authorship and the artistic techniques of drama and
dialogue he employed. These studies assist our appreciation of Updike's
understated drama here and the crucial, though ambiguous, character of
the "Moment."

Gregor Malantschuk in his study of Kierkegaard's dialectical method
argues that *The Concept of Dread* ought not to be considered as an isolated
work. Rather, he sees it as a dialectical twin to Kierkegaard's *Philosophical
Fragments*, which was published four days before it in 1843.[35] As we mentioned above, *Philosophical Fragments* is Kierkegaard's attempt to emphasize
that Christian truth is not recollected but comes "from above," in that
the Eternal (Christ the Teacher) breaks into human time in "the Moment," called also "the Fullness of Time" when God reveals Himself to
man. Where *Philosophical Fragments* described the downward movement,
the Moment coming from above, *The Concept of Dread* moves in the
opposite direction. Beginning "from below," as it were, with an analysis
of man's dread, it moves upward in argument to lead the reader to a
confrontation with Christianity, to lead the reader to realize that the
"dread-ful moment" can be preparatory for the desire for a revelation, that
the "Moment" *can* be filled and become a meeting-point with "the Fullness
of Time." Consequently, although dread and Christian faith are *theologically* different for Kierkegaard, they are *psychologically* the same in that the
dread-ful moment is pivotal for both the acceptance or rejection of faith.[36]

Updike's imagery in the closing sections of the story captures well
Kierkegaard's descending-ascending, finite-infinite dialectic, the differ-

ence in *theological* perspective, and the time-eternity paradox, while at the same time he dramatizes effectively the psychologically similar reaction to "the Moment" for both the believer and non-believer. And yet that "moment" is hauntingly ambiguous in the story. Note that Bela's expression is "bestowed in silence" and that the story ends in mutual silence. In *The Concept of Dread* such silence is the ambiguous outcome of the dread-ful moment since, for the believer, his ineffable, private relationship to God must issue in silence and, for the non-believer, his refusal to go further into faith also issues in silence, or what Kierkegaard calls "shut-up-ness."

Malantschuk's study of the dialectical method is complemented by Louis Mackey's brilliant book, *Kierkegaard: A Kind of Poet.*[37] There Mackey argues that Kierkegaard's choice of so many pseudonyms, a perplexing point for some critics, was rooted in his conviction that all truth is perspectival, that no human attitude, even religious faith, ever attains absoluteness, and so truth is inevitably refracted into many relative and distinctive standpoints. Hence, form and content are one in Kierkegaard's authorship in that the pseudonyms represent his technical instrument for communicating his own dialectical perception of the relativities within human existence. Kierkegaard will not only invent his own dialectical images, but he will deliberately invert familiar ones in order to frustrate, as it were, any univocal purchase on his thought. Kierkegaard's goal here was what he called "indirect communication."[38] As artist, he would so arrange opposing points of view in dialogue, dramatizing each in such a way that the perplexed reader would be distracted away from the debate itself and be compelled to reflect upon the argument in terms of his own life and seek resolution *there* since the book itself provided none. For this reason, Kierkegaard's "aesthetic" works are deliberately ambiguous and thus demand a "subjective" reading in the sense of a personal engagement with the problem.

This technique of an ambiguously designed indirect communication, as Mackey insists, is primarily an artist's technique and is an apt description of Updike's own, not only here in this story, but throughout much of his fiction. Updike has admitted that "everything unambiguously expressed seems somehow crass to me," that his "sense of life [is] multilayered and ambiguous," and that "I feel that to be a person is to be in a situation of tension, is to be in a dialectical situation."[39] He chose as an epigraph to *A Month of Sundays* Tillich's comment that "This principle of soul, universally and individually, is the principle of ambiguity." What some critics find frustrating in Updike's work is precisely this principle of ambiguity which is the soul of his fictional world and, as in Kierkegaard, is central to his art of communication.

The ending to "The Astronomer" is ambiguous, not because of fuzziness or imprecision, but because it develops "Kierkegaardian sensations into real fiction." Those "sensations" heighten the drama and illuminate the imagery at the story's close. The next-to-last paragraph describes the silence that ensues after Bela's mute "confession," and the mixture of cosmic and earthly images of debris corresponds with the "dread-ful" moments both men have shared.

> On the table, below our faces, the cups and glasses broken into shards by shadows, the brown dregs of coffee and wine, the ashtrays and the ashes were hastily swept together into a little heap of warm dark tones distinct from the universal debris. (p. 129)

Finally, without these "Kierkegaardian sensations" the story's last paragraph might sound like wispy romanticism. With them, however, one appreciates how these lines not only recapitulate the recurring images by transforming them into personal referents, but how the "Kierkegaardian sensations" bestow an ironic dimension to the questionable nature of memory/recollection and to the significance of isolated "moments" which glimmer in the temporal flow of one's life.

> In memory, perhaps because we lived on the sixth floor, this scene— this invisible scene—seems to take place at a great height, as if we were the residents of a star suspended against the darkness of the city and the river. What is the past, after all, but a vast sheet of darkness in which a few moments pricked apparently at random, shine? (p. 129)

C. KARL BARTH AND THE POWER OF NOTHINGNESS

Since its publication in 1677, John Bunyan's *Pilgrim's Progress*, with its tale of Christian's flight from the City of Destruction and his quest for the Celestial City, has provided the classical structural movement and perhaps even the standards of expectation for any fictional account of a Protestant Christian's spiritual journey in a world bounded by the obstacles of evil. It is noteworthy, then, that in his most obviously "Christian" novels (*The Poorhouse Fair, Rabbit, Run, The Centaur*, and *A Month of Sundays*), Updike, who is a Protestant traditionalist in so many ways, should create central characters who are not on pilgrimage but are, as it were, imprisoned. These characters are on spiritual pilgrimage, true enough, but each novel's redemptive progress is defined less by action than by reflection, argument, and confession. Unlike *Pilgrim's Progress*, these novels emphasize not so much the goal, the Celestial City, as the starting point, the City of Destruction, which holds these characters captive. Immobility rather than movement characterizes these novels. It appears that to Updike the great ironic consequence of Man's Fall is that one is inevitably led into protracted speculation, debate, and denial concerning its many possible meanings. That knowledge of good and evil, so hard won by the Fall, is both hindrance and help, for such knowledge simultaneously both imprisons us and discloses our only possible path toward true redemption. Every Pilgrim's progress or regress in Updike's fiction starts with this realization and its exploration.

Several years ago during an interview John Updike observed: "My books are meant to be moral debates with the reader, and if they seem pointless—I'm speaking hopefully—it's because the reader has not been engaged in the debate. The question is usually, 'What is a good man?' or 'What is goodness?' and in all the books an issue is examined."[40]

Updike's comment was made in reference to his earlier fiction, but it is also pertinent to an appreciation of his latest novels. One of the comic highlights of *A Month of Sundays* is Marshfield's extended conceit conjoining the history of ethics and opinions about its central problem, "Is the good just the pleasurable or what?" with the history of his own seduction of the woman who will be his wife. There the moral debate is satirized, but in *Marry Me* it is treated more seriously. Almost every love encounter in *Marry Me* is marked by the lovers' dialogue about "right" and "wrong." Thus, the artistic device of concluding the novel with three equally feasible endings no doubt is intended to induce us, the readers, to reflect upon the issues of their on-going debates. John Bunyan's claim that through reading *Pilgrim's Progress* "This Book will make a traveler of thee" is also an apt description of Updike's intentions here and in all of his novels.

However, as Updike's own comment indicates, the writer-reader engagement not only takes place on the moral level of debate, but it necessarily involves a more basic, *ontological* question: "What is goodness itself?" By ontological I mean that the primary question at issue concerns *reality* itself, the exploration of *what is*; therefore, the question is a philosophical or theological one at root. All other questions (social, psychological, moral) are secondary insofar as their specific inquiries relate to and are dependent upon one's response to this more radical question. For example, Updike's corollary question, "What is a good man?," which his fiction probes in dramatic form, derives its own ontology from this more radical question about goodness itself. Furthermore, since such a debate is dialogic and dialectical, the antithetical question which is necessarily implied is: "What, then, is evil? and what, then, is an evil man?"

Updike's perceptions concerning this antithetical question are well documented and illuminate, by contrast, his perceptions about the nature of goodness. In his personal memoir of 1962 called "The Dogwood Tree: A Boyhood," Updike admitted that, although he was now a Congregationalist and no longer a Lutheran, his throat still "goes grave" whenever the congregation sings Luther's hymn: "For still our ancient foe/Doth seek to work us woe;/His craft and power are great,/And armed with cruel hate,/On earth is not his equal."[41] After reflecting on this peculiarly visceral reaction, he continued:

> The immense dirge of praise for the Devil and the world . . . nourishes in me a seed I never knew was planted. How did the patently vapid and business-like teachings to which I was so lightly exposed succeed in branding me with the Cross? And a brand so specifically Lutheran, so distinctively Nordic; an obdurate insistence that at the core of the core there is a right-angled clash to which of all the verbal combinations we can invent, the Apostles' Creed offers the most adequate correspondence and response. (p. 143)

The positive assertions of the Apostles' Creed as a counter-balance to negative associations of the Devil and the world became, in fact, the foundation of Updike's faith, for as his memoir expresses it: "when [doubts of faith] came, they never roosted in the branches of the tree, but attacked its roots; if the first article of the Creed [I believe in God, the Creator of heaven and earth] stands, the rest follows as water flows downhill. That God, at a remote place and time, took upon Himself the form of a Syrian carpenter and walked the earth . . . appeared to me quite in the character of the Author of the grass." (p. 143)

I have returned to this early memoir because the convictions expressed there are not only iterated but developed *in the same order of argument* ten years later in Updike's six-page introduction to Frank Sheed's collection *Soundings in Satanism*.[42] Updike begins this introduction rather apologetically, situating himself with other contemporary Protestants for whom the question, "Can evil be a personal, dynamic principle?" seems "clownish" and too "supernatural." He wonders whether Protestants have become "more virtuous than the myths that taught us virtue"; instead, "we magnanimously grant our Creator His existence by a 'leap' of our wills, incidentially reducing His 'ancient foe' to the dimensions of a comic strip." (p. 87)

After posing those questions, Updike goes on to suggest that these questions themselves are rooted in man's ambivalent reactions to Creation itself.

> Yet these grand ghosts did not arise from a vacuum; they grow . . . from the deep exigencies and paradoxes of the human condition. We know that we live and we know that we will die. We love the creation that upholds us and sense that it is good, yet pain and plague and destruction are everywhere. (p. 87)

At this point in his reflections Updike returns to that central conviction about the first article of the Apostles' Creed that he expressed in his earlier memoir. Here he says that he would "timidly open the question of the devil as a metaphysical possibility, if not necessity." Why? Because he feels that "the assertion 'God exists' is a drastic one that imposes on the universe a structure; given this main beam, subordinate beams and joists, if reason and logic are anything, must follow." (p. 88)

It comes as no surprise to readers of Updike that, after these personal musings, he should step aside and, as he puts it, "let a true theologian speak." That true theologian is, of course, Karl Barth; and the rest of Updike's essay, for the most part, consists of his selective quotation from Barth's analysis of Evil abridged in *Church Dogmatics: A Selection*.[43]

Unfortunately, in the essay we are considering, Updike apparently presumes that the reader shares his own expertise in Barth's theology and thus can appreciate his extensive quotation from it. Since this, admittedly, is rarely the case, perhaps a brief exposition of Barth's thought in this particular context is more desirable than direct quotation from the essay itself.

In a sense Barth's theology rests upon his understanding of what Updike also feels is central to Christian faith-understanding, namely: the first article of the Creed. We saw Updike state above that "the assertion 'God exists' is a drastic one that imposes on the universe a structure; given this main beam, subordinate beams and joists, if reason and logic are anything, must follow." However, Barth will emphasize boldly that the first article of the Creed (God's existence as Creator of heaven and earth) can be understood *only* in the light of Jesus Christ as He is revealed to us in Scripture. The meaning and import of that first article is *revealed*; any other approaches in attempting to understand it, according to Barth, are at best empty efforts at speculation. For Barth, from eternity God's intention in creating the world was to reconcile Himself with Man in the God-Man, Jesus Christ, Who would embody this union between Creator and Creation. Christ is the goal and meaning of creation, and that goal is a Covenant union of God and Man. Creation thus reflects God's power and His *positive* will and contains the indelible character of God's Yes of blessing to Creation since He has willed Creation to be the theatre where this drama of reconciliation takes place.

It is important to note, then, that it is within this positive, affirmative context that Barth addresses the question of Evil in his dogmatic chapter on "Nothingness" from which Updike chooses his citations. Barth's idea of *das Nichtige*, translated sometimes as the *Nihil* or, here, as Nothingness, is the logical consequence—the subordinate beam or joist, as it were—of his Christocentric theology of Creation. Creation reflects God's positive will, His Yes of blessing; the power of Evil is only indirectly derived from this positive power. Since only Creation, positively willed by God, is "something," Evil, strictly speaking, is "nothingness."

Barth has to resort to paradoxical language in describing Nothingness. Descriptions like "unreal," "an impossible possibility," "an ontological impossible" are awkward and often confusing, but Barth never denies that Evil has an ontic existence or actuality. What he is stressing is that Evil, by not being part of God's positively willed creation, exists only relatively. Its No exists only by reason of the exclusion that the power of God's Yes entails, the way a shadow exists only by reason of light. Without the light there would be no shadow; the shadow cannot exist by itself and yet the shadow now *is* and can still produce *actual* effects since it can plunge other "things" into darkness, separating them from light. Finally, since Evil is negative (i.e. *is* no-thing in itself) and so fundamentally irrational, its origin and existence cannot be explained, for, as Barth says, "it would not be evil if it could be explained."[44] Rather, Nothingness can only be treated intelligently through fantasy, art, poetry, or, as in Barth's own example, in music like Mozart's where the negativity that is Nothingness is contrasted with and absorbed by the positive creative act and not *vice versa*.[45] Nothingness is by no means a personal being or a positive power for Barth, some "thing" that pre-exists the world's creation—all those properties traditionally associated with Satan; at best "Satan" can become, in Updike's phrase, "a myth to teach us virtue." Updike apparently shares this perspective; consequently, we do not find thoroughly Satanic figures in his fiction—like Apollyon in Bunyan. Instead, we confront the more impersonal forces of Nothingness as they intermingle with and obscure human creation.

This brief excursion into the high ground or ethereal realm of Barth's theology is, I believe, a necessity for any reader who desires to probe Updike's fictional vision. The heights, as well as the language, are admittedly often rarefied; but, like meandering through the muddle of Mme Blavatsky to appreciate Yeats or confronting the opacity of Swedenborg to appreciate Blake, a plunge into the cold water of Barth's theology freshens and deepens one's understanding of Updike. More importantly, it is the Barthian vision of Creation that clarifies and corrects certain misreadings of Updike that critics are heir to. The examples of such misreadings are many, but here I shall cite merely two major ones.

1) One representative criticism is well expressed by Wilfred Sheed in his review of *Couples*.

> Updike is not a humanist. Man is too small to fuss over inordinately
> . . . the only question that counts is whether God exists and whether
> His intentions are friendly—for us and for our brothers, the rocks.
> . . . Existence is tragedy enough for a Calvinistic temperament like his
> own; and nothing that happens to anyone in particular can add very
> much to that.[46]

It is true that Barth is in the theological tradition of Calvin—as was John Bunyan—but his divergence from the pivotal tenet of Calvin, i.e. predestination, reshapes in a drastic way Calvin's rather dour vision.

In Calvin's doctrine of predestination the fact that God "elects" some individuals for salvation implies that others are not so elected, thus leading to the gloomy speculations about God's intentions that Sheed refers to. But Barth, as a consequence of the theological logic that we have seen, completely upends Calvin's idea of election-predestination. For Barth, Christ, the God-Man, is the key to any theology of election, and a positive key at that. Subjective concerns about one's salvation such as Bunyan's Christian exemplifies are, in a sense, out of order for a true Barthian; only by concentrating on the objective revelation about Jesus Christ do we find God's intentions. These intentions are revealed and not hidden as a Calvinist would claim. What is revealed? That God from eternity had predestined *Himself* to unite with Man in the God-Man. The Electing God is not separated from Man or hidden, for the Electing God becomes the Elected Man in Jesus. This election is unique in Jesus Christ; but all men and all creation are elected *in* Him, for He has taken upon Himself any reprobation for sin and evil. Since the Cross, reality *is* grace; one's act of faith is precisely one's acknowledgment of God's election of man in Christ, the acceptance of reality as it is really revealed.[47]

Even those, and there are many, who find Barth's theology of election insupportable must concede its ultimate optimism and very positive view of man and the world. That Updike, an acknowledged Barthian, finds Barth so compatible is a significant determinant in grasping Updike's repeated reassurances that "everything is infinitely fine and any opinion is coarser than reality," that he "loves his characters," and that his books have "happy endings."[48] On the other hand, of course, Updike will remain suspicious of any "easy humanism" and, as artist, will dramatize the darker aspects of humanity that, of itself, is not necessarily contrary to an ultimately positive vision.

In the concluding paragraph to that introductory essay to *Soundings in Satanism*, Updike makes clear his basically positive sentiments despite those "absences" that indicate the power of Nothingness.

> . . . I call myself Christian by defining a Christian as "a person willing to profess the Apostles' Creed. . . ." I know no other combination of words that gives such life, that so seeks the *crux*. The Creed asks us not to believe in Satan but only in the Hell to which Christ descends. That Hell, in the sense at least of a profound and desolating absence, exists I do not doubt; the newspapers give its daily bulletins. And my sense of things, sentimental I fear, is that wherever a church spire is raised . . . this Hell is opposed by a rumor of good news, by an irrational confirmation of the plenitude we feel is our birthright. The instinct that life is good is where natural theology begins. (p. 91)

2) Barth's idea of Nothingness is a drastic departure from the philosophic analyses of Nothingness offered by such Existentialists as Sartre or the early Heidegger. For Barth, Nothingness is not simply a consequence of creaturely contingency and finitude. Rather, God created the world *good;* thus the inevitable *creaturely imperfections* (since only God is perfect), although they manifest what Barth calls the "shadow side of creation," should never be identified with Nothingness. Creaturely imperfections or the shadow side of creation are willed by God for His service and can be evidence of His Yes of blessing; but Nothingness, on the other hand, is that which is excluded by God's No, a Nothingness totally alien to the work of creation, shadow side included.

According to Barth, to confuse these two (the imperfections of creation and Nothingness) is man's great error and is, in fact, an example of the triumph of Nothingness. Such a confusion, says Barth, is not only a slander on creation and an erroneous indictment of the Creator but also leads to a subtle concealment of the *real* Evil that is Nothingness as it becomes incorporated into one's philosophic outlook or is justified as an essential or even salutary aspect of creation.[49] Nature might *seem* evil to us but it *is* not in itself, for nature always embodies God's gift of creative grace. Nothingness is the negation of grace, the antithesis to the Creator and creation. Only God and His creatures properly *are*; nothingness *is* not.

An understanding of this pivotal element in Barth's theology, i.e. the strong possibility of confusing Nature with Nothingness and its inevitable consequences, is almost essential in order to grasp *the* thematic debate that arises continually throughout Updike's fiction. There that "possibility" or temptation becomes actual. Even in that introductory essay we are considering, we see Updike's instincts *as artist*, i.e. as one who describes the human condition as it both *seems* and *is*, challenge the presumptions, albeit affirmative, of Barth insofar as we humans *experience* reality.

> Barth's formulas fit: man is a battlefield, and Satan is best "behind" one. But what of creation in general? Does a black-and-white *opus proprium* [God's Yes] and *opus alienum* [God's No] really satisfy our perception of the universe as a curious explosion, a chaos wherein mathematical balances achieve momentary islands of calm? Man as organism is beset not by "Nothingness" but by predators and parasites themselves obeying the Creator's command to survive and propagate . . . Nature—Nature, whom we love more than our own bodies, from whose face we have extracted a thousand metaphors and affectionate messages—cares nothing for us. Is this the Satanic nothingness? In fact, it has been taken as such; the Christian West, with its myth of the devil, has taken the fight to Nature with a vengeance, has . . . invented the machines that now threaten to scrape Nature into the infernal abyss. . . . Yet we wonder, as now our human species like some giant brand of bacteria fills every vacuum and recreates chaos artificially, if this was intended. Or if the essence of our creaturehood is cooperation, even with the devil. (p. 90)

Karl Barth enjoins us not to enter upon such speculations; of course, these are precisely the "confused" questions that are the stuff of Updike's fiction.

D. THE POORHOUSE FAIR AND RABBIT, RUN

The characters in Updike's novels are decidedly un-Bunyanesque in that they rarely travel any distances—with the exception of Henry Bech and Ellellou and, briefly, of Rabbit in *Rabbit, Run*. For the most part theirs is a more constricted universe and their pilgrimages are *interior* journeys, quests to discover a gracious *something* in a world apparently bounded by Nothingness. And yet, although their travel is an interior one, their pilgrimages will be punctuated in the fashion of Bunyan by significant moments of dialogic exchange and will sometimes be assisted by the directives of Evangelists along the way. However, unlike the resolution or final "conversion" that a Bunyan pilgrim might seek and find, Updike's pilgrimages will be dialectical in character and ambiguous concerning any "resolution." Updike's pilgrims set out upon what Joseph Waldmeir describes well as a "questing non-quest," and this structural movement is part and parcel of Updike's artistic technique. By "questing non-quest," Waldmeir means that Updike's fictional mode of inquiry, which becomes each novel's structural motif, is a dialectical probing, an intellectual examination of opposing problems and solutions.[50] In a sense, then, character, theme, and technique are all ever on pilgrimage in Updike; this necessarily results in ambiguity and ambivalent conflict because the process of affirmation/negation, something/nothing, question/answer/ further question are intrinsic to it.

For example, in Updike's first novel, *The Poorhouse Fair* of 1959, several themes concerning good and evil are explored, especially those of a politico-social cast (secular humanism vs. transcendent hopes; Utopian faith vs. traditional Christian beliefs; progressive socialism vs. reverence for America's past), but fundamental to these is that *ontological* question about Something and Nothingness. A confirmation for this assertion is found in Updike's own excellent introduction to the new 1977 edition of *The Poorhouse Fair*. There Updike acknowledges his debt to H. G. Wells, George Orwell, and Henry Green in its inspiration and composition, but he offers this important addendum.

> There is, then, a philosophical ambition here; an attempt, no less, to present the meaning of being alive, as conveyed by its sensations. Our eager innate life, rebounding from the exterior world, affirms itself, and the quality of the affirmation is taken to be extrinsic, immanent, divine. I needed God to exist. . . . Like a Thomist proof the novel moves from proposition to objections to counter-objections. The dis-

tinction between essence and being (*essentia* and *ens*) I took from St. Thomas; with his help I sought to consecrate, to baptize into American religiosity, these three very atheistic Englishmen, Wells, Orwell, and Henry Green.[51]

Updike's intentions, as expressed here, are manifest throughout the novel. Several commentators have offered fine explications of the novel's imagery and themes,[52] but none has given sufficient attention to the fact that the crucial series of debates between the secularistic prefect Conner and the 94-year-old Christian believer, Hook, essentially hover about an ontological question. (pp. 67-81)[53] As Updike indicated, these debates take on a Thomistic (and one might add Barthian) mode of argument and are dialectical in structure.

Conner the secularist recognizes evil only in its human manifestation as pain, and so he despises Creation itself. In his concentration on the shadow side of creation and the emptiness of Chaos, Conner fails to comprehend the ontological implications of his own thinking. However, in the following exchange Hook, who begins his defense with a combination of the Thomistic First Cause argument and Kant's moral argument for God's existence, comes to realize the more *positive* implications of the argument, namely that the light must precede the shadow.

> "Now, what makes you think God exists?" As soon as he pronounced the ominous hollow noun, Conner knew absolutely he could drive the argument down to the core of shame that lay heavily in any believer's heart.
>
> "Why, there are several sorts of evidence," Hook said . . . "there is what of Cre-ation I can see, and there are the inner spokesmen."
>
> "Creation. Look at the smoke of your cigar: twisting, expanding, fading. That's the shape of Creation. You've seen, in the newspapers you've just said you've read, photographs of nebulae: smears of smoke billions of miles wide. What do you make of their creation?"
>
> "I know little of astronomy. Now a flower's creation—"
>
> "Is also an accident."
>
> "An ac-cident?" Hook smiled softly. . . .
>
> "Lightning struck certain acids present on the raw earth. Eventually, the protein molecule occurred, and in another half-billion years the virus and from then on its evolution. Imagine a giant tossing rocks through eternity. At some point, he would build a cathedral."
>
> "It seems implaus-ible."
>
> "Its mathematics. The amount of time it takes is the factor that seems implausible. But the universe has endless time. . . ."

"I don't quite see how any amount of time can generate some things from nothing."

"Presumably there always was something. Though relatively, very little. The chief characteristic of the universe, I would say, is emptiness. There is infinitely more nothing in the universe than anything else."

"Indeed, you propose to extinguish religion by measuring quantities of nothing. Now why should no matter how much nothing be imposing, when my little fingernail, by being something, is of more account?"

"The truth is, Mr. Hook, that if the universe was made, it was made by an idiot, and an idiot crueler than Nero. There are no laws. Atoms and animals alike do only what they can't help doing. Natural history is a study of horrible things. You say you read the papers; but have you ever walked around the skeleton of a brontosaurus? Or watched microbes in a drop of water gobble each other up?"

"No, but I have seen a lobster being cooked."

"These are our Fathers, Mr. Hook. Monsters. We are mostly monsters. People speak of loving life. Life is a maniac in a closed room."

"Now it has never been claimed," Hook said, "that the Creator's mind is a book open for all to read." (pp. 79-81)

At the close of their debate, Hook's final assessment ("There is no goodness, without belief. There is nothing but busy-ness.") brings goodness to an ontological plane where its opposite is not immorality but Nothingness. "Belief" here is not to be identified with a religious faith in the strict sense, but with a more fundamental faith in Creation itself on which other "beliefs" are founded. Updike has noted in his work "a recurrence of the concept of blessing, of approval, of forgiveness,"[54] and this novel ends with Hook's desire to communicate a Yes of blessing to Conner as a testament (in the Biblical sense of a covenant-bond) between them.

[Hook] stood motionless, half in moonlight, groping after the fitful shadow of the advice he must impart to Conner, as a bond between them and a testament to endure his dying in the world. What was it? (p. 127)

The admixed imagery of light and shadow suggests well Hook's human condition; because he experiences *both* the shadow side of dying creation and its Yes of blessing, his ambiguous condition leaves him finally tongue-tied. And yet, that question "What was it?" reflects his perception that all such "testaments" begin with the realization that *something was*.

Perhaps the "it" for which Hook was groping had already been expressed by the blind old woman Elizabeth Heinemann in her description of the Heaven she anticipated. Elizabeth said:

"The things you see, are to me composed of how they feel when I touch them, and the sounds they make, for everything has a sound, even silent things; when I draw near an object it says 'yes' before I touch it, and walking down a corridor the walls say 'yes, yes' and I know where they are and I walk between them. They lead me, truly. At first, when this sense began to grow, I was afraid to have these voices come into my darkness; that is before I had forgotten what darkness was, when I still remembered the light. You see, I could hear the walls talking, but I didn't understand that they said, 'Don't be afraid, Elizabeth; I'm here, yes,' like Mr. Conner speaking a moment ago. I believe . . . we live in a house with a few windows, and when we die we move into the open air, and Heaven will be, how can I say, a *mist* of all the joy sensations have given us. (p. 69)

The *Poorhouse Fair*, like most Updike novels, is basically static in dramatic movement. One exception is *Rabbit, Run*, which, only by comparison, is truly Bunyanesque. In fact, Bunyan's description of Christian's tale is not an inexact summary of *Rabbit, Run*.

This Book it chalketh out before thine eyes
The man that seeks the everlasting Prize.
It shews you whence he comes, whither he goes,
What he leaves undone; also what he does:
It also shews you how he runs and runs. . . .[55]

Like *The Pilgrim's Progress*, *Rabbit, Run* is replete with allegorical names and places. Rabbit's first name is that of a harried Harry; his last name Angstrom (a stream of anxiety in German) describes his plight. He is trapped like a rabbit by his marriage to a Springer; his boyhood mentor was Tothero, who is now, effectively, a *Tod* or dead hero; he briefly revives by meeting a sad and sorrowful Ruth, who lives on Summer St. in a house where the Pellegrinis (pilgrims) live; upon leaving her, he becomes Ruthless and eventually Mr. Death, being indirectly responsible for his daughter's death. On his opening "pilgrimage" he flees the shadows of Mt. Judge, which he sees as part of a City of Destruction, and travels—literally at first and then symbolically—through towns like Bird-in-Hand, Intercourse, Paradise, New Providence, Mechanics Grove, Unicorn in search of a mandala-like Sun of the south, only to realize that he is traveling in a circle and is, in fact, returning. All his subsequent pilgrimages will be similarly circular, questing non-quests.

Ironically though, despite these Bunyanesque motifs, most critical interpretations of this novel have been almost entirely dependent on the critical assessment of Rabbit's *character*. Such assessment, in turn, is often determined by the individual critic's emphasis on one aspect of the novel's epigraph taken from Pascal: "the motions of grace, the hardness of heart, external circumstances." The first phrase, "motions of grace," elicits assessments that are often pious in sentiment or that depict Rabbit as a "saintly figure" whose obvious irresponsibility is transposed into more positive Existential language. The result is that Rabbit becomes a Camus-like Rebel-Hero who must spurn the claustrophobic pressures of society in order to pursue "motions of grace" from *within* that compel him toward some higher ideal.[56]

The "scoundrel" reading of Rabbit's character will, instead, emphasize his "hardness of heart." Rabbit is one who is oblivious of the sacral dimensions of the world; hardly a saint, he is seen as an anti-hero as well.[57] Others choose to emphasize the "external circumstances" and read the novel as a social satire or, in Richard Gilman's phrase, "a grotesque allegory of American life with its myth of happiness and success."[58]

Each of these readings is no doubt legitimate and each highlights important considerations suggested by this complex novel. My quarrel is not with such laudable efforts, which have enlightened us all. Rather, my contention is that we might well return to Updike's own contention, quoted earlier, that each of his novels engages a moral debate about goodness and that a Barthian understanding of Pascal's epigraph can connect all *three* phrases in a thematic unity. For example, when the phrase "external circumstances" is understood in Barthian terms, the point at issue becomes an ontological one and not merely societal. Ontological in the sense that Something vs. Nothingness is at issue; "motions of grace" and "hardness of heart"—like subordinate beams and joists—reflect differing perspectives or responses to these radical issues.

My contention rests upon the significant, though brief, appearance of the Lutheran minister Fritz Kruppenbach in almost the exact middle of the novel. Like Evangelist in *The Pilgrim's Progress*, it is Kruppenbach who offers thematic direction and delineates the issues of the novel's ongoing debate. Kruppenbach's appearance is unusual in that he is the only character whom Rabbit does not encounter directly in the novel; he appears, instead, from off stage as it were, entering like a Greek chorus to add clarifying comment upon the dramatic proceedings, thus embodying that "main beam" of the Apostles' Creed that supports all else.

For some time I have been surprised to find that most critics of *Rabbit, Run* have either ignored the figure of Kruppenbach or dismissed him as something of a buffoon, perhaps because of the etymology of his name. In a personal reply to my inquiries about him, Updike confirmed my suspicions about his Barthian character and significance by stating that he is "the touchstone of the novel as I intended it. His life, including the motorcycles, is meant to be Barth in action."[59]

The setting for Kruppenbach's appearance is important. Eccles, the liberal Episcopalian minister—a figure who is a bit like Pliable or Worldly-Wisdom in Bunyan or, as his name implies, like Ecclesiasticus (The Book of Sirach), the author of conventional non-Christian wisdom—reluctantly visits Kruppenbach, Rabbit's nominal pastor, to explain the situation of Rabbit's separation. A true Barthian, well aware of the inroads the shadow side of Creation can make, Kruppenbach's lawn is "graded in fussy terraces, has the unnatural chartreuse evenness that comes with much fertilizing, much weed-killing, and much mowing." (p. 140) Eccles discovers Kruppenbach, as usual, mowing, and he dreads this encounter. "Of all the ministers in town, he likes Kruppenbach least. The man is rigid in his creed and a bully in manner.   . Yet Kruppenbach's son must not have found it so: witness the motorcycle." (p. 141)

Eccles' fears are justified because, as soon as he tries to offer a psychological interpretation of Rabbit's difficulties, he is interrupted by an Evangelical harangue. Kruppenbach's criticism of Eccles is effectively a criticism of Rabbit as well since he and Rabbit are often depicted as pilgrim counterparts even during their golf games where it seems "as if they are together engaged in an impossible, startling, bottomless quest set by a benevolent but absurd lord." (p. 140) Kruppenbach's harangue is not a sermon in the strict sense but, like Barth, his every talk inevitably becomes sermon-like. In fact, his words here are a paraphrase of one section from Barth's own sermon-like talk entitled "The Task of the Ministry," which appears in the collection that Updike himself has recommended as "quite the best introduction to Barth's work."[60]

Kruppenbach reminds Eccles of the true "task of the ministry" they share; any other task is the "Devil's," "nothing," or "busyness" (echoing Hook's pronouncement in *The Poorhouse Fair*). Kruppenbach's perspective is evident:

. . . What do you think it looks like to God, one childish husband leaving one childish wife? Do you ever think anymore of what God sees? . . .

It seems to you our role is to be cops, cops without handcuffs, without anything but our human good nature. . . . Well, I say that's a Devil's idea. . . . If Gott wants to end misery He'll declare the Kingdom now. . . . I say you don't know what your role is or you'd be home locked in prayer. *There* is your role: to make yourself an example of faith. . . . In running back and forth you run from the duty given you by God, to make your faith powerful, so when the call comes you can go out and tell them, "Yes, he is dead, but you will see him again in Heaven. Yes, you suffer, but you must *love* your pain, since it is *Christ's* pain." When on Sunday morning then, we must walk up not worn out with misery but full of Christ, *hot* with Christ, on *fire*: burn them with the force of our belief. . . . There is nothing but Christ for us. All the rest, all the decency and busyness, is nothing. It is the Devil's work. (p. 143)

At first glance Kruppenbach's fiery exhortation seems rooted in certain dualistic excesses often attributed to Barth. For Kruppenbach it appears that there is a cosmic opposition: the gracious concerns of God the Wholly Other vs. man's puny ineffectual efforts; the only bridge between them is established by man's humble submission in faith. But, as we have seen in our exposition of Barth, Kruppenbach's emphasis on Christ ("hot with Christ," "There is nothing but Christ for us") is not a gloomy pietism derogating humanity but is rooted in a positive vision of the world. Just as man is elected in the Man Jesus, so too the reprobation that man deserves falls on Jesus. This, for Kruppenbach-Barth, is *the* meaning of the Cross in that Christ has borne condemnation for us all; on the Cross Christ encountered the powers of Nothingness and overcame them. Consequently, Kruppenbach enjoins our concentration on Christ since "all the rest" is "nothing," "the Devil's work," and actually draws our attention away from the positive meaning of Christ and Creation.

The significance of Kruppenbach's perspective is demonstrated by contrast with Eccles' own sermon later in the novel. Where Kruppenbach stressed "burning with the force of belief" (ironically, Rabbit admires only people with "force"), Eccles' words lack precisely such force; and so Rabbit "scarcely listens to the sermon at all," a sermon that is so impersonal that, pointedly, it is recounted in the third person.

It concerns the forty days in the Wilderness and Christ's conversation with the Devil. Does this story have any relevance to *us*, here and now? In the Twentieth Century, in the United States of America. Yes. There exists a sense in which *all* Christians must have conversations with the Devil, must learn his ways, must hear his voice. . . . Its larger significance, its greater meaning, Eccles takes to be this: suffering, deprivation, barrenness, hardship, lack are all an indispensable part of education; the initiation, as it were, of any of those who would follow Christ. (p. 197)

It is ironic but not unsurprising that, despite his liberal humanism, Eccles' sermon should be so *negative* in viewpoint; the truth, we are told, is that "he doesn't believe anything." (p. 130) His encouragement of conversations with the Devil lacks force because it lacks the positive substratum of Kruppenbach's perspective. In such a context Rabbit's reaction to Eccles' sermon is noteworthy:

In his robes [Eccles] seems the sinister priest of a drab mystery. Harry has no taste for the dark, tangled visceral aspect of Christianity, the *going through* quality of it, the passage *into* death and suffering that redeems and inverts these things, like an umbrella blowing inside out. He lacks the mindful will to walk the straight line of paradox. His eyes turn toward the light however it glances into his retina. (p. 197)

Critics who cite this passage generally see it as a description of Rabbit's religious pusillanimity, and this is true to some extent. However, Rabbit's perception of Eccles' Christianity as a "drab mystery" and his contrasting instinct to "turn toward the light" suggest more: that his conflicting instincts here make *him* the focal point of the novel's debate about Something vs. Nothingness; light vs. drabness; Kruppenbach vs. Eccles.

Rabbit's pilgrimage is unlike that of Bunyan's Christian who flees *this* world of sin in quest for a sinless city elsewhere; Rabbit's quest must take place *within* the world of Creation. Christian's pilgrimage is a forward movement; Rabbit's is backward or, better, circular. Christian seeks goodness and desires freedom from sin; Rabbit cannot define goodness in the first place nor can he adequately realize his sinfulness. It is Barth's definitions of sin that characterize Rabbit's peculiar problem as pilgrim: Sin is "the self-surrender of the creature to Nothingness," "the irruption of chaos into the sphere of creation"; "sin is that which is absurd, man's choice and decision for that which is not."[61]

Barth has also described well the strange power of Nothingness, a power whose strength is rooted in falsehood and is dependent upon its ability to *mimic* the good, thereby intertwining with it. Barth's description of these "powers" effectively summarizes the major themes of the novel and the dramatic ambivalence of Rabbit's character.

> Where are the powers of Nothingness? They are there in the depths of the soul. They are there in the relationships between man and man, and especially between man and woman. . . . They are there in that in which man seeks his satisfaction or which he would rather avoid as undesirable, in his care and carelessness, in the flaming up and extinguishing of passion, in his sloth and his zeal, in his systemization and anarchy. . . . in, with, and under all these things there is constantly played out the mimicry of nothingness—the play of that which is absolutely useless and worthless, yet pretends to be vitally necessary and of supreme worth.[62]

Just as the opposite of goodness is Nothingness, so too the opposite of a good man is a Nothing-man. The Nothing-man is one who is fascinated with Nothingness or who confuses creation with Nothingness or who mimics and thus distorts goodness: Rabbit Angstrom.

Rabbit, of course, is not a totally Nothing-man. Again and again throughout the novel he asserts that he is searching for "something"—for example, saying to an uncomprehending Eccles that "somewhere behind all this . . . there's something that wants me to find it." (p. 107) Furthermore, most of Rabbit's actions are propelled by his very dread of Nothingness. In Barth's theology such dread can transcend the Existential or psychological version of dread that humankind is heir to; for Barth, dread of Nothingness can, in fact, be a "motion of grace" as Pascal's epigraph puts it. Existential dread is "mere" dread, an act that takes place *within* man himself; "engraced" dread is God's action, not man's, and can overcome mere dread because it arrives as the *positive* realization of *something* missing that is now offered—a positive component present that is absent from mere dread.[63]

Unfortunately, though, Rabbit finds himself plunged into a world of Nothingness; he dreads it but it is the only "thing" he knows. As Fred Standley has observed, "Rabbit has no focal point—no clearly conceived object outside of himself with which he can affirm the reality of his own existence either in affinity for or in rebellion from. . . ."[64] Consequently, Rabbit must say No, at least implicitly, to everyone and everything; caught in Barthian chaos, he cannot say Yes. When others ask where he is going, his answer is generally "nowhere." (pp. 26-27, 86) "Goodness" for him will be associated inextricably with doing "nothing." Late in the novel, at the grave scene, he will feel exculpated because he did not *do* anything regarding his baby's death. When others are shocked at his reaction, he is surprised and flees, running nowhere in particular.

As he runs and meets dead-ends, he eventually returns to Ruth. It is noteworthy that their brief conversation is characterized almost entirely by negatives and denials. Its tone is captured well by Ruth's assessment of him: "You're Mr. Death himself. You're just not nothing, you're worse than nothing. You're not a rat, you don't stink. You're not enough to stink" and "No, you don't do anything. You just wander around with the kiss of death" and "Maybe once you could play basketball but you can't do *any*thing now. What the hell do you think the world is?" (pp. 251-52)

Rabbit's ironically honest answer to that last question is: "All I know is what feels right. You feel right to me. Sometimes Janice used to. Sometimes nothing does." Earlier, Rabbit had been attracted to Ruth, who experienced sex as a "falling through to . . . nowhere," (p. 73) precisely because of "Ruth's delicious nothing, the nothing she told him she did," (p. 83) for, as he muses, "in all the green world nothing feels as good as a woman's good nature." (p. 79) Significantly enough, after he leaves her, he is only buoyed up by the hope that she will not abort their child, that "something" will perdure.

We cited above Barth's description of the "power" of Nothingness in terms of its effects. The two major fascinations of Rabbit—basketball and sex—are always intermixed in his mind with the imagery of Nothingness, emptiness, darkness, holes, and the like. Even his positive instincts reflect the grip of the powers of Nothingness.

At the end of the novel, as he runs he suddenly meets a fork in the goal-less pilgrim's road he has begun, a fork created by his memory of his son Nelson, the only "something" to which he can cling. But, as he foresees the probable end of the two roads off that fork, his imagination is gripped by images of Nothingness.

> Nelson remains: here is the hardness he must carry with him. On this small fulcrum he tries to balance the rest, weighing opposites against each other: Janice and Ruth, Eccles and his mother, the right way and the good way. . . . He tries to picture how it will end, with an empty baseball field, a dark factory, and then over a brook into a dirt road, he doesn't know. He pictures a huge vacant field of cinders and his heart goes hollow. (p. 254)

Hence, even memory of Nelson is not enough; he feels betrayed by the outside world, for he has found no "goodness" there. The book ends with Rabbit beginning a new pilgrimage; defeated without, he will seek "goodness" within. Once again, however, prospects for this pilgrimage issue in images of Nothingness.

> Goodness lies inside, there is nothing outside, those things he was trying to balance have no weight. He feels his inside as very real suddenly, a pure blank space in the middle of a dense net. . . . It's like when they heard you were great and put two men on you and no matter which way you turned you bumped into one of them and the only thing to do was pass. So you passed and the ball belonged to the others and your hands were empty and the men on you looked foolish because in effect there was nobody there. (p. 255)

By dramatizing Rabbit's confusion at the novel's end, Updike invites us, his readers, to engage in this moral debate about goodness and its opposite. Rabbit's pilgrimage continues and, in fact, becomes ours as well.

2: *The Centaur*

In 1964 Updike won the prestigious National Book Award for his third novel, *The Centaur*. In his acceptance speech, later entitled "Accuracy," he said this:

> Fiction is a tissue of literal lies that refreshes and informs our sense of actuality. Reality is—chemically, atomically, biologically—a fabric of microscopic accuracies. Language approximates phenomena through a series of hesitations and qualifications; I miss, in much contemporary writing, this sense of self-qualification, the kind of timid reverence toward what exists that Cézanne shows when he grapples for the shape and shade of a fruit through a mist of delicate stabs. The intensity of the grapple is the surest pleasure a writer receives. Though our first and final impression of Creation is not that it was achieved by taking pains, perhaps we should proceed in the humble faith that, by taking pains, word by word, to be accurate, we put ourselves on the way toward making something useful and beautiful and, in a word, good. [1]

Updike has called *The Centaur* "my gayest and truest book." It is also his finest to date; one might say it is something useful, beautiful, and very good. In his acceptance speech Updike uses the language of Thomas Aquinas' "transcendentals" to describe the ideal of a work of art. For Aquinas, the transcendentals (so called, because they were categories that went beyond Aristotle) were held to be those properties that were common to all existing things, including God Himself. Aquinas listed six such properties that made up the Great Chain of Being: *res* (reality), *ens* (being), *verum* (truth), *bonum* (goodness), *pulchrum* (specific beauty), and *unum* (unity or identity). For Aquinas, since such properties are common both to God and other existents, the transcendentals could be a means for an analogical knowledge of God. Later, Kant's distinction between the noumenal and phenomenal realms made the word "transcendental" descriptive of the noumenal, the *Ding-an-sich* or Thing-in-itself, that cannot be perceived or explored by human cognitive faculties. It is appropriate that Updike's acceptance speech should evoke the transcendentals, understood in both their Thomistic and Kantian senses, since *The Centaur* evokes a dramatic confrontation between these two opposite understandings of what the word "transcendental" means.

In a sense *The Centaur* is a bridge novel in Updike's *corpus* and contains thematic material, dramatic dilemmas, and familiar characters found in the earlier novels and stories, and yet it points forward, not only more obviously to *Of the Farm* which follows it, but to the adult tensions and themes developed in the later work. Furthermore, as his address suggests, it manifests the fruit of taking pains, of being accurate, and reveals a stylistic sureness on Updike's part less evident in his previous work. In *The Centaur* he experiments with another mode of narrative or, better, other modes. The familiar realistic story-telling proper to the Olinger stories is present, but conjoined with it is a mythological focus wherein the Olinger events are seen from an Olympian perspective and the characters, ostensibly ordinary, take on the god-like qualities of Olympians. In addition, this paralleling of realism with myth at times takes on a double-focus, a simultaneity of the two perspectives that is itself a fine stylistic achievement.

Simultaneity and double-focus in theme and structure are the key to the novel. Nothing in it is just one thing: each event, each personality, each image or symbol takes on multiple referents. What the philosophers call the "coincidence of opposites" is ever at work here.

As a consequence, *The Centaur*, more explicitly than the preceding fiction, is able to unite the three secret things, Sex, Religion, and Art. For example, one of its controlling images, the tree, will subtly be identified with each of the secrets: the fixity of Art (p. 62), the stirrings of Sexuality (p. 118), the Passion of Christ (p. 217).[2] So too will other images and symbols in varying degrees: clocks, staircases, celestial cities and the underworld, downhill and uphill roads, and so on.

This novel is so rich and complex that it admits of many critical entries. Robert Detweiler concentrates on the novel's shape and patterned structure, a structure he feels can only be appreciated by an analogy with painting. "The intention and the effect of the double narrative in *The Centaur* are to expand literal reality through distortion—as in Surrealism (with its accompanying psychological modes)—and through the simultaneous projection of many facets of a personality or action, as in Cubism."[3] Detweiler finds the techniques of Surrealism operative especially in the dream sequences, in the novel's absence of logical sequentiality, and in the recurring device of the intermingling of animal, mechanical, and human qualities (e.g. in the merger of Caldwell's person and body with his Buick car throughout). The Cubist influence he discovers in the "use of simultaneous perspective, in the strategy of 'situating' the story between fact and fiction, in the dependence upon camouflage and counterfeit, and in the collage technique."[4] Since the Cubist focus is that of simultaneous perspectives, Detweiler defends what some readers find perplexing in the novel, namely: from whose point of view is the story being told? Most critics presume that it is Peter's point of view that prevails, that it is *his* story alone. But Detweiler argues that, since its formal structure is analogous to Cubism, *The Centaur* admits of no one formal point of view. Instead, the reader is impelled himself to grasp the *Gestalt* of the novel in its totality of complex and multi-referential relationships whereby individual scenes, particular memories, seen *a distans*, stand revealed not as separate aspects but as interrelated facets of one, all-embracing configuration.

Closer to Detweiler's analogical approach is that offered by Larry Taylor, who sees the novel as a "pastoral elegy" in the tradition of Milton's *Lycidas*.[5] Taylor proposes that, just as Milton transformed the scholar Edward King into the simple shepherd Lycidas in order to aggrandize him, *The Centaur* elevates the teacher Caldwell into the Centaur Chiron, making him into a sacrificial "hero." By drawing upon the resources of this pastoral tradition, Updike is able to unite the earthly with the heroic and celestial, to catalogue commonplace flowers, herbs, trees with an epic paean.

Suzanne Uphaus' argument is exactly opposite to Taylor's.[6] She takes the novel to be a mock-epic, i.e. one based on the fundamental disjunction between heroic allusions and the mundane. This mode, she feels, reflects Peter's adult sense of realism and his loss of faith in any "classical" beliefs. The effect is de-mythologization and the death of all heroic vision whether Classical or Christian. Perhaps Taylor and Uphaus are both correct—contradictory though that might seem—since this novel is many things.

Joyce Markle and the Hamiltons stress thematic considerations, especially that of Caldwell's altruism and sacrifice.[7] However, by doing so, both critics give scant attention to the mythological elements so significant in the novel. In fact, the Hamiltons go so far as to call *The Centaur* "basically another Olinger story" where the mythological sequences "serve chiefly to give us insight into Updike's belief that the truth about any landscape does not lie on the surface but is found when observation deepens into vision."[8]

Since I feel that *The Centaur* is even more complex, not only in structure but also in theme, than even these perceptive critics have granted, my analysis will be divided into four sections in the hope that that complexity and subtlety might be more manifest.

A. VACILLATION: THE THREE SECRET THINGS

Although there is a contention we have noted among critics as to whether Peter Caldwell's is the unifying point of view throughout the whole of *The Centaur*, nevertheless it is clear that Peter's is at least one perspective and that his own acknowledged narratives dramatize the tension among the three secret things. Peter, an aspiring and then mature artist, is drawn, on the one hand, to Sex, Sex as both radically natural and as the elusive mystery of Nothingness. (". . . where her legs meet there is nothing. Nothing but silk and a faint dampness and a curve. This then is the secret the world holds at its center, this innocence, this absence. . . ." [p. 246]) On the other hand, he is drawn toward Religion and the sensibility and questioning that his father displays, i.e. to Religion as transcendent to Nature and as elusive supernatural mystery. Peter's admission that, now an adult, he has become a "second-rate abstract expressionist" painter living with a mistress in New York (the paradise of his boyhood) intimates his present resolution of the tension; yet his recollections about his father reinstate his ambivalence about that choice. Consequently, to engage this tension once again, to recollect upon that choice, he must proceed as artist. Art has been his refuge and his support; he will use its techniques— myth, surrealism, expressionism, landscape, pointillist—in order to re-enter that conflict and transform it.

At issue is the mystery of Time itself, as the recurring symbolic references to clocks, seasons, and the sun suggest. Sex, so obviously linked with Nature and its urgencies, is dramatically indicative of the life-cycle and man's temporal finitude. Religion's claim is that Time has been conquered in Christ, that the Eternal is not only possible but present—yet religious men like George Caldwell live in time and must die. For Peter, Art alone seems the bridge of permanence, the fixing of Time, the conquest, though partial, of Nature and past time—but is it?

Here Peter's vacillation is reminiscent of major themes found in the last poems of William Butler Yeats, in the collections *The Winding Stair* (1933) and *Last Poems* (1936-39). One might even call his particular narratives Peter's "The Municipal Gallery Revisited" in that the Olinger populace, like the gallery pictures in Yeats, are the images to be confronted anew by him while, simultaneously in that encounter, they become the work of his imaginative re-making of them into heroic, mythic figures. Memory and imagination merge.

In the poems "Vacillation" and "A Dialogue between Self and Soul," Yeats composes a debate between one aspect of himself, his "soul," which, drawn by the higher promptings of the spirit, desires to ascend the celestial stairs and enter the sacral sphere, and that other aspect, his "self" or "heart," which is still fascinated by the downward vision of Nature and its cycle of death and rebirth. The mystical Christianity offered by Von Hugel is most attractive to Yeats' "soul" and so he "vacillates." Yet, despite nostalgic regrets, the "heart" prevails and Yeats, the artist, chooses the downward descent into Nature, the imaginative source for Homer and all pagan mythology, which is the groundbed for earthly poetic themes.

> I—though heart might find relief
> Did I become a Christian man and choose for my belief
> What seems most welcome in the tomb—play a predestined part.
> Homer is my example and his unchristened heart.
> The lion and the honeycomb, what has Scripture said?
> So get you gone, Von Hugel, though with blessings on your head.[9]

The recurring imagery of ascending and descending stairs, the confusion concerning clocks, his ambivalent attraction and repugnance toward his father and what he represents, symbolize Peter's similar vacillation. His vacillation reaches its Yeatsian climax in the final paragraph of Peter's narrative in his last boyhood recollection in Chapter 8. The description of the landscape is almost an exact repetition of that found at the opening of Peter's first narrative in Chapter 2 (p. 48), thereby suggesting a cyclical movement to Peter's perspective.

> I turned my face away and looked through the window. In time my father appeared in this window, an erect figure dark against the snow. His posture made no concession to the pull underfoot; upright he waded through our yard and past the mailbox and up the hill until he was lost to my sight behind the trees of our orchard. The trees took white on their sun side. The two telephone wires diagonally cut the

blank blue of the sky. I knew what this scene was—a patch of Pennsylvania in 1947—and yet I did not know, was in my softly fevered state mindlessly soaked in a rectangle of colored light. I burned to paint it, just like that, in its puzzle of glory; it came upon me that I must go to Nature disarmed of perspective and stretch myself like a large transparent canvas upon her in the hope that, my submission being perfect, the imprint of a beautiful and useful truth would be taken.

Then—as if by permitting this inchoate excitement to pass through me I had done an honest piece of work—I went weary and closed my eyes. . . . (p. 293)

The climactic force of this passage is necessarily lost, of course, when it is examined in isolation from the rest of The Centaur. Throughout the novel Caldwell expresses his distaste for Nature, for it "reminds him of death," is just "garbage and confusion and the stink of skunk"—a repugnance that Peter often shares. Here he is glimpsed transcending Nature, "making no concession to the pull underfoot," while Peter imaginatively descends to Nature, desirous of her embrace. The tree image, which earlier is associated with Sexuality and the pagan natural cycle of life and death, here in its connection with Caldwell takes on associations of ascent, of life-giving potential, and, as we shall see, Christological sacrifice. The color white, which before this has been the symbol of death, now is transformed into images of glory, purification, and, anticipating the last chapter, renewal and resurrection. However, Peter himself remains "soaked in a rectangle of colored light."

Young Peter's desire to resolve his own vacillation is converted instead into his artistic desire to merge the sacral, spiritual sphere his father represents with Nature and the temporal, rather than acknowledge their tension. With evident irony, the adult Peter describes this youthful desire in cruciform imagery. He wishes by "stretching" himself to receive an artistic "stigmata" of the scene "in its puzzle of glory." But his desire is frustrated and so he eventually grows weary, proleptically prey to the frustration of being the abstract expressionist and atheist he will be as an adult.

Peter's duplicate role as Prometheus points up the Religion, Art, and Sex "vacillation" that his character embodies. Throughout the classical and post-classical tradition Prometheus himself has been a figure representing multiple roles that are emblematic of the conflicts of Religion, Art, and Sex. In the simplest version of the myth, that found in Aeschylus'

Prometheus Bound, Prometheus is a demi-god who thwarts Zeus' plan to end the human race by stealing fire, concealing it in a stalk of fennel, and giving it to man. This gift of fire represents all the benefits that issue from human self-consciousness: reason, astronomy, divination, metallurgy, in short "every art possessed by man." In Hesiod's *Works and Days* we are told that Zeus, enraged at the theft, counterbalanced this gift of fire by fashioning and then sending the alluring Pandora so that men might embrace their own destruction. Prometheus, anticipating Zeus' revenge, shut up in a casket all the evils that might plague the world, but Pandora, his brother's wife, out of curiosity opened it and misfortune has been man's lot ever since.

However, even without the more evident ills released through the agency of the alluring Pandora, it is obvious that Prometheus' original gift to man is itself an ambiguous one for man. Denis Donoghue's excellent essay in his *Thieves of Fire* addresses well the kind of "Promethean" ambiguity that one finds in those reflections offered by the adult Peter-Prometheus throughout *The Centaur*. Donoghue observes:

> It is proper to say of the Promethean intervention in human history that it was a once-for-all affair, as a result of which we know we can't go home again: the intervention is historical and irrevocable, its chief characteristic is that it cannot be deleted. Theft of the divine fire of knowledge made reflection possible and therefore necessary; it made men self-aware, self-conscious, it made the human race a multitude of reflexive animals. But because the gift of consciousness is stolen, it introduces into consciousness itself, as a mark of guilt, the "unhappy consciousness" which Hegel describes in *The Phenomenology of Spirit*. Consciousness is stolen fruit or stolen fire, in either form the original sin, source of corresponding original guilt. Men take the harm out of it by converting some of its energy to a pious end, the knowledge of God, or in its secular form, the knowledge of Nature. But forgiveness is never complete. One of the consequences of the theft is that man knows his attributes and is guilty in possessing them. . . . But the theft also gave man the power and the habit of self-expression by recourse to symbols; it allowed them to use symbols to mediate between the two kinds of experience lately sundered—nature and man. (pp. 25-26)

Donoghue's remarks on Promethean fire describe well the shifting themes in Peter-Prometheus' narratives: his nostalgia for an irretrievable past, his divided consciousness, his sense of guilt about stolen gifts, his desire to "take the harm out of it" by "converting" his energies to a knowledge of Nature, his recourse to symbols, and finally and more subtly his preoccupation with reconciliation with the "gods." The adult Peter's concern is with the cost of knowledge and self-consciousness, with the prideful nature of the artistic impulse, and he now finds himself in a no man's land "on the boundary between heaven and earth." In his boyhood New York was the "throat of Paradise" but now, because consumed by Promethean fire, it is his private hell instead. For, as a boy, he had made an ironic "conversion" of religious symbols into artistic ones. In one narrative he recounts his anticipation of a visit to a museum as a child, a visit undertaken as a kind of odd parody of a religious pilgrimage and recalled in imagery echoing the stark discovery of the doubting Thomas at the end of John's Gospel.

> The one called the Frick contained the Vermeer of the man in the big hat and the laughing woman whose lazily upturned palm unconsciously accepts the light, and the one called the Metropolitan contained the girl in the starched headdress bent reverently above the silver jug whose vertical blue gleam was the Holy Ghost of my adolescence. That these paintings, which I had worshipped in reproduction, had a simple physical existence seemed a profound mystery to me: to come within touching distance of their surfaces, to see with my eyes the truth of their color, the tracery of the cracks whereby time had inserted itself like a mystery within a mystery, would have been for me to enter a Real Presence so ultimate that I would not be surprised to die in the encounter. (p. 85).

As an adult Peter has apparently completed the "conversion" and is a Promethean abstract expressionist. His childhood passion for Vermeer reasserts itself in his narrative, though, through his attempt to render with delicacy and simplicity the ordinary domestic scenes of his boyhood; and, as in Vermeer, the dominant colors for evoking such scenes will be yellow, blue, and grey. But, significantly, he has chosen that most Promethean of painterly roles, that of the abstract expressionist. Gaston Bachelard's definition of Promethean is most pertinent to *The Centaur*, for he has called Promethean "all those tendencies which drive us to know more than our fathers." Thus the adult Peter's vocation is an apt one, for common to the diversity among abstract expressionists is their spirit of revolt against traditional styles and technical procedures, their emphasis on improvisation and self-determination.

Ironically, though, Peter admits that he is a "second-rate" abstract expressionist, and his narratives betray this truth. Even as an artist, he vacillates. Drawn to the formal problems of space and time as was Vermeer, his contentious impulse as an abstract expressionist testifies to his desire to break the bonds of finitude and deny the limits of space and time and, by doing so, "know more than our fathers." The brilliance of the novel's ultimate structure, however, is meant to remind us that Peter's Promethean task is impossible. Zeus' "laws" are arbitrary and fixed; even Prometheus is enclosed within a grander, more comprehensive myth. In light of that grander myth (that of Chiron) he is a mere actor and somehow even less than that: a Prometheus bound, a victim whose freedom is won only through another's sacrifice, redeemed not by those gifts proper to fire but by the generous gesture of another intermediary between the gods and men who has accepted the design of Zeus' universe. That very "conversion" which this vacillating Prometheus seeks is upended in the novel, and the earlier Religion into Art conversion Peter has made is subtly reversed—as we shall see—by the conversion of Promethean recreative analogies into those of a religious resurrection.

That Peter is not the formal controlling point of view that unites the novel, as Detweiler contends, seems well taken. The adult Peter's narratives are generally acknowledged by him to be inadequate and incomplete; his viewpoint is too partial in perspective. Consequently, even his hesitant, frustrated efforts at recovering memory must become themselves mythicized and incorporated into a larger mythic structure that is the completed novel. In other words, his own "mythic" narratives are subsumed within a more comprehensive mythic structure that, in turn, complements them. It is this comprehensive mythic structure that frees the novel from any of its apparently realistic perspective, from any need for narrative consistency in both spatial and temporal modes, and from the necessity for any exact correspondence between personal memory and Classical mythology. The novel itself vacillates.

Updike has said that "the book as well as the hero is a centaur,"[10] and this is central to its understanding. Like a centaur, it is, to all appearances, disjoined, generated in rapacious and haphazard fashion, and essentially divided in impulse and aspiration. Yet, when its shape is complete, the novel, centaur-like, attempts a dramatic reconciliation of the tensions between the gods and men, between Nature and spirit, between the city of the gods (Olympus) and the city of men (Olinger), between Caldwell-Chiron and Peter, young and old.

It is only after completing it and reflecting on its many diverse parts that the reader realizes that The Centaur is not only fiction, but partakes in the somewhat trendy post-modern technique called, among other things, meta-fiction. In his later fiction, especially in *A Month of Sundays* and *The Coup*, Updike will give a nod toward meta-fiction, which, briefly, is fiction that calls attention to itself as fictive. Here perhaps an illustration will serve better than a definition. Critics have not noted the similarities between *The Centaur* and John Barth's *Chimera*. Perhaps the reason is that Updike and John Barth are considered poles apart: Updike is relegated to the tradition of nineteenth-century psychological realism whereas Barth is elected as America's most representative "fabulator," i.e. our most obvious exponent of self-conscious, playful maker of fictions (in the plural). Yet, like *The Centaur*, *Chimera* is mythicized autobiography, is concerned with the act of composing fictions and its limitations, contrasts two mythic figures in terms of success (Perseus, like Chiron, finally dwells among the stars) and failure (Bellerophon, like Prometheus, remains earth-bound), and engages the issue of competing "immortalities," that of the Hero and the Artist. Also, each "novel" ends amid the stars "where the constellations represent a kind of continually repeated narrative."[11] Throughout both *The Centaur* and *Chimera*, the antic behavior of the characters and the intrusions of authorial playfulness signal to the reader that the *whole* text must be read as fictive and mythic.

John Barth's "signals" are more obvious than Updike's; yet in both books such signals are introduced to transfer the reader's attention from the tales of the heroes to the writer's efforts at composing his multifarious tales. Northrop Frye reminds us that such a transfer is, in fact, the first step in the recovery of myth.[12] The next step takes place when the writer, in effect, entrusts his work to the reader. The reader thus becomes the "mental traveller," the "hero" of what he has read. Precisely because of the very complexity of the text, the reader of *The Centaur* is lured into participating in the process of mythic self-creation and self-identity, of the acceptance of meaningful "roles," of attempts at reconciling those conflicting impulses that engage both Caldwell and Peter, Caldwell from an ethico-religious perspective and Peter from his triple perspective regarding the Three Secret Things.

In Peter's boyhood narratives, the fascinations and promptings of sex are associated inevitably with death. Each of his encounters with Penny (Pandora) engage this subject. (pp. 118-19, 181, 246) Like Pandora in mythology, she apparently brings those evils that are reprisals commensurate with Prometheus' gifts to man. Elsewhere, when Dedman (Daedalus) shows Peter the pornographic playing cards, at first the Jack of

Hearts card seems "very beautiful, a circle completed, a symmetry found," but its very beauty reminds him sorrowfully of his father. (p. 181) Sex and Nature can be made beautiful through artistic symmetry, yet death touches both. Even as an adult, while extolling the charms of his sleeping Negro mistress, he asserts, "I love you, I want to be a Negro for you. . . . But I cannot, quite. I cannot quite make that scene. A final membrane restrains me. I am my father's son." (p. 269) Then he reflects about their "rather wistful half-Freudian half-Oriental sex mysticism" and wonders, "*Was it for this that my father gave up his life?*" (p. 270)

Peter's only recourse will be a Yeatsian one. As Northrop Frye describes it in his essay, Yeats sought "redemption" from the pressures of time, sexuality, and chance through the exercise of imagination. By way of imagination the artist can render Nature no longer hostile, but enabling, a part of one's vitalizing creative power.

> Redemption is secured by the poet's identifying himself with Man through the discovery of personal archetypes, daimons, and moods, aspects of the greater form of himself; in this perspective the whole cycle of nature, of life and death and rebirth which man has dreamed, becomes one single gigantic image, an image the imaginary poet, its 'maker' has conquered. The poetic process, we might say, thrives on a conflation, or confusion, of the actual world and the world of imagination; the creation of an imaginary world . . . empowers the poet and absolves from the pain of the actual.[13]

Yeats will identify himself with Timon and Lear and other heroes; Peter will make himself Prometheus and populate Olinger with gods.

B. Sacred and Secular Scriptures

Inspired by the groundbreaking success of the modern "greats" like Joyce, Faulkner, and Mann, several contemporary American authors in the past twenty years have returned to tap the two basic mythological resources of the Western tradition: Classical Greek myth and Biblical myth. John Barth, Richard Brautigan, and James Dickey have made subtle and explicit use of Greek myth in order to counterpoint their contemporary fables; Robert Coover, Bernard Malamud, and John Gardner, by contrast, have employed the images and structures of Biblical myth for similar purposes. The success or failure of each enterprise lies not so much in the myth as in its vitalization, in what Updike called in his National Book Award speech "the intensity of the grapple."

In his Norton Lectures at Harvard in 1975, Northrop Frye introduced an important distinction between these two mythological sources by designating the one "secular" and the other "sacred" scripture.[14] According to Frye, the stories proper to Biblical myth do not differ in structure or development from those of Greek myth but differ in regard to their claim to authority and import in social function. Biblical myth, even for today's unbeliever, still retains the claim-character of Revelation. That is, it is regarded as a *received* imaginative structure that is related to belief and worship—in short, it is traditionally viewed as "sacred" scripture. Even though many of its stories originated in man-centered concerns, the Bible is seen more as an epic of the Creator, with God as its hero rather than man, while its construct is that of a "vast mythological universe, stretching in time from creation to apocalypse, and, in metaphoric space, from heaven to hell."[15] For the believer, the Biblical stories are perceived as *logoi* (i.e. "true" stories in the sense that they are revelatory of the crucial issues that concern human existence) and not just *mythoi* (i.e. profane stories with no such crucial referents). Therefore, even though *mythoi* and *logoi* are similar in structure and origin, the latter derive their authority and impact from the act of faith and from theological doctrine; hence, their "sacred" character.

By contrast, Frye categorizes Greek myth (and with it all other non-Biblical fables, legends, etc.) as "secular" scripture. Secular scripture is viewed as admittedly self-created and not received; its narratives are essentially man-centered, involving man's self-understanding in relation to *this* world. Sacred and Secular Scriptures accent, by way of contrast, two competing perceptions proper to man. Secular scriptures point up the verbal part of man's own act of creation via the imagination, Sacred Scripture his "received" awareness of some uncreated force or power beyond himself, an otherness of spirit. Frye suggests that Romance is the genre that best reminds us of these contrasting preceptions and he concludes by observing:

> It is quite true that if there is no sense that the mythological universe is a human creation, man can never get free of servile anxieties and superstitions, never surpass himself, in Nietzsche's phrase. But if there is no sense that there is also something uncreated, something coming from elsewhere, man remains a Narcissus staring at his own reflection. Somehow or other, the created scripture and the revealed scripture,

or whatever we call the latter, have to keep fighting each other like Jacob and the angel. . . . The improbable, desiring, erotic, and violent world of romance reminds us that we are not awake when we have abolished the dream world: we are awake only when we have absorbed it again.[16]

Frye's distinctions provide a welcome preface for *The Centaur*, which, I believe, is the most complex and successful demonstration of the interaction of Sacred and Secular Scripture in contemporary literature. Initially overpraised, often for the wrong reasons, and now perhaps too casually dismissed by critics, *The Centaur*, because of its unique wedding of the two scriptures and its employment of Romance, demands a critical rereading as well as a clarification of previous misreadings.

The initial critical difficulty has been that the novel is composed in four different narrative modes, some overlapping. First, there is the apparently "realistic," objective narrative, written in the present tense, about the vicissitudes of George Caldwell, a science teacher, and his teen-aged son Peter (Chapter 7). Secondly, there is a first person narrative of the events occurring in the same three-day period told in the past tense from a perspective fifteen years later by the adult Peter; this account, usually straightforward, is occasionally interwoven with Classical mythology (Chapters 2 and 4; Chapter 8). Thirdly, there is a double-focus narrative that combines the mythological perspective with the "realistic" story about Caldwell-Chiron (Chapters 1 and 9) or about Peter-Prometheus (Chapter 6). Fourthly, there is a straightforward parody of a newspaper obituary (Chapter 5).

The novel makes explicit and consistent reference to the characters of Greek myth, and Updike has included a mythological index should the reader go astray. The central myth is the story of the wise, immortal centaur Chiron, who, wounded by a poisoned arrow, longs for death and, since Prometheus is being punished for his theft of fire, begs Zeus to allow himself to be a substitute for Prometheus. Zeus hears Chiron's plea, takes away his pain and immortality, and sets him among the stars as Sagittarius. On the novel's apparently realistic level, the wise, kindly Chiron corresponds with the befuddled and impulsive science teacher Caldwell; and the rebellious Prometheus, for whom he sacrifices his life, corresponds with his adolescent son Peter. The other characters (e.g. the wife and mother Cassie is likened to Ceres, Mother Earth; Zimmerman the principal to Zeus, and so on) correspond with the varied gods of Olympus.

The interplay between realism and myth has become commonplace enough in recent literature, and literary success in such ventures is generally measured against Joyce's *Ulysses*. Such seems to be the criterion critics and reviewers applied to *The Centaur*, thereby finding it wanting since, ironically, Joyce himself has become mythologized. Updike, however, has given us another lead; he has said that this novel is "an experiment very unlike that of *Ulysses*, where the myth lurks beneath the surface of events. In a way, the natural events in my books are meant to be a kind of mask for the myth."[17]

Consequently, the multiple mythic dimensions to *The Centaur* are more central to its appreciation than are occasional clever correspondences between "realistic" details and the mythic overlay. In a sense, there is no realism in the novel at any point; all is myth or, better, multimyth. Hence, Frye's categories of the sacred and secular scriptures become appropriate guides. In discussing his novel Updike made this observation, almost echoing Frye, "I think that initially art was tied in with theology and has to do with an ideal world: the artist is in some way a middleman between the ideal world and this, even though our sense of the ideal—and I'm speaking here of our gut sense, regardless of what we think we believe—is at present fairly dim."[18] In the novel this "ideal" world is comprised not only of the idealized transformation of the Olingerites into Olympians but also of the received "ideal" world of Christian faith and its Biblical cosmology as a counterpoint to it. As they were initially, Art and Theology are tied together.

When Updike was asked why he chose this mythic form for *The Centaur*, he replied, "I was moved, first, by the Chiron variant of the Hercules myth—one of the few classical instances of self-sacrifice, and a name oddly close to Christ."[19] Later in the same interview, he pointed out other underlying myths in other novels.

> . . . there is the St. Stephen story underlying *The Poorhouse Fair* and Peter Rabbit under *Rabbit, Run*. Sometimes it is semi-conscious. . . . And in *Couples*, Piet is not only Hanema/ anima/ Life, he is Lot, the man with two virgin daughters, who flees Sodom, and leaves his wife behind.[20]

Elsewhere, Updike described the shape of the novel "as a sort of sandwich." The two mythic "slices" that enclose it are introduced in the book's Foreword and in its epigraph. The Foreword summarizes the original Chiron myth as I have recounted it. Yet, it is significant that, with so many other sophisticated versions available, Updike chose that by Josephine Peabody in her *Old Greek Folk Stories Told Anew*, published in 1897.[21] Peabody's eminent Victorian version recasts the Chiron story in language quite resonant with Christological overtones: "it was still needful that a life be given to expiate that ancient sin"; "Chiron, noblest of all the centaurs . . . was wandering the world in agony from a wound he had received by a strange mischance"; "Chiron, blameless as he was . . . begged that he might be accepted as an atonement for Prometheus."

The novel's epigraph is a quotation from Karl Barth that reads: "Heaven is the creation inconceivable to man, earth the creation conceivable to him. He himself is the creature on the boundary between heaven and earth." Critics of *The Centaur* have analyzed exhaustively the implications of this epigraph in relation to the novel.[22] Still, no critic has pursued the profound implications of the *source* and *context* of the epigraph. It is taken from Barth's *Dogmatics in Outline*, his exposition of the Christocentric character of the Apostles' Creed.[23] As we have noted, Updike then and now considers himself "theologically a Barthian," and so his ideal of Sacred Scripture should possess a Barthian cast and structure.

Hence, the source and context of the Barth epigraph ought not be ignored. Updike's quote of Barth is taken from a summary epigraph that introduces the ninth chapter of *Dogmatics in Outline*, entitled "Heaven and Earth." This chapter is an important bridge between Barth's preceding chapter entitled "God the Creator" and the following entitled "Jesus Christ." Updike quotes only the first two sentences from that summary epigraph; the omitted third sentence reads: "The covenant between God and man is the meaning and the glory, the ground and the goal of heaven and earth and the whole creation." (p. 59)

Since the word "Creation" admits of many meanings, Barth's understanding of it in this context is important for an intelligent grasp of Updike's epigraph. Not unlike Northrop Frye, Barth sees Creation "stories" as distinguished by their sacred (revelatory) or secular (man-centered myth) character. Furthermore, Barth's remarks about Creation myths anticipate in outline some dramatic episodes in *The Centaur*:

> If we take this concept [of Creation] seriously, it must be at once clear that we are not confronted by a realm which in any sense may be accessible to human view or human thought. Natural science may be our occupation with its view of development; it may tell us the tale of the millions of years in which the cosmic process goes on; but when

could natural science have ever penetrated to the fact that there is one world that runs through this development? Continuation is quite a different thing from this sheer beginning, with which the concept of creation and the Creator has to do. It is assuredly a basic error to speak of creation myths. At best myth may be parallel to exact science. . . . Myth considers the world, as it were, from its frontier, but always the world that already exists. There is no creation myth because creation as such is simply not accessible to myth. . . . At most we can say that certain mythical elements are found [in Genesis 1 & 2]. If we are to give the biblical narrative a name, or put it in a category, then let it be that of a saga. (p. 51)

Barth's theology of Creation, as we have noted earlier, is characterized by its rigorous Christocentrism; because of this, the Genesis narrative of Creation is not a myth, but rather a saga since it is a familial story about the love of a Father for His Son and those He represents. For Barth, Creation is inaccessible to man since only the revelation about Jesus Christ found in the New Testament is the key to the mystery and purpose of Creation. From eternity, God the Creator intended through Jesus Christ to unite Himself with man, His creature, in a covenant of love—a covenant that would reflect God's own inner love-relationship. "Creation is the temporal analogue, taking place outside God, of that event in God Himself by which God is Father of the Son . . . what God does as the Creator can in a Christian sense only be seen and understood as a reflection, as a shadowing forth of this inner divine relationship between God the Father and Son." (p. 52) Consequently, since the Covenant-Creation story begins in eternity and not time, neither science nor myth has access to it; only the saga of God the Father and the Son's love-relationship can make it known in all its mystery.

When one turns from this Barthian context and source to the novel itself, subliminal quaverings begin, for the critical episode in both the first and the third chapters involves Caldwell's lecture to his science class (his occupation, *vide* Barth above) about the origin and evolution of the universe. Significantly, from a Barthian viewpoint, the first lecture is delivered in the language of modern science; the second, its retelling, in the language of myth. In the first lecture on the age of the universe, Caldwell realizes that the number of zeros in five billion makes the universe's dating unintelligible to his class, so he is forced to reduce that mind-boggling statistic to a comprehensible scale of three days by our clock-time. Proceeding from the big bang to the formation of the stars and earth, he finally reaches the most crucial stage prior to man's emergence in life: the indispensable activity of the volvox.

> . . . the volvox of these early citizens in the *kingdom of life*, interests us because he invented death. There is no reason intrinsic in the plasmic substance why life should never end. Amoebas never die; and those male sperm cells which enjoy success become the *cornerstone of new life* that continues *beyond the father*. But the volvox, a rolling sphere of *flagellating* algae organized into somatic and reproductive cells *neither plant nor animal*—under a microscope it looks just like a *Christmas* ball—by pioneering this new idea of *cooperation*, rolled *life into the kingdom*—as opposed to *accidental*—death. For while each cell is potentially *immortal*, by volunteering for a specialized function within an organized society of cells, it enters a *compromised* environment. The strain eventually wears it out and kills it. It dies *sacrificially*, for the *good of the whole*. These first cells who got tired of sitting around *forever* in a blue-green scum and said, "*Let's* get together and *make* a volvox," were the first *altruists*. The first do-gooders. If I had a hat on, I'd take it off to them. (pp. 41-42)

Not only does the lecture foreshadow Caldwell's own sacrificial activity, but I have italicized certain key words because, interwoven with the scientific terminology, a thread of Biblical language descriptive of Christ's role in redemption emerges. The activity of the volvox capsulates Pauline and Barthian theology: like the volvox, Christ comes into the kingdom, to become the new cornerstone and offer a share in His Father's life, to bring new creation via His death (which involved flagellation), a life based on cooperative love in order that in the new kingdom each one, once potentially immortal, might really be so; yet, because He entered the compromised environment of sin, this new life was won only by sacrifice for the good of the whole. Furthermore, the shared decision to make and send the volvox-Christ was an eternal one and entirely altruistic because motivated only by goodness and love, thus deserving man's spontaneous and unconditional praise.

In the novel's third chapter, this lecture on the genesis of all things is retold by Chiron in the language of the Classical Orphic myth of creation which Updike borrows verbatim from Robert Graves' *The Greek Myths* 1.[24] In this mythic explanation of creation, Night laid a silver egg in the womb of Darkness and from it was hatched Love (Eros) which set the universe in motion, thereby making the things of heaven and of the earth her children. Under her reign men lived without cares and death to them was no worse than sleep. But Chiron, upon reaching this idyllic situation, suddenly trails off from this mythic narrative with the words: "Then her scepter passed to Uranus. . . ." (p. 99)

Barth's theology of Creation, like the myth of Eros, makes Covenant-love the motivation for the origin and goal of Creation, but he emphasizes that this is inaccessible to both science and myth and can be understood only in the light of the Father-Son relationship revealed in Christ. Chiron-Caldwell's incomplete sentence, "her scepter passed to Uranus," hints at this. The patriarchal myth of Uranus (the Sky-Father), that of a planned intelligence guiding the world, eventually replaced the Eros and Mother Earth myths as the mythic description of Creation.[25] In the earlier Eros and Mother Earth sexual myths, death and evil are part of a natural process and need not be explained. As the grandfather Kramer-Kronos puts it in the novel, "Nature . . . is like a mother; she com-forts and chas-tises us with the same hand." (p. 291) However, in the later Sky-Father myth of Creation, the world is made by an intelligence, not born "naturally," and so, since an intelligent Creator is presumed, the existence of death and evil must be explained. Where the Sky-Father myth is operative, as in both late Classical myth (the Prometheus-Chiron tales) and in Biblical myth (the stories of Creation and Covenant), such an explanation demands a complementary myth of a "fall." The word "fall" itself connotes a descent from a higher realm; in Greek myth this realm will be the Golden Age (which Kramer-Kronos represents throughout) and in the Bible, Eden.

The central characters in The Centaur, Caldwell and Peter, are both from different perspectives troubled by the realization of such a fall, a disparity between heaven and earth, a break with some Edenesque Golden Age, forever irretrievable. Both perceive this dislocation within the parameters of the Sky-Father myth, whereas the next novel, Of the Farm, will engage the Mother Earth-Eros myths.

Such structural similarities between Classical and Biblical myth will give Updike the opportunity to interweave them thematically with multiple variations. At the same time, though, like a true Barthian, he will remind us implicitly that all mythic creation and redemption stories are ultimately inadequate; only the complex saga of a Father-Son love-relationship can disclose such mysteries. What seems at first blush secular might be sacred after all.

C. ROMANCE: BOUNDARY FICTION

In order to convey man's "boundary" situation described in the Barth epigraph, Updike was compelled to resort to that "border" fiction called Romance. This resort to Romance is fitting in a way since, as Frye points out in his *Anatomy of Criticism*, "the romance, which deals with heroes, is intermediate between the novel, which deals with men, and myth, which deals with gods. Prose romance first appears as a late development of Classical mythology. . . . The novel tends rather to expand into a fictional approach to history."[26]

Consequently, the structural techniques proper to Romance will furnish Updike with the imaginative leeway *simultaneously* to tap the resources of both the accepted conventions of the novel and the conventions of Classical mythology that inform it, and have them function as a bridge or boundary between the apparently realistic episodes historically framed by 1947 (the novel) and the book's final shape (myth). Just as Caldwell-Chiron in his lecture had to compress into a three-day time period the seemingly timeless process leading up to man's creation, so too Updike will compress a similar "creative" process (the complex story itself) into a three-day representative period. Such compression corresponds with the conventions of Romance and its three-day rhythm of death, disappearance, and revival.

True to the tradition of Romance, Caldwell and Peter are presented as being continually caught between two worlds represented by cities: 1) the worlds of Olympus and Olinger in 1947; 2) the past world of a now mythicized Edenesque Olinger and Peter's present world in New York, the city that, as a boy, he mythicized as "the throat of Paradise" (pp. 84, 86, 163, 165), and now sees as indicative of his "fall" instead; 3) the realms of heaven and earth suggested by the Christ-associated cities of Bethlehem and Jerusalem.

The descent-struggle-ascent transitions proper to Romance also characterize the dramatic movement of *The Centaur*. The explicitly mythological chapters (1 and 9) describe Caldwell-Chiron's descent into the underworld and culminate in his apotheosis. It is important to note that these events, in a sense, take place *outside* the three-day time frame, suggested by the fact that Caldwell's clock-time is ever ahead of the more realistic clock-time throughout. The apparently "realistic" or, better, "Novelistic" sections begin in chapter 2 with Peter's descent from his bedroom, describe the adventuresome struggles he shares with his father in the underworld, and end with his return and ascent to his bedroom at home. For Peter the process marks a rite of passage or what Wheelwright terms the three "ceremonies of transition": 1) separation (Peter is separated from his "Mama" as Caldwell calls Cassie, who is also Ceres and Mother Earth); 2) marginal experiences where one is plunged into darkness and anonymity "between two worlds" (the main body of the story); 3) attainment, a stage that is marked by ceremonies of acceptance and rejoicing.[27]

The adventures that make up the central narrative begin with both Caldwell and Peter suffering from stomach hurts (the "snake" the father calls it); like his father, Peter-Prometheus is suffering from a wound and a curse. Peter's humiliation is that of psoriasis, which is "not a disease because I generated in out of myself," but an affliction he accepts, convinced that "God, to make me a man, had blessed me with a rhythmic curse that breathed in and out with the seasons." (pp. 52-53) Only the spring sun promises a cure for him; but this is January, "a hopeless time," for his scabs "ran together in a kind of pink bark," suggestive of Eden's second tree. Nevertheless, as in the Fisher-King Romances, a curse and a disease provide the occasion for adventure, and so they must begin their journey. As in the natural cycle proper to Romance, winter here, with its associations of darkness, confusion, sterility, and moribund life, will take on the features of an enemy. Upon their return home as "heroes," which is Cassie's greeting (p. 286), solar imagery will come to the forefront, indicating a cyclic return. Cassie once again sees Peter as her "little sunbeam," and Pop Kramer wonders whether Caldwell had brought back the *Sun* (pun on the local newspaper). Caldwell has not but he returns with the good news that the X rays were clear.

Caldwell's, the wise Chiron's, descent into the underworld is motivated by his search for truth (p. 83), another characteristic motif of romantic descent. Northrop Frye in discussing this theme in Romance clarifies Caldwell's motives: "When it is wisdom sought in the lower world, it is almost always wisdom connected with the anxiety of death and the desire to know what lies beyond. Such wisdom is usually communicated in some kind of dark saying, riddle, or oracular utterance."[28] In his endless conversations with the Olympians of Olinger, Caldwell is told several such maxims. The first two he rejects: Kramer-Kronos' "Time and tide wait for no man," and Doc Appleton-Apollo's "Know thyself." Instead, he will seize upon the saying opposite to the Delphic Oracle's "Know thyself," namely "Ignorance is Bliss," and he will finally arrive at wisdom when, in the final chapter, he recalls his minister-father's utterance that "all joy belongs to the Lord," marking a shift from the Classical oracular to the Biblical and Christian.

Caldwell's search for wisdom is linked with his concern about his imminent death, a concern shared by his son. He is fearful of stomach cancer and perceives it as "like a poisoned snake wrapped around my bowels," "a spider in my big intestine." Such imagery is significant, for Frye observes:

> In romance where descent themes are common, the hero often has to kill or pacify a dragon which guards a secret hoard of wisdom. The descent is often portrayed as a mimic temporary death of the hero; or he may be swallowed by the dragon, so that his descent is into the monster's belly. In medieval treatments of the Christian story some of these themes reappear. Between his death on the cross and his resurrection Jesus descends into hell, often portrayed as the body of a huge dragon or shark. . . .[29]

As Frye points out here, descent-ascent themes in Romance are structurally the same when found in both sacred and secular scriptures. By capitalizing on this similarity in structure, Updike is able to: 1) interweave via allusion Classical and Biblical themes as parallels in the story's movement; 2) maintain a contrast—despite their common quest and shared descent-ascent movement—between Peter's secular perspective as artist and Caldwell's perspective as ethico-religious. Through such techniques, by The Centaur's end in its final chapter, Updike is able both to interlock the sacred and the secular and to sustain their difference in perspective. Frye describes well the difference between Caldwell's sacred, upward movement and Peter's secular, artistic ascent.

> In traditional romance, including Dante, the upward journey is the journey of a creature returning to his creator. In most modern writers, from Blake on, it is the creative power in man that is returning to its original awareness. The secular scripture tells us that we are the creators; other scriptures tell us that we are the actors in a drama of divine creation and redemption. . . . Identity and self-recognition begin when we realize that this is not an either-or question, when the great twins of divine creation and human recreation have merged into one, and we can see that the same shape is upon both.[30]

The Romantic journey begins with the Caldwells' downhill trip through Firetown, past the cemetery, through Galilee, the Seven-Mile Tavern (Emmaus?) until they meet a hitchhiker at a point where "the road then knifed between two high gashed embankments of eroding red earth." (p. 97) The hitchhiker (Hermes) appears to Peter "like some primeval monster coming to life again out of a glacier" and "as if we were, my selfless father and my innocent self, a treacherous black animal he was capturing." (pp. 80-81)

Eventually they reach Olinger High School where Caldwell-Chiron's classes are ironically described as taking place in an Olympian clearing reached after a trek through a forest wilderness. After school Peter and Caldwell begin their second descent, first through Hades (Heller's basement), then through Vulcan's realm (Hummel's garage), only to separate with Peter entering Minos' labyrinth (Minor's soda-shop) where he is tempted by Pandora (Penny) and taunted by his Titan classmates, with Caldwell, meanwhile, visiting Apollo (Dr. Appleton) at whose office they reunite. Peter sees the doctor's stethoscope lying "like a slain rubber serpent," and in his fear he realizes that "like an encircling serpent my father's death seemed to tighten its coil." (pp. 128, 136) Afterwards, they again separate briefly: Peter enjoys the Elysian Fields of Alton, while Caldwell, the swimming coach, enters the Styx of Alton's Y.M.C.A. pool. Their efforts to return home are thwarted because their black Buick (its mechanical body is identified with Caldwell's body throughout) has an "attack," and so they are compelled to stay in Tartarus (Alton). There, as in the Orpheus legend, Caldwell charms Rhadamanthus, Dionysus, and Charon and temporarily finds rest for Peter and himself in *The New Yorker Hotel* (the city of paradise for Peter). As they are led up the narrow stairs to their room, Peter realizes that "Here was our destination: all night in ignorance we had been winding toward this room. . . ." (p. 162)

After school on the following day, during a basketball game, Peter-Prometheus challenges Zeus (the principal Zimmerman) and Caldwell-Chiron challenges Ares (the Rev. Marsh), winsome parodies of "classical" confrontations. Meanwhile, snow has fallen, and its arrival functions, not only as symbol for Nature's purification and the unification of heaven and earth, but as the occasion for an explicit coupling of Classical with Biblical language. Furthermore, it recalls and so alters the scientific description of Creation ("out of zero all has come to birth") that we heard before, and the use of the present tense conveys an eternal aspect to the scene.

Those who step outside discover that it is snowing. This discovery is ever surprising, that Heaven can so prettily condescend. Snow puts us with Jupiter Pluvius among the clouds. . . . Olinger under the vast violet dome of the stormstruck night sky becomes yet one more Bethlehem. Behind a glowing window the infant God squalls. Out of zero all has come to birth. The panes, tinted by the straw of the crib within, hush its cries. The world goes on unhearing. The town of white roofs seems a colony of deserted temples . . . the alterations of density conjure an impression of striding legs stretching upward into infinity. The storm walks. The storm walks but does not move on. (pp. 328-39)

But, as Peter and his father actually enter the snow to get their car, this vision of snow as beneficent and as reminiscent of Bethlehem changes, in Peter's perspective, into something "ghostly." He sees the snow as "an immense whispering whose throat seems to be now here, now there," as "an entire broadening wing of infinitesimal feathers," until he feels "the universe in all its plastic and endlessly variable beauty pinned, stretched, crucified like a butterfly upon a frame of unvarying geometric truth." (pp. 255-56) He experiences this commingled vision of shadow and light, of infinite and finite, of birth and crucifixion, as a series of "revelations." (pp. 255-57) Such a vision is appropriate because the car cannot ascend the hill because of the snow, and so they must spend the second night with Vera Hummel (Venus).

At this point in the narrative, the visitation to Venus, Peter's adult voice obtrudes and he reminisces about another journey in his childhood, this an artistic one to the Alton Museum. This briefly inserted reminiscence, overlooked by critics, is not a purple patch but is central to the novel's shape and significance. For this museum-memory functions on several levels: 1) as an artistic adventure, it parallels the adventurous ascent he and his father share both realistically and mythically on this third day; 2) it encapsulates the "topocasm" or four levels of existence that are thematically interwoven throughout; 3) it becomes the objective correlative for Peter's Promethean artistic effort to capture, in narrative, an unceasing "moment" in the flow of his and his father's adventures.

The reminiscence begins with Peter's recollection of his and his mother's entering the museum grounds where "an even older world, Arcadian, would envelope us." (p. 266) Once there, his mother would, Adam-like, name every plant and bird and tree for him; and in this Eden, as they passed, "a linked pair of humans would break apart and study our passing with darkened, rounded eyes." Once inside, they would "pass up the wide stairs" and "into the high religious hall of the museum itself." The museum consisted of three levels plus a skylight, and the boy's Dantesque ascent within it corresponds with what Frye has delineated as the "topocasm" of Christian myth, those four levels of existence especially evident in Dante and Milton. 1) The lowest level is that of the demonic world of sin, violence, and corruption; 2) the second is the world of physical nature into which fallen man is born but to which he cannot adjust and in which he must die; 3) the third is that of a "timeless" Eden or of Eliot's "garden world" of residual memory where human nature seems innocent and unfallen; 4) the fourth is Heaven, the Sky and its Light, where God's presence manifests itself as grace and providence.[31]

Peter tells us that it was in the museum's basement where classes in nature appreciation were held, and that he enrolled but, after watching "a snake in a glass cage swallowing a chattering field mouse whole," he never returned. On the second level, the main floor, were the scientific exhibits: "stiff stuffed creatures" and "a noseless mummy." He tells us that this "floor filled [him] with dread," for he wondered, echoing Dante and Eliot, "who could believe there could be such a quantity of death?" However, the next floor, the third level, was devoted to art and "radiated the innocence and hope of seizing something and holding it fast that enters whenever a brush touches canvas." Peter is entranced by this third level, for Sexuality and Art meet in a moment arrested by the imagination.

> There were also bronze statuettes of Indians and deities, and in the center of the large oval room at the head of the stairs a naked green lady, life size, stood in the center of a circular black-lipped pool. She was a fountain. She held to her lips a scallop shell of bronze and her fine face was pursed to drink, but the mechanics of the fountain dictated that water should spill forever from the edge of the shell away from her lips. . . . The patience of her wait, the mildness of its denial, seemed unbearable to me then, and I told myself that when darkness came . . . then her slim bronze hand made the very little motion needed and she drank. In this great oval room which I conceived of as lit by the moon through the skylight above, the fall of water would for a moment cease. In that sense, then—in the sense that the coming of night enwrapped the luminous ribbon of downfalling water and staunched its flow—my story is coming to its close. (pp. 267-68)

This recollection that begins Chapter 8, like the chapter's closing paragraph that we quoted earlier, culminates in an act of imaginative faith and hope, the artistic equivalent of religious commitment. Yet, immediately after this museum-memory, the adult Peter turns toward his own "worthless canvases" and toward his mistress, a sleeping innocent like the fountain lady, and realizes that he is inadequate in capturing the mysteries of this saga of father and son. The conclusion of his narrative of their return trip reflects this realization.

In the morning at Vera Hummel's house (Venus), Peter is depressed by his father's absence and yet exhilarated by the awakening of his sexual identity in Vera's presence. When his father comes back, they start retracing the route they descended two days before, but "Halfway up Fire Hill (above us the church and its tiny cross were inked onto an indigo sky), a link snapped," (p. 283) and they are forced to walk home up the hill through the snow. When they arrive, they are met by a downstairs light, "an ambrosial smell of warm apples," and his mother's greeting them as "heroes." There Peter learns that the X rays show nothing of his father's illness—the snake has been tamed and the dragon defeated—and hears his father say, "God takes care of you if you let him." The romantic cycle is completed, and Peter's narrative ends as it began—in a state between waking and sleeping, that realm peculiar to Romance, the boundary fiction.

D. THE FINAL CHAPTER: APOTHEOSIS AND APOCALYPSE

In *The Hero with a Thousand Faces*, Joseph Campbell provides an outline for the hero's achievement that is unwittingly descriptive of Caldwell-Chiron's destiny in the novel's last chapter.

> The mythological hero, setting forth from his commonday hut or castle, is lured, carried away, or else voluntarily proceeds, to the threshold of adventure. There he encounters a shadow presence that guards the passage. The hero may defeat or conciliate this power and go alive into the kingdom of the dark (brother-battle, dragon-battle; offering, charm), or be slain by the opponent and descend in death (dismemberment, crucifixion). Beyond the threshold, then, the hero journeys through a world of unfamiliar yet strangely intimate forces, some of which severely threaten him (tests), some of which give magical aid (helpers). . . . The triumph may be represented as the hero's sexual union with the goddess-mother of the world (sacred marriage), his recognition by the father-creator (father atonement), his own divini-

zation (apotheosis) . . . intrinsically it is an expansion of consciousness and therewith of being (illumination, transfiguration, freedom). The final work is that of return. If the powers have blessed the hero, he now sets forth under their protection (emissary). . . .[32]

The Centaur's final chapter is an apotheosis in the Romantic and Classical senses, and Caldwell-Chiron embodies these archetypes. Furthermore, his growing realizations, as recorded in the chapter, correspond with the ascending imagery proper to the more Biblical Apocalypse. There, his ruminations begin with reflection upon the mineral world (limestone), move to reflection upon the vegetable world (plants), to the animal world (dogs), the human (his son and his father), and, finally, the divine world (Lord and Zeus).[33] The chapter thus becomes, as apocalypse, the Biblical inverse to the opening chapter which contains two Genesis accounts, that of the creation of man (via the volvox) and the creation of Chiron.

In that chapter we are told of Chiron's birth. His mother, Philyra, repelled by her monster son, prayed to be metamorphosed into a linden tree rather than suckle him. Chiron in his youth often went to "examine linden trees" and "standing embraced by the tree's wide soft shade had believed himself to discover . . . some hope of return to human form." He later realizes that the "linden tree has many healing properties." (pp. 22-23)[34] This ambivalent significance of the tree as both symbol of maternal rejection and symbol of healing, which is here grounded in Classical myth, will later take on Christological resonances.

Mircea Eliade points out that Christianity appropriated the symbolism of the Tree of the World, that Cosmic Tree which is so situated in the Center of the Universe that it upholds and unites the three cosmic regions of Hell, Earth, and Heaven as on one axis. The Cosmic Tree thus becomes the pillar of communication between Heaven and Earth for the sacrificial hero who climbs it.[35] Eliade goes on to say that "Christianity has utilized, interpreted, and amplified the symbol. The Cross, made of the wood of the tree of good and evil, appears in the place of this Cosmic Tree; the Christ himself is described as a Tree."[36] The Cosmic Tree's roots are in Hell but its branches touch the Heavens; Christ's death on the Tree was simultaneously a descent into Hell and a Resurrection.

In the novel Caldwell's visit to the dentist for an extraction will be described in language reminiscent of Christ's suffering on the tree at the place of the Skull, Calvary.

A tree of pain takes root in his jaw. . . . Truly, the pain is unprecedented: an entire tree rich with bloom, each bloom showering into the livid blue air a coruscation of lucid lime-green sparks. . . . Caldwell recognizes the pain branching in his head as a consequence of some failure in his teaching, a failure somewhere to inculcate in this struggling soul consideration and patience; and accepts it as such. The tree becomes ideally dense; its branches and blooms compound into a silver plume, cone, column of pain, a column whose height towers heavenward from a base in which Caldwell's skull is embedded. It is pure shrill silver with not a breath, not a jot, speck, fleck of alloy in it. (pp. 217-18)

The significance of this episode is anticipated shortly before it by Peter's account of a boyhood dream, a nightmare about his father undergoing the start of a Christ-like Passion.

Face-ashen, his father, clad in only a cardboard grocery box beneath which his naked legs showed spindly and yellowish, staggered down the steps of the town hall while the crowd of Olingerites cursed and laughed and threw pulpy dark objects that struck the box with a deadened thump. In a way that we have in dreams, where we are both author and character, God and Adam, Peter understood that in the town hall there had been a trial. His father had been found guilty, stripped of everything he owned, flogged, and sent forth into the world lower than the hoboes. (p. 210)

As this nightmare suggests, Peter's roles throughout *The Centaur* are multiple, extending beyond the Classical mythic correspondences. There he is both Prometheus and Ocyrhoe, the daughter of Chiron; but within the book's Biblical framework, he at times plays God, i.e. author of his narrative creations, at other times actor, like an unredeemed Adam or denying Peter. But in all these permutations he finds himself both cause and beneficiary of Caldwell-Chiron-Christ's "sacrifice" for him.

While other characters offer variations of Classical riddles and historical clichés, Caldwell alone will continually quote Jesus' parables without irony. "The man with two talents didn't get sore at the man with five." (p. 106) "Don't bury your talent in the ground. Let your light shine." (p. 206) Peter will describe him in Christological language reminiscent of St. Paul in Colossians 1:13-20 (the hymn to Christ): "My father provided, he gathered things to himself and let them fall upon the world." (p. 92) The climax of Caldwell's obituary will be the simple assertion, "Here was a man," echoing Pilate's pronouncement. (p. 174) Even a casual scene, such as the occasion where Peter is teased by his classmates about his father, takes on Biblical overtones. Peter realizes that beneath their mockery "an emotion of fermented guilt and fondness would seek to purge itself upon me, the petty receptacle of a myth . . . being Caldwell's son lifted me from the faceless mass. . . ." (p. 121) Also, the mocking memories of his classmates are replete with resonances of Christ's Passion. (pp. 121-22)

However, as the episode of Peter's fumbling translation of Vergil's *Aeneid* suggests, Peter, like Aeneas who only recognized his goddess-mother Venus as she was *avertens*, turning to leave him, will only recognize his father's true "glory"—as did the disciples in the Resurrection narratives—after Caldwell is *avertens*, departing.

This symbolic departure takes place at the end of chapter 8 where Peter tells us that his father "was lost to my sight behind the trees of the orchard." The ninth and final chapter begins with Caldwell, out of sight and in despair, as he wanders outside on the wintry farmland. The snow-whitened coldness of Nature repels him at first. Then, suddenly, his thoughts and reactions to it are transposed and described in mythic fashion; but, in addition, we hear language reminiscent of Christ's Agony in the Garden and of imagery found in Psalm 22. Psalm 22 figures prominently in the liturgy of Good Friday; furthermore, its opening lines, "My God, my God, why have you forsaken me?," are Jesus' last words on the Cross in both Mark and Matthew's gospels.

> In this season [the plants] were barren of virtue and the ground of blank snow made them calligraphic. He searched their scribble for a word and found none. There was no help. There was not one of the twelve he had not consulted and not one had given the answer. Must he wander forever beneath the blank gaze of the gods? The pain in his tissues barked like a penned pack of dogs. Set them free. *My Lord, set them free.* As if in fury at his prayer there poured through his mind like the foul congested breath of Hecate the monstrous tumble of aborted forms and raging giants that composed the sequence of creation: a ferment sucked from the lipless yawn of Chaos, the grisly All-father. (p. 295)

The novel's next paragraph dramatizes Caldwell's Barthian realization that man is also "the place where God wishes to be praised within creation," for he suddenly perceives in the "No" of withering natural creation hints of a "Yes" of renewal and rebirth. It is through memories of religious associations that his own private yes is confirmed.

Yet even in the dead of winter the sere twigs prepare their small dull buds. In the pit of the year a king was born. Not a leaf falls but leaves an amber root, a dainty hoof, a fleck of baggage to be unpacked at a future time. Such flecks gave the black thatch of twigs a ruddy glow. Dully the centaur's litmus eye absorbed this; slowly the chemistry of his thought altered . . . and he remembered walking on some Church errand with his father down a dangerous street in Passaic; it was a Saturday and the men from the sulphur works were getting drunk. From within the doubled doors of a saloon there welled a poisonous laughter that seemed to distill all the cruelty and blasphemy in the world, and he wondered how such a noise could have a place under the sky of his father's God . . . he remembered his father turning and listening in his backwards collar to the laughter from the saloon and then smiling down to his son, "All joy belongs to the Lord."

It was half a joke but the boy took it to heart. *All joy belongs to the Lord.* Wherever in the filth and confusion and misery, a soul felt joy, there the Lord came and claimed it as his own. . . . And all the rest, all that was not joy, fell away, precipitated, dross that had never been . . . the time left him possessed a skyey breadth in which he swam like a true grandchild of Oceanus; he discovered that in giving his life to others he entered a total freedom. Mt. Ide and Mt. Dikte from opposite blue distances rushed toward him like clapping waves and in the upright of his body Sky and Gaia mated again. Only goodness lives. But it does live. (pp. 295-97)

I have included the whole of these paragraphs because they and especially the closing phrases of the second ("In giving his life to others he entered a total freedom," "in the upright of his body Sky and Gaia mated again," and "Only goodness lives")—have been characterized as "mummifying rhetoric" and "stippled preciosity" by Richard Gilman. One becomes more generous toward their hieratic tone, however, upon returning to Barth's *Dogmatics in Outline* and particularly to that section from which Updike chose his epigraph. There the sequence of Barth's theological argument reads as a parallel to Caldwell-Chiron's realization about creation-freedom-joy-goodness, and the abstract phrases take on theological import. Since we cannot include the whole chapter, a mosaic of quotes must be sufficient evidence.

The world with its sorrow and its happiness will always be a dark mirror to us, about which we may have optimistic or pessimistic thoughts; but it gives us no information about God as the Creator. But always, when man has tried to read the truth from sun, moon, and stars or from himself, the result has been an idol. But when God has been known and then known again in the world, so that the result was a joyful praise of God in creation, that is because He is to be sought and found by us in Jesus Christ. (p. 52)

For if we are free, it is only because our Creator is infinitely free. All human freedom is but an imperfect mirroring of the divine freedom. . . . Man is not made to be Hercules at the crossroads. Freedom to decide means freedom to decide toward the Only One for whom God's creature can decide, for the affirmation of Him who has created it, for accomplishment of His will; that is, for obedience. (p. 56)

. . . this whole realm that we term evil—death, sin, the Devil, and hell—is *not* God's creation, but rather what was excluded by God's creation, that to which God has said "No." And if there is a reality of evil, it can only be the reality of this excluded and repudiated thing, the reality behind God's back, which He passed over, when He made the world and made it good. (p. 57)

And if we inquire into the *goal* of creation, the object of the whole, the object of heaven and earth and all creation, I can only say that it is to be the theater of God's glory. The meaning is that God is being glorified. . . . Whatever objections may be raised against the reality of the world, its goodness incontestably consists in the fact that it may be the theater of His glory, and man the witness to this glory. (p. 58)

The novel's epigraph appears on the next page, (p. 59) following upon these assertions by Barth. Just as Caldwell actualizes them sequentially, so too he embodies the epigraph itself: "in the upright of his body Sky and Gaia mated again." We must emphasize, however, that Caldwell's experience does not make him a "Christ-figure" in the strict sense. Rather, as Barth's argument here and above makes clear, Caldwell, as man "on the boundary between heaven and earth," can through his gestures of praise, sacrifice, and joy be "a *sign* and an *indication*, a promise of what ought to happen in creation and to creation—the meeting . . . and, in Jesus Christ, the oneness of Creator and creature." (p. 64) Although the primary mythological framework is that of Greek myth, the Christological allusions, so often interwoven with it, introduce an optimistic dimension to the Caldwell-Chiron narratives. This is especially evident at the novel's close, which records Chiron's suffering, sacrifice, and eventual exaltation. There Caldwell-Chiron's acceptance of death not only is described according to its classical mythological parallel, but it includes an underlying insinuation of the Passion narrative as well.

It is significant, therefore, that Updike should deliberately attach an epilogue to the novel. The story proper ends with Caldwell-Chiron's acceptance of death; the epilogue is added to record Chiron's exaltation by Zeus whereby he receives an honored place in the heavens. This is Chiron's final destiny. For Karl Barth, the goal of Christ's life is reached in a similar ascension and exaltation, for Barth argues:

> What is the meaning of the Ascension? According to what we have said about heaven and earth, it means at any rate that Jesus leaves earthly space, the space, that is, which is conceivable to us and which He has sought out for our sakes. He no longer belongs to it as we belong to it. That does not mean that it becomes alien to him, that this space is not His space too. On the contrary, since He stands *above* this space, He fulfills it and He becomes present to it. (p. 125)

When these remarks of Barth are read in tandem with Updike's epilogue, a striking configuration emerges. Furthermore, when one includes the epilogue with the preceding narrative about Caldwell-Chiron's suffering, generous sacrifice, and acceptance of death, the whole final chapter reads like a re-casting of the mighty hymn to Christ found in Philippians 2:5-11. This hymn, a favorite of Barth, is the most famous of the kenotic texts describing God's descent and ascent in Christ; therefore, it seems fitting that we close this investigation by suggesting that it be read as a parallel text to Updike's epilogue which reads:

> Zeus had loved his old friend, and lifted him up, and set him among the stars as the constellation Sagittarius. Here, in the Zodiac, now above, now below the horizon, he assists in the regulation of our destinies, though in this latter time few living mortals cast their eyes respectfully toward Heaven, and fewer still sit as students to the stars. (p. 299)

> In your minds you must be the same as Christ Jesus:
> His state was divine,
> Yet he did not cling
> to his equality with God
> but emptied himself
> to assume the condition of a slave,
> and become as men are;
> he was humbler yet,
> even to accepting death,
> death on a cross.

But God lifted him up
and gave him the name
which is above all other names
so that all beings
in the heavens, on earth, and in the underworld,
should bend at the name of Jesus
and that every tongue should acclaim
Jesus Christ as Lord,
to the glory of the Father.[37]

3: Of
the Farm

The novel *Of the Farm*, written in the late summer and early autumn of 1964, is a pivotal work in Updike's writing career. Up to 1964, with some few exceptions to prove the rule, his fiction is located in Eastern Pennsylvania, in fictional towns like Brewer, Alton, and especially Olinger, inhabited by characters and occasioned by events familiar for a Shillington boyhood in the 1940's. As he himself has said, "I was full of the Pennsylvania thing that I wanted to say." All these early works represent such a nostalgic return.

Earlier in 1964 Updike had written a foreword to his collected Olinger stories with the intention of saying farewell to Pennsylvania:

> I bind these stories together as one ties a packet of love letters that have been returned. Olinger has receded from me. Composition, in crystallizing memory, displaces it, and town and the time it localizes have been consumed by the stories bound here. Not an autobiography, they have made one impossible. In the last of them, Olinger has become "like a town in a fable," and in my novel *The Centaur*, by turning Olinger explicitly into Olympus, I intended to say the final word, and farewell.[1]

Of the Farm demonstrates that Updike both did and did not fulfill that intention. Its setting is not too far distant from Olinger perhaps, but is creeping closer to the urban sprawl of the Northeastern corridor. After 1965, Updike's fictional locale moves from Pennsylvania to New England. The travel chapters of *Bech: A Book*, the return of Rabbit to Brewer in *Rabbit Redux*, and the desert setting in *A Month of Sundays* are the exceptions; however, they too, despite the different locales, explore the same post-1965 themes: sex, marriage, and divorce. Updike has noted that "The difference between Olinger and Tarbox is much more the difference between childhood and adulthood than the difference between the two geographical locations. They are stages on my pilgrim's progress, not spots on a map."[2]

As *The Music School* collection will also illustrate, *Of the Farm* marks a crucial stage in that pilgrim's progress. Critics have been quick to point out that its characters are already familiar to readers of Updike. The protagonist Joey Robinson seems a clone of Peter Caldwell and of the sensitive, morally haunted boys found in the early stories. His mother, Mrs. Robinson, is a recognizable older version of Cassie Caldwell and of Mrs. Dow in "Flight" and Mrs. Kern in "Pigeon Feathers." Joey's second wife Peggy has also appeared earlier, but generally in near-ripe, not fully mature, permutations. Her son Richard is a more precocious, urbanized version of some earlier heroes; and so on. Such correspondences perhaps delight the detective within us, but they are not necessary for an appreciation of the fiction. They are threads merely, not tapestry; and Updike has said in this connection:

> Threads connect it to *The Centaur*: the farm is the same, and the father, even to his name, George, seems much the same in both books. . . . In a sense this novella is *The Centaur* after the centaur has died; the mythical has fled the ethical, and a quartet of scattered survivors grope with their voices toward cohesion. And seek to give each other the stern blessing of freedom mentioned in the epigraph from Sartre.[3]

The plot of *Of the Farm* is easy to summarize. As in *The Centaur*, the action is restricted to three days, here a weekend in August when Joey Robinson drives from his residence in New York City to visit his widowed mother who still lives on the farm of his boyhood. Joey has recently divorced his first wife Joan, and now, newly married, he makes the trip with his wife Peggy and her son by her previous marriage, 11-year-old Richard.

The purpose of the visit is to "get acquainted," an objective soon achieved but in surprising fashion. Joey is now 35, an advertising consultant and not the poet his mother hoped he would be, and he dreads the visit. Even though he is memorialized everywhere in mementoes and photographs, he, like his father and grandfather before him, has resented the farm, especially so now since he associates it with his mother's undermining of his first marriage and the subsequent loss of his children. His dread is realized: throughout the three days his mother and Peggy spar verbally over Joey and the issue of his manhood, over Richard and his upbringing, and over the roles a "real" woman and wife should have. These debates dredge up within Joey memories of ghosts who are absent yet eerily present: his dead father and grandmother, his first wife and his abandoned children, as well as his most vivid and unresolved boyhood experiences.

There is little external action to speak of. Since it is "a farm where no one farms," Joey must mow the untended field with his mother's tractor lest she be fined; later he, his mother, and Richard visit a local shopping center. On Sunday mother and son attend the local church and hear a sermon on the creation of Eve which Joey appraises as "excellent" and his mother as "young." The novel's climax occurs on their return home when Mrs. Robinson suffers a heart seizure; after their initial anxiety about her is stayed, the visitors return to New York.

Updike himself has described the novel's unique texture and rhythm better than anyone else in his preface to the Czech edition.

> Like a short story, it has a continuous action, a narrow setting, a small cast. I thought of it as chamber music, containing only four voices— the various ghosts in it do not speak, and the minister's sermon, you will notice, is delivered in close paraphrase, without the benefit of quotation marks. The voices, like musical instruments, take turns dominating, embark on brief narrative solos, and recombine in argument or harmony. The underlying thematic transaction, as I conceived it, was the mutual forgiveness of mother and son, the acceptance each of the other's guilt in taking what they had wanted, to the discomfort, respectively, of the dead father and the divorced wife.[4]

The evolution of the novel into this final form is a fascinating one and points up other crucial themes which critics have, for the most part, overlooked. In December 1963 Updike was contacted by an editor of *The Ladies' Home Journal* and was asked to submit one in a series of essays offered by celebrated American novelists on the subject: Woman. Updike completed his essay by May 1964 but the *Journal's* project was abandoned, so he submitted it to *New Yorker* magazine which rejected it for being "too young." It is fitting (and perhaps an inside joke) that this last appraisal should echo Mrs. Robinson's verdict on the minister's sermon since Updike's original essay on Woman is precisely, except for slight changes, the minister's sermon in the novel. Updike admitted, "I wrote the sermon first as an essay no one would print, and then wrote the novel as a mounting for it."[5]

Within that essay, besides the sermon material, one already finds other ideas and imagery, like ribs and stays, that facilitated such a mounting. The essay begins with Updike's admission that he starts it with only two items on his desk: a Bible and a slip of paper on which are jottings for an unwritten story whose theme was to be the "obdurate mystery of Woman." The slip of paper reads:

> Love-making, done between waking and sleeping, captive of fantasy; sometimes the woman a negress, the touch of her spine, the shape of her turns negroid; other times Spanish, mesas, wrought iron balconies, olive trees fill the mind. . . .

Compare this with Joey's lyric description of Peggy in *Of the Farm*:

> My wife is wide-hipped and long waisted, and surveyed from above, gives an impression of terrain, of a wealth whose ownership imposes upon my body a sweet strain of extension; entered, she yields a variety of landscapes, seeming now a snowy rolling perspective of bursting cotton bolls seen through the Negro arabesques of a fancywork wrought-iron balcony; now a taut vista of mesas dreaming in the midst of sere and painterly ochre; now a grey French castle complexly fitted to a steep green hill whose terraces imitate turrets; now something like Antarctica; and then a receding valleyland of blacks and purples where an unrippled river flows unseen between shadowy banks of grapes that are never eaten.[6]

Updike has transformed and unified the disparate imagery on the slip of paper in the light of the farm-woman-landscape themes that will pervade the novel. However, the rest of the original essay, including the lengthy quote from Genesis, will become the minister's sermon in an abbreviated form.

Although *Of the Farm* was greeted with rather tepid reviews when it first appeared, subsequent close critical readings have explored and exposed its remarkably subtle artistry. In fact, alone among Updike's fiction, it has generated very fine academic criticism. Robert Detweiler concentrates on the novel's unifying design in the shape of an "X."[7] He sees this "X" serving as "the model for metaphors of intersection and interaction, as the representative structure for characterization, as the unifying figure in the manipulation of time and space, and as both the integer and the unknown quantity of the story's problem." Detweiler's "X" explication is most persuasive. It represents well the "crux" of the story (Joey's emotional and ethical dilemma) and the fact that this return to the farm brings together two divergent lines of his existence (boyhood, first marriage with adulthood and second). Furthermore, the "X" pattern points up the recurring geometric images (triangles, hour-glasses, curves, etc.) and unites them in tension. Even better, as Detweiler suggests, the algebraic "X" as the unknown quantity signifies well both Joey himself and the mystery of Women in his life. Thus the mouseketeer's injunction in *Rabbit, Run* to "know yourself" is here expanded beyond the self toward encounter with another mystery.

Larry Taylor[8] focuses, instead, on the novel's link with the pastoral tradition dating back to Theocritus. He finds much of the ornate, allusive language that Joey employs in describing Peggy's charms reminiscent of the pastoral love-lyric. Its lush, celebratory style—which could and did invite parody[9]—is itself, according to Taylor, a parody of such an idyll. Both Joey and Mrs. Robinson find it difficult to distinguish the ideal from the real, and their language reflects this. She idealizes her farm while he idyllizes his farm or field, Peggy. One is a pastoralist by instinct; the other is an urban anti-pastoralist who, ironically, must resort to pastoral images in order to laud his ideal.

Joyce Markle's analysis attends more to psychological themes, especially the Oedipal conflicts between mother and son and Joey's Thanatos-Eros relationship with Peggy.[10] The Hamiltons, on the other hand, emphasize the theme of freedom, which is introduced immediately in the novel's epigraph taken from Sartre.[11] It reads:

> Consequently, when in all honesty, I've recognized that man is a being in whom existence precedes essence, that he is a free being who, in various circumstances, can only want his freedom, I have at the same time recognized that I can only want the freedom of others.

The Hamiltons note that it is the subject of freedom and the search for its meaning that dominate all the conversations, arguments, and recollections in the novel. But they argue cogently that Updike is not discussing Sartre's notion of freedom with its existentialist ontology, but, rather, that idea of freedom proper to Karl Barth's theology and referred to in the minister's sermon. For Barth true freedom issues from the right relationship of a man and a woman, a rightness established by God's order in creation. This point is well taken, I think, and I shall return to it.

These and other studies have proven invaluable for deepening one's appreciation of the novel's artistic complexity. My remarks will not be an effort to supplant these readings but to explore further those artistic elements that have been either overlooked or touched upon too lightly.

For example, the minister's sermon, perhaps too casually dismissed by critics, embraces the novel's major themes and is central in understanding its unity of tone and texture. Its text from Genesis and the subsequent commentary also fuses those Three Secret Things: Religion by way of the right order of Nature and Creation; Sex in its description of the creation of Eve and the resultant import for the mystery of male-female relations; and Art in that Creation reveals God's handiwork whereas man's handiwork is found in his toiling together with others and in his husbandry of language.

Admittedly, that third secret, Art, is not quite so apparent a motif as in Updike's other fiction. However, it is important to be aware ever that this story is told by Joey, the failed poet, and only from his perspective. It is Joey who shapes the story: his mythic viewpoint overarches and encloses the other competing myths offered throughout. Joey reveals that he is faced with the threefold challenge as to the full meaning of the word "husband." Now divorced from his boyhood farm and from his first wife, he must face the responsibility to be the guardian and conserver of all the many things that the farm represents and also be the "helpmeet" to his second wife if he is to define his manhood. The completed story will represent another husbandry, the "husbandry of language," that duty the minister will mention, and so the very act of composing his story will be an event of self-discovery, that more subtle act of husbandry. Norman Mailer once observed that "as he writes, the writer is reshaping his character. He is a better man and he is worse, once he has finished a book."[12] Although Mailer's remark is somewhat dubious for general application, it is pertinent in Joey's case, for the process of writing his story does coincide with the process of his maturation and self-acceptance. The varied stylistic modes (pastoral lyric, fairy tales, mini-dramas, dreams, confessional monologues) capture well his disjointed pilgrim's progress.

Updike has commented on the novel's title, indicating that he intended "to mean that the book was *about* the farm, and the people belong *to* the farm, were of the earth, earthy, mortal, fallen, and imperfect."[13] The farm, then, is both setting and symbol. Each of the characters is identified with the farm at various points and its earthy embrace, in turn, will define symbolically their characters. Furthermore, each character is in some respect a counterpart for the other characters; the farm, as focal point in setting, provides a dramatic focus for the qualities they share.

At the center of the novel, however, is Joey; Joey *is* the farm in that the farm represents his past, present, and future. (cf. pp. 5, 15, 18-19,

38, 173) Given such identification, the farm becomes the fitting symbol for his psychic exploration, that movement toward growth and maturity which results in the "freedom" alluded to in the Sartre epigraph. As we shall see, the farm becomes an "individuating symbol" in Jung's sense, so that by the novel's close—after ambivalent moments of regression and progress—he is able to accept the farm (admitting in the last line, "Your farm. I always thought of it as our farm."), and to be "free" of it as well and ready to return to his new home in New York.

We quoted above Updike's own comment that in comparing *The Centaur* with *Of the Farm*, "the mythical has fled the ethical." Not so. True, the more obvious mythic superstructure is gone; but, since Joey's quest is for psychic maturity, his search will necessarily involve the probing of those more subtle mythic symbols proper to the unconscious. The farm is already a mythic place when he arrives because of his conscious recognition of his mother's genius for mythologizing everything connected with it. But his challenge will be transcend her mythology, first by incorporating it and then by transforming it in the light of his own psychic struggle.

The farm is, indeed, abundant with myths. But the myths proper to Mrs. Robinson and Peggy are of a more conscious sort, easily detectable to an outsider. Such myths correspond with Mark Schorer's more general definition: "Myths are instruments by which we continually struggle to make our experience intelligible to ourselves. A myth is a large, controlling image that gives philosophical meaning to the facts of ordinary life, that is, which has organizing value for experience.   "14

Joey's mythicizing, though, will be somewhat different in kind because different in direction. His concern is less that of coming to terms with the ordinary external world—though partially that—than with the process of understanding himself. As we shall see later in our analysis of *A Month of Sundays*, Joey's goal is that of psychic integration, of becoming a "whole man" according to Jung's psychology. This process involves that "of becoming the independent personality who is (relatively!) free from the domination of the parental archetypes and independent of the supportive structures of the social environment. He can therefore establish his own individual values and relationships which are valid because they are based on the reality of his self-knowledge and not on a system of illusions or rationalizations."15

Consequently, the varied competing myths that animate the story will interact on multiple levels; the story itself, as shaped by Joey, will attempt to integrate them as, concomitantly, it describes Joey's striving for self-integration.

Throughout their verbal exchanges, Peggy and Mrs. Robinson concentrate on their different interpretations of the meaning of Manhood, Womanhood, and Freedom. (pp. 31-32, 112, 134) Both, however, resort to an unexpressed private mythology. Of Mrs. Robinson: ". . . my mother's description of my father's anguished restlessness as 'his freedom' was beautifully congruous. My mother within the mythology that she had made of her life was like a mathematician who, having decreed several limited assumptions, performs feats of warping and circumvention and paradoxical linkage. . . ." (p. 31) Of Peggy, "I saw that in my mother's describing as a gift her failure to possess my father had angered her; it had touched the sore spot within her around which revolved her own mythology, of women given themselves to men, of men in return giving women a reason to live." (p. 31) And together: "deeper and deeper their voices dived into the darkness that was each to the other, in pursuit of shadows that I supposed were my father and myself." (p. 134)

While the women argue publicly about these issues, Joey's psychic journey will engage them on a more private level. With Richard as interlocutor, Joey, his mother, and his wife will each offer differing mythic sagas of the farm, an artful reinterpretation that, for each of them, will be a mode of expiation for the humanly disruptive choices each has made.

Joey remains, in a sense, ever the conventional "hero" of the narrative. Like the male hero in all classic myths he is directed in his unconscious quest toward the simultaneous discovery of three great mysteries: of Woman, of Earth, and of the Self. Joseph Campbell in *The Hero with a Thousand Faces* unwittingly summarizes this novel's development.

> Woman, in the picture language of mythology, represents the totality of what can be known. The hero is the one who comes to know. As he progresses in the slow initiation which is life, the form of the goddess undergoes a series of transfigurations . . . by deficient eyes she is reduced to inferior states; by the evil eye of ignorance she is spellbound to banality and ignorance. But she is redeemed by the eyes of understanding. The hero who can take her as she is, without undue commotion but with the kindness and assurance she requires, is potentially the king, the incarnate god, of her created world.[16]

Initially, Joey's perspective toward Woman (and Earth and Self) is fragmented, like that of a hero given a riddle-laden task. At the story's start, he and his family are greeted as "Pilgrims!" by his mother, evoking our expectation of an adventure. As they leave the car to enter the house, Joey finds himself prey to an odd double perspective.

> I seemed to see [Peggy] with my mother's eyes, as a tall and painted woman toppling toward me, and simultaneously with my own, from the rear, as a retreating white skirt whose glimmering breadth was the center, the seat, of my life. (p. 8)

He then recalls a similar splitting of attention at his second wedding where "I was conscious of [my mother's] presence even at the pinnacle of the rite, when in the corner of my eye I saw Peggy's firm chin recede. . . ." (p. 10)

One could comment on these scenes from a Freudian vantage point, pointing up its possible Oedipal undertones, but the farm-related imagery descriptive of Joey's women throughout suggests more, namely: that just as *The Centaur* dealt with the Sky-Father myth, this novel presents the hero's encounter with the Earth-Mother myth on multisignificant levels.

Mrs. Robinson, approached in mythic terms, is like the nourishing and devouring Mother of Myth, both benign and dangerous like the Earth itself. But so too are Peggy and Joan, as we shall see. Yet, because Mrs. Robinson herself is so closely identified with the farm—in fact her own memories of her life's stages are consciously linked with the history of the farm (p. 32)—she represents more obviously the Earth-goddess undergoing, as in Campbell's phrase, "a series of transfigurations." For example, by taking Joey's recorded perceptions of her in sequence, a striking complex of images emerges.

> "as if in being surrounded by her farm we had plunged into the very territory of her thoughts." (p. 13)
>
> "my mother's voice alone, rising and falling, sighing itself away and wishing itself reborn, letting itself grow so slack and diffuse it seemed the murmur of nature. . . ." (p. 28)
>
> "My mother's silences . . . revisited the darkness in which, but for her grace, I would be buried unborn, were as terrible as ever." (p. 31)
>
> "With her hair down she had seemed witchlike to me ever since as a child. . . ." (p. 40)
>
> "Behind the mesh her face was almost featureless, the head of a goddess rescued from the sea." (p. 74)
>
> (As Richard and Joey discuss moon-geography) "She did not respond, and I knew, knew on my prickling skin, that she had clouded, having felt, in our digression away from her earth, a personal affront." (p. 111)
>
> (Joey's boyhood memory) "I seemed to be in bed, and a tall girl stood

above me, and her hair came loose from her shoulder and fell forward filling the air with a swift liquid motion, and hung there, as a wing edged with light, and enclosed me in a tent as she bent lower to deliver her goodnight kiss." (p. 127)

In Mrs. Robinson's own mythology, true to her Mother-Earth role, the farm is continually "humanized." She will call her farm a "people sanctuary" and will observe that "Land is like people, it needs a rest. Land is *just* like a person, except it never dies, it just gets tired." (p. 24) Joey will do the opposite: in his mythmaking he will "farmicize" the human, thereby encountering Woman in her more universal, earthly manifestation. As Campbell points out, when the hero comes to know woman, he learns through her the natural world which she possesses as an extension of herself. She is the portal through whom the green world of Nature and Earth is perceived.[17] In like manner, our hero Joey by knowing Woman learns to know the farm (the mystery of Earth) and his farm (his self). To the hero, Nature, Woman, and the Self are correlative goals.

This awakening realization on Joey's part is evident from his lyric descriptions of Peggy in similar Mother-Earth imagery. Even Mrs. Robinson's less lyrical assessment of Peggy in a bikini is appropriate: "I'm all for Nature, the more of it the better." (p. 79) But, just as was true of his perceptions of his mother, his attitude toward Peggy as Woman will betray a shifting ambivalence.

". . . the space of the bed was totally obscure: a rich hiatus, a velvet lake. . . . The mysterious space of the bed creaked and Peggy asked. . . ." (p. 45; cf. also p. 143)
(The beginning of this passage was quoted in full above) "My wife is wide-hipped and long-waisted, and, surveyed from above, gives an impression of terrain. . . . Over all, like a sky, withdrawn and cool, hangs—hovers, stands, is—is the sense of her consciousness, of her composure, of a non-committal witnessing that preserves me from claustrophobia through any descent no matter how deep." (pp. 46-47)
"Perhaps I imagined the whorish little hitch of her hips as she stood erect. . . ." (p. 79)
"She acknowledged me only by following the tractor, eyes downcast, like a concubine in processional chains. . . ." (p. 97)
(On Peggy hoeing in a bikini) ". . . her figure which tapered to ankles that seemed to vanish in the earth." (p. 88)
"There are moments when she seems to be an abyss. She can be terribly stupid." (p. 138)

Joey asks, "Are you bleeding?" "Abundant. I think I'm sympathetic with the rain." (p. 144) To which Joey responds, "It's stupid Nature."
"Peggy, bare-shouldered in her bikini, was up to her hips in brambles . . . she seemed a doe of my species . . . seemed in the centaurine costume more natural, more practically resolved to give herself . . . to the farm." (p. 161)
Peggy to Joey: "You like [the farm] the same way you like me. It's something big you can show off." (p. 102)
(Joey, after tracing the length of her spine with his hand) "I felt this long living line as a description of grief—as in those new paintings whose artists, returning to nature from the realm of abstraction, render the sky an impossible earth-red which nevertheless answers to our eyes as sky." (p. 162)

As these examples manifest, subtly the competing and also conflicting images of Peggy and his mother as Earth-figures unite and separate in Joey's perception. A pivotal meeting takes place in the extended scene where Joey mows the meadow. Significantly, it is his mother who must start the tractor, then yield her seat to him. Later he must wear her coolie hat to protect himself from the sun, for "Within the hat there was a perpetual shade and the rustle of shelter." (p. 96) As he begins, feeling like a "king" enthroned (recall Campbell's hero above), Joey recalls how different his method of mowing is from hers. Her method "was to embrace the field, tracing its borders and then in a slow square spiral closing in until one small central patch was left. . . . Mine was to slice, in one ecstatic straight thrust, up the middle and then to narrow the two halves. . . . I imitated war, she love." (p. 58) Both, of course, as the sexual connotations suggest, imitate love, but the difference lies between War and Love, Ares and Aphrodite whose torrid affair gave birth to both Eros (Love) and Anteros (unrequited Love). But, during this symbolic act of mowing, Joey's attention shifts from one Aphrodite-Earth figure (his mother) to another (Peggy). Let us recall that one of Aphrodite's epithets is "Foam-borne" and that Ares was captivated not only by her but also by his love of combat itself.

The tractor body was flecked with foam and I, rocked back and forth on the iron seat shaped like a woman's hips, alone in nature, as hidden under the glaring sky as at midnight, excited by destruction, weightless, discovered in myself a swelling which I idly permitted to stand, thinking of Peggy. My wife is a field. (p. 59)

An ironic counterpoint to Joey's ecstasy is provided by Richard's observation that "Tractors are slow, aren't they?" To which Mrs. Robinson replies, "That's because they're like dying people, they have their feet in the ground instead of on top." (p. 61).

Tractors and Joey are slow because "the field was vast, yet the very slowness of my progress . . . subdued it." As the Earth-figures here intuit, at issue is Joey's manhood and his realistic contact with the earth. However, the women will concentrate attention on the more conscious stereotypes of masculine-feminine diversity. Mrs. Robinson will assert that "I didn't want my only child to be an Olingerite, I wanted him to be a *man*." (p. 30) Later she and Peggy have this exchange:

> "As to Joey and me," [Peggy] said, "I'm the first woman he's ever met who was willing to let him be a man." This was the secret song, the justification with which she had led me into divorce.
> "Maybe," my mother said, "we mean different things by the word 'man.' " (p. 112)

Joey's efforts at achieving manhood are more complex, however, than such conscious *machismo*-tainted contrasts indicate. True, throughout he admits his weakness, his conspiratorial disloyalties, his failures and nasty suspicions, his submission to petty tyrannies—in short, the case book of a mama's boy who ought to get with it. Yet, as we mentioned earlier, Joey's most significant undertaking is not that of acquiring a hairier chest or of only cutting apron strings, but that of a private, personal—and so more universal—search for what Jung calls "individuation." This is the result of a complex psychological process that makes a human being "an individual," a "whole man," not in terms of external deportment but on the deepest levels of interiority. This process, as in Joey's case, entails, first, the encounter with one's primal unconscious imaginative impulses (the earthly given), and, secondly, the engagement with that unifying symbol which arises from such an encounter. For Joey, the farm itself and his subsequent story about its multiple associations become at once a unifying and transforming symbol for his psychic quest and self-discovery.

Superficially, *Of the Farm* appears to be merely a chatty domestic drama written from the point of view of a hypersensitive, over-sexed, middle-aged boy. And yet, closer investigation reveals that this story of a spiritual search also contains all the major motifs of religious mythology: initiation, death and rebirth, sin, expiation, and redemption—that is, an archetypal quest. Even the sexual passages found throughout which have distracted a number of critics enjoy a broader significance than a Freudian would find. For Jung, unlike Freud, the *libido* has a wider meaning than sex, for it comprehends the sum total of energetic life processes, those vital forces of which sexuality is but one area. Power, hunger, hatred, sexuality, and religion are all manifestations of the libidinous instinct for Jung: their integration marks a person's effort toward true "manhood."[18]

In the novel Joey records two significant dreams. The first is a recurrent one of Peggy who, like a beckoning siren, invites Joey, here simultaneously boy and man, to enter the farm, a farm now redeemed by her forgiveness.

> I was home, on the farm. I stood at the front of the house looking up over the grape arbor, where the grapes were as green as the leaves, at the bedroom windows, like a small boy, too shy to knock at the door, come to call on a playmate. Her face appeared at the window, misted by the screen. Peggy . . . as she bent forward to call me through the screen, her smile was wonderful; she was so happy here, so full of delight at the strangeness of the place, so in love with the farm, and so eager to redeem, with the sun of her presence, the years of dismal hours I had spent there. Her smile told me to come up . . . it knowingly conveyed, through itself, from elsewhere, forgiveness—and it was so gay. (p. 48)

The second dream is ostensibly more chilling and less gay. Joey dreams that while he is mowing, his tractor stumbles over something, so he stops, dreading that he has destroyed some pheasant eggs. Dismounting, he discovers himself in a strange landscape, vacant, swampish, and smouldering like a dump.

> Something curled up was lying caked with ashen dirt. Abruptly anxious, overswept with pity, I picked it up and examined it and discovered it to be alive. It was a stunted human being, a hunched homunculus, its head sank on its chest as if shying from a blow. A tiny voice said, "it's me." The face beneath the caked dirt was, though shrunk, familiar. Who was it? "Don't you know me, Daddy? I'm Charlie." I pressed him against my chest and vowed never to be parted from him. (p. 146)

Both these dreams can be easily and justly interpreted as guilt-dreams, indicative of unresolved feelings of resentment and dependency (dream #1) or of paternal abandonment (dream #2). Such an interpretation accords well with Joey's moral conflicts as recorded consciously throughout this story. However, as Jung makes clear in his discussion of "The Psychology of the Child Archetype,"[19] such dreams are not wholly negative in meaning but, instead, can dramatize a most positive psychic transition for the dreamer. For example, dreams of a "child" (oneself as a child, a child related to the dreamer, an unknown child, no matter) often intimate the dreamer's unconscious striving for further growth, the vague realization of the possibility for a new wholeness. As Jung said, "One of the essential features of the child-motif is its *futurity*. The child is a potential future . . . the child-motif signifies as a rule an anticipation of future developments, even though at first sight it may seem like a retrospective configuration."[20] Furthermore, the child-motif can manifest itself as a dwarf, elf, or homunculus as in Joey's second dream. In any case, the child-motif arises when one's conscious mind is beset by a conflict of opposites to such a degree that *consciously* one sees no way out: when the conscious Ego is thus stymied, deeper images from the unconscious well up. As Jung said, "The child-motif represents the pre-conscious, childhood aspect of the collective psyche."[21] Jung continues:

> Abandonment, exposure, danger etc. are all elaborations of the child's *insignificant beginnings* and its *mysterious and miraculous birth*. This statement describes a certain psychic experience of a creative nature, whose object is the emergence of a new and, as yet, unknown content.
> . . . Because the symbol of the "child" fascinates and grips the conscious mind, its *redemptive* effect passes over into consciousness and brings about that separation from the conflict-situation which the conscious mind was unable to achieve. The symbol anticipates a nascent state of consciousness. So long as this is not actually in being, the "child" remains a mythological projection which requires religious repetition and renewal by ritual.[22]

At the risk of overemphasizing a Jungian reading, such considerations do clarify certain structural and thematic elements in the novel. Why, for example, the "child" dreams both involve the transforming symbol that the farm becomes for Joey. Why Joey, upon awakening from that second dream, agrees to go to Sunday religious service with his mother (renewal by ritual for Jung) and admits he "needed to test my own existence against the fact of their faces and clean clothes and hushed shoulders, to regather myself at a vacant hour." (p. 148) Why his subsequent passionate desire to "rescue" both his mother and his wife coincides with his horrific vision of the farm (p. 160), so reminiscent of the child-hero's redemptive rescue of Woman in mythology. Why also Joey should feel compelled to tell his child-counterpart Richard—who, throughout, apes his boyhood interests in science fiction, moon exploration, and Wodehouse, and is described as "Cupid interviewing Venus" and has eyes with a "froglike shininess"—a fairy tale about a frog who descended to find a treasure, but grew smaller and smaller, until first he disappears, only to eventually awake with renewed vision. (pp. 129-31)

Finally, such considerations clarify the novel's closing dialogue where, superficially, the women's assessment of Joey reads as irony or condescension. In fact, it is *Joey's* account of the dialogue that reunites the three women in his life and suggests a more subtle, implicit resolution to the story's many conflicts.

> "Don't worry about the mowing," [Mrs. Robinson] said. "Sammy can finish it someday. You did the man-sized part." She turned her head to Peggy. "He's a good boy and I've always been tempted to overwork him."
> "He *is* a good boy." Repeating this, Peggy voluntarily grinned, grinned at me as in my dream or as she had the first time we met.
> . . . at my approach, the two women, Joan in blue and Peggy wheat-yellow, had turned to face me, and when Joan said, *This is my husband,* Peggy's hand stabbed mannishly toward mine and grinned with startling width, as if incredulous.
> "That's the smile," my mother said. (p. 173)

Ambiguity, of course, remains. The reasons are not only artistic but psychological as well—and here they are as one. Joey's efforts at self-discovery and an integrated manhood involve his confrontation with his *anima,* that multifarious image which represents the feminine aspect of a man's psyche. Joey is 35, the usual age for such a critical encounter; without it, further maturation is impossible. Jung explained, "Every man carries within himself the eternal image of a woman, not the image of this or that particular woman. This image is fundamentally unconscious . . . an imprint or archetype of all the ancestral experiences of the female, a deposit, as it were, of all the impressions made by a woman. . . . Since this image is unconscious, it is always unconsciously projected upon the person of the beloved, and is one of the chief reasons for passionate attraction or repulsion."[23]

It is important to recall that Joey sincerely still loves all the significant women in his life: mother, Peggy, and first wife Joan. Each represents some aspect of his *anima* image and yet, being but an aspect, ushers in contradictory reactions. Joan's "defect"—an improper word for unconscious impulses—is that she offered an ethereal, poetic image for Joey. As he admits, "I think I married Joan because, when I first saw her wheeling her bicycle through the autumnal dusk of the [Harvard] Yard, she suggested, remote and lithe and inward, the girl of 'The Solitary Reaper' and, close-up, seemed a cool Lucy whose death might give me cause to sing." (p. 109) Since all his memorable descriptions of her are of a similiar, non-earthly, ethereal kind, it is no surprise that he still loves her *a distans*. Even when pregnant and full of new life, as her photograph reminds him, she still carried it as a secret.

But both Peggy and his mother in differing ways represent to him a mother image in the archetypal sense. "Mother" here is not to be taken literally but is a universal symbol for an enveloping, embracing presence that, as devouring, he hopes to flee and, as nourishing, he wishes to welcome. If a male represses such ambivalent feeling, he begins to live regressively, seeking his childhood and his mother, yet hating it. Jung describes the situation in phrases remarkably similar to the novel's imagery:

> There is in him a desire to touch reality, to embrace the earth and fructify the field of the world. But he makes no more than a series of impatient beginnings, for his initiative as well as his staying power are crippled by the secret memory that the world and happiness may be had as a gift—from the mother. It makes demands on the masculinity of a man, on his ardor, above all on his courage and resolution, when it comes to throwing his whole being into the scales.[24]

At this stage of the myth, the Mother-image, as we have seen, is both old and young, both Mother-Earth as Ceres and Goddess of Death as Persephone, while the son is simultaneously spouse and infant. As Jung warns, an unfortunate result, as in Joey's case, can be the son's erroneous projection of the mother "image" onto his actual mother.

> This projection can only be dissolved when he comes to realize that in the realm of the psyche there exists an image of the mother and not only of the mother, but also of the daughter, the sister, the beloved, the heavenly goddess, the earth spirit. . . . Every mother and every beloved is forced to become the carrier and embodiment of this omnipresent and ageless image which corresponds to the deepest reality in a man.[25]

The extraordinarily complex *content* of the male's unconscious Woman-image cannot be directly known to the conscious mind but its import can be so integrated. *Anima* "figures represent *functions* which filter the contents of the collective unconscious through the conscious mind."[26] One such mode of conscious integration, as we shall see also in *A Month of Sundays*, takes place when a man fixes those feelings, moods, fantasies sent by his *anima* in some specific art-form, such as writing, painting, or sculpture. This creative effort taps the more primal unconscious impulses and attempts to shape them by way of intellectual or ethical or religious evaluation. Joey Robinson's own story, the novel itself, represents precisely such an effort.

It is owing to the fact that Joey's personal psychic venture is so multi-leveled, involving sexual, ethical, and religious concerns, that the minister's sermon is so climactic and important. It recapitulates almost all of the novel's previous themes and yet organizes them from a revelatory and more universal perspective— as universal, one might suggest, as the collective unconscious to which it is indebted.

Earlier in the novel we hear Mrs. Robinson recount the classical myth about the creation of male-female differences taken from Plato; as in *The Centaur*, once again the Secular and Sacred Scriptures are proposed.

> "Plato says," my mother told the boy, "that God made people absolutely round, with four arms and four legs and two heads, and they would roll everywhere with terrific speed. In fact people were so happy and powerful that God grew jealous and split them in half, with a little difference, so that everybody keeps looking for their other half. That's what love is." (p. 69)

A discussion ensues as to whether the "little difference" is only the penis or whether there are psychological differences as well. Peggy thinks so; Mrs. Robinson does not, yet later she remarks that she would like to see the farm as a place where people could come and become "round" again, a contextual irony of the first order.

Plato's myth captures the novel's central themes of Nature-Creation, Sexual Differences, and the Search for the Self. However, it omits the major theme of Freedom-Responsibility, keynoted by the Sartre epigraph. The Biblical myth includes this theme. Rather appropriately, therefore, the minister's text is Genesis 2:18-23.

> And the Lord God said, It is not good that man should be alone; I will make him a helpmeet for him.
>
> And out of the ground the Lord formed every beast of the field, and every fowl of the air; and brought them unto Adam to see what he would call them: and whatsoever Adam called every living creature, that was the name thereof.

And Adam gave names to all the cattle and the fowl of the air and to every beast of the field; but for Adam there was not found a helpmeet for him.

And the Lord caused a deep sleep to fall upon Adam, and he slept; and he took one of his ribs and closed up the flesh instead; and the rib, which the Lord God had taken from man, made he a woman, and brought her unto the man.

And Adam said, This is now bone of my bone, and flesh of my flesh; she shall be called Woman, because she was taken out of Man.

As we indicated above, this text and reflections upon it constituted Updike's original, unpublished essay, fated to become the minister's sermon here. Its content was derived from Updike's selective use of material found in Karl Barth's *Church Dogmatics: A Selection*, Chapter VII, "Man and Woman."[27] As the title indicates, the chapter itself is a selection from Barth's more extensive treatment of Man's Creation found in his *Church Dogmatics* III, 1 and III, 4.

It might be well, then, to review briefly in this context the importance of Creation in Barth's theology. As we have seen, for Barth Jesus Christ is the key to the mystery and purpose of Creation. From eternity, God the Creator intended through Jesus Christ to unite Himself with Man, His creature, in a Covenant of Love: this is what the revelation of and about Christ makes known. This Covenant of Love, with Christ as goal, is the internal basis of Creation, and Creation is the external basis of the Covenant. In other words, Creation is the theater, the place where the history of God's Love-Covenant is enacted, while that Love-Covenant is the dynamic within Creation, the force that gives Creation purpose and meaning.[28]

This, then, is the theological basis for Barth's treatment of human sexuality. He will argue that, since the Covenant rests upon and is the goal of Creation, the outlines of the relationship between Creation and Covenant can be discerned in the story of the creation of Adam and Eve. Their creatureliness will reflect God's Covenant with Man, for that Covenant is constitutive of their very created being and sexuality. The definitive revelation about Jesus Christ shows that Man is created by God to be a Covenant-partner and is only truly a man in relation and not in solitariness, i.e. Man is meant to manifest that kind of relation to God and his fellow man which Jesus revealed. Consequently, to be a fellow man is a decisive determination of Man's nature; in fact, Man's very bisexuality as male and female, according to Barth, is evidence of this relative status toward God and one's fellow man.

Furthermore, since Man is ever in dialectical tension, being as he is "a creature on the boundary between heaven and earth," the sexual encounter between male and female will manifest this dramatic tension and will mirror the dialectical encounter and boundary between creature and Creator. In short, Man "in his divinely created sexuality is a similitude of the Covenant."

The minister's sermon presumes this theology of sexuality, and he, following Barth's own procedure, will offer reflections on each paragraph taken in sequence from the Biblical text.

In his commentary on the second verse, concerning the creation of animals and Adam's naming them, the minister alludes to "the eternal pact" of God's covenant with Creation and also suggests an appropriateness to Joey's own imaginative efforts at later composing his story—recalling, thereby, imagery to be found in the novel.

> Has not Man, in creating civilization, looked to the animals not only as beasts of burden and sustenance but for inspiration, as in the flight of birds and the majesty of lions. Has not, in honesty, an eternal pact been honored and kept? . . . Is not language an act of husbandry, a fencing-in of fields? . . . language aërates the barren destiny of brute matter with the penetration of the mind, of the spirit. (pp. 150-51)

The minister then goes on to the next verse, which describes Eve's creation from Adam's rib. Reminding us of Plato's parable, he describes the rib as "rounded" and his commentary continues in language replete with Jungian resonances.

> God . . . imparted to Woman a creaturely shapeliness. A rib is rounded. Man, with Woman's creation, became confused as to where to turn. With one half of his being he turns toward her, his rib, as if into himself, into the visceral and nostalgic warmth wherein his tensions find resolution in dissolution. With his other half, he gazes outward toward God, along the straight line of infinity. He seeks to solve the riddle of death. Eve does not. In a sense she does not know death. Her very name, Hava, means "living." Her motherhood answers concretely what men would answer abstractly. But as Christians we know there is no abstract answer, there is no answer whatsoever apart from Christ.
>
>   And third, Woman was made while Adam slept. Her beauty will have in men's eyes a dream-like quality. Each day we awake like Adam

> puzzled to find ourselves duplicated—no, not duplicated, for the ex-
> pectant softness and graceful patience of the other stands in strange
> contrast to us. In reaching out to her, Adam commits an act of faith.
> (pp. 152-53)

In Barth's theology of sexuality, Christ is the key or the "concrete answer" for any understanding of Creation and Covenant. And yet, as the minister indicates, whenever a man reaches out toward Woman who represents to him the mysteries of Life, Nature, and his own creation, he is implicitly placing his faith in Creation itself and in God's Covenant. Man can only achieve true self-knowledge, that is, make a turn inward toward self-discovery, by turning outward to Woman (which, in a sense, is a re-turn for him), thus embracing the mystery of Creation. God has *ordered* His Creation thus; no one can escape that right order. Despite the fact that Man will always be puzzled and unsettled by Woman and *vice versa*, "Man can be and speak and act as a true man only as he realizes that in so doing he must answer the question of woman, i.e. give an account of his own humanity. . . . They elude themselves if they try to escape this orientation toward one another, i.e. the fact that they are ordered, related, and directed to one another."[29] Man, like Adam now minus a rib, first sees Woman as a grievous wound he has suffered and so a foretaste of death's nearness; but, on seeing that rib rounded, he thinks of the wound as healed, as a protection from death.

For this reason, the minister will stress the key lines from the next verse, Adam's words "This is now bone of my bone and flesh of my flesh," and will quote directly from Karl Barth.

> Karl Barth . . . says of Woman, "Successfully or otherwise she is in
> her whole existence an appeal to the kindness of man. . . ." "For kind-
> ness," he goes on to say, "belongs originally to his particular respon-
> sibility as a man." . . . In designating her with his own generic name,
> Adam commits an act of faith, "This is *now* bone of my bones, flesh
> of my flesh." In so declaring, he acknowledges within himself a re-
> sponsibility to be kind. He ties himself ethically to the earth. . . . But
> kindness needs no belief. It is implicit in the nature of Creation, in
> the very curves and amplitudes of God's fashioning. Let us pray.
> (pp. 153-54)

The minister's sermon thus capsulates the crucial dramatic moral di-lemmas, psychological ambivalences, and central themes found elsewhere in *Of the Farm*. Above we discussed the development of Joey's psychic freedom. Here the inclusion of Barth's theology raises the question of ethical freedom to which it is related. In Barth's theology, ethics is a *theological* category, not a morally philosophic one: Man's proper moral conduct is determined by Revelation, specifically the revelation about Jesus Christ Who is the goal of Creation, the criterion for what is right or wrong in Creation. Ethical action is a response to God's command, then; in the context of the minister's sermon, it is the responsible response to God's right order in His Creation as revealed in that text of Genesis. Consequently, Man is truly "free" and "ethical" only when he accepts in faith his creaturehood and his place in God's plan of creation.

> Because [Man and Woman's] freedom is that which they have from and before and for God, therefore it can take shape only in their fellowship with each other, and their humanity can consist concretely only in the fact that they live in fellow-humanity, male with female, and female with male.[30]

Jung, Barth, and the minister all agree: Woman ties Man "ethically to the earth" (and psychologically, and religiously) and Man's responsibility is to be kind. For Barth, as for Jung, the figure of Woman is *not* restricted to wife or erotic partner. Each woman Man encounters, says Barth, "is Woman for him too, whether as mother, sister, acquaintance, friend, or fellow-worker."[31]

After hearing this sermon, Joey will attempt to become not only an integrated man but a kindly and responsible one as well. The novel's last line reveals this new effort at kindness and responsibility when he assures his mother, "*Your* farm?, . . ." "I've always thought of it as our farm." With such an admission, he accepts his past, his present, and his future, his women, his self in the freedom described in Sartre's epigraph. He becomes a "hero" and enters what Kierkegaard calls the ethical, the second sphere of existence.

4: *The Music School*

John Updike remarked in a 1968 interview that "Nothing that happens to us [novelists] after the age of twenty is as free from self-consciousness, because by then we have the vocation to write. Writers' lives break into two halves. At the point you get your writerly vocation you diminish your receptivity to experience."[1] In a 1974 address he returned to this conviction and elaborated upon it by saying:

> A writer begins with his personal truth, with that obscure but vulnerable and, once lost, precious life that he lived before becoming a writer; but, those first impressions discharged—a process of years—he finds himself, though empty, still posed in the role of a writer, with it may be an expectant audience of sorts and a certain habit of communion. It is then that he dies as a writer, by re-submitting his ego, as it were, to fresh drafts of experience and refined operations of his mind. *To remain interested*—of American novelists, only Henry James continued in old age to advance his art; most, indeed, wrote their best novels first, or virtually first. Energy ebbs as we live. . . . Almost alone the writer can reap profit from his loss.[2]

Updike's remarks resonate with a most personal ring, for a retrospective look at his writing career discloses, not only a life, but a career itself broken into "two halves." Updike has been a professional writer for two decades. His first decade's work, for the most part, records the strife, observation, and feeling of that pre-twenty-year-old wherein nostalgic recollections of boyhood are transmuted by an adult's imagination and youthful autobiography is altered into art. In his Foreword to *Olinger Stories* (1964) he characterized his early stories as "crystallizations of memory," a most apt description of most of the stories collected in *The Same Door* (1959) and *Pigeon Feathers* (1962). But it is also an appropriate

103

designation for his novels, not only for the more obviously autobiographical *The Centaur* (1963) and *Of the Farm* (1965), but even for the futuristic *The Poorhouse Fair* (1959) and the contemporary *Rabbit, Run* (1960). As he later remarked, "I was full of a Pennsylvania thing I wanted to say," and it is evident that the "Pennsylvania thing" of his youthful memory informs almost all the fiction of that 1955-65 decade.

Updike wrote that Foreword to *Olinger Stories* in 1964 with the intention of saying farewell to Pennsylvania and to his boyhood memories. Except for brief returns in *Rabbit Redux* (1971) and *Buchanan Dying* (1974), he has sustained that intention. After the novel *Of the Farm* (1965), his favorite fictional locale moves from Pennsylvania to New England (often Tarbox) and his themes no longer reflect boyhood recollections but adult concerns. In the decade 1965-76 the tensions of marriage, the process of aging, and the varied losses of "faith"—religious, political, sexual—become his central themes. However, he himself observed that "the difference between Olinger and Tarbox is much more the difference between childhood and adulthood than the difference between two geographical locations. They are stages on my pilgrim's progress, not dots on a map."[3]

The years 1964-66, therefore, mark an important transitional stage in Updike's pilgrim's progress and so are of crucial significance for a complete understanding of his writing career. Unfortunately, this pivotal period has been the most neglected one in Updike criticism because most critical attention has been devoted to his novels to the neglect of his short stories.[4] After the publication of *Of the Farm* in 1965, however, there was a gap of three years before the publication of *Couples* in 1968, and so one must turn to the short stories, especially those collected in *The Music School* (1966), for the material that records this period of transition.

The Music School collection holds a distinctive place in the Updike corpus because it contains several stories that, in addition to more familiar Updike themes, specifically engage the issues of artistic self-consciousness and the act of composition itself. In the story "The Bulgarian Poetess," published in March 1965, Updike created a spokesman who would explicitly engage these issues, Henry Bech. In 1970 he told an audience why he felt compelled to invent Henry Bech:

> Now, as for the Bech stories. . . . For a writer, life becomes overmuch a writer's life. Things happen to you that wouldn't happen to anybody else, and a way of using this to good advantage, of course, is to invent another writer. At first, he is very much an alter ego, but then, in the

end, not so. At any rate I have used the writer in *Bech* as a subject in order to confess sterility in a truthful way. . . . In my book, I tried to—and I believe I did—package and dispose of a certain set of tensions and anxieties which I have as a practicing writer.[5]

But Bech's character is only the most obvious alter ego in *The Music School* collection. Most of the remaining stories reveal a narrator or character wrestling with similar "writerly" problems of sterility and creativity and the tensions that result. A cursory reading, though, might miss this artistic aspect. The primary and ostensible theme of almost every story is that of the mystery of sexuality and sexual relationships examined in the light of their sterility or vitality. Subordinate, but concomitant with it, is the secondary theme of the mysterious relationship between the imagined and the real, between artistic re-creation and Creation, between the sterile and vitalizing processes of the mind. Updike's later story "Museums and Women," published in 1967, will explicitly conjoin these two "mysteries," but several stories in this collection do so with greater subtlety. The most obvious clue, however, that Updike is addressing these twin themes is found in the epigraph chosen for *The Music School*, a quotation from Wallace Stevens' poem, "To the One of Fictive Music":

Now, of the music summoned by the birth
That separates us from the wind and the sea,
Yet leaves us in them, until earth becomes,
By being so much of the things we are,
Gross effigy and simulacrum, none
Gives motion to perfection more serene
Than yours, out of our imperfections wrought,
Most rare or ever of more kindred air
In the laborious weaving that you wear.[6]

These lines represent well Stevens' continuing poetic theme: that the apparent dichotomy which exists between the realm of reality, disorder, and the actual (earth) and the realm of the imagination, order, and the ideal (music) is bridged only through Art. The "One" addressed in the poem is the Muse of poetry who personifies man's power of imagination and memory. The "birth" referred to in the first line is that of human consciousness which separates us from nature (wind and sea) "yet so leaves us" in it that we see in nature a "gross effigy" of ourselves. But "the music summoned by the birth" of consciousness is Art which tries to unite man and nature, and none is more perfect and "rare" than poetry. Yet poetry is of a "kindred air" since as the bridge between, the more the poem retains of ourselves, the closer it brings us to nature.[7]

Updike's choice of this epigraph is most apt since most of the stories deal with the "Stevensian" theme of re-creating reality and the past via imagination and memory. The intractable "natural" reality that challenges this re-creative effort is that of Woman in the mystery of her sexuality. This is most apparent in "The Stare," "In Football Season," "The Morning," "Leaves," "Harv is Plowing Now," and "The Bulgarian Poetess." In each of these stories the sexual challenge is associated with the artistic challenge to *imagine* and so re-create the object of pursuit; implied in this effort, furthermore, is the narrator's desire for a new form of union, so that, in a Stevens-like way, the story not only recounts that effort but *becomes* the new form of union as well.

At first the brilliantly designed story "The Music School" seems excepted—until we note that the adulterous narrator, now "unfaithful" to his wife and "faltering toward divorce," had been "unfaithful" to the novel he once planned to write and so now, "though unmusical," he waits in a music school attempting to sort out answers to both infidelities. In this and the other stories, composition and theme, frame and form are one in that each story's inner dynamic is heuristic in a composite way. We find the narrator, explicitly or not, seeking "connections" amid remembered or imagined events so that the resultant structure (i.e. where these connections intersect) both shapes and is shaped by this heuristic movement. Throughout, there is threefold pursuit, as there is continually in the poetry of Wallace Stevens:[8] 1) pursuit of the elusive, disordered reality (Nature and Woman); 2) the conscious effort to draw upon the resources of the imagination through the medium of metaphor; and finally, 3) the heuristic movement outward which becomes simultaneously a search for the self, the symbolic center of the pursuit. But the goal and instrument of these three quests are the same: recovery and re-creation.

The dense and difficult story "Harv is Plowing Now" illustrates well this triple-layered attempt at recovery. In it the controlling metaphor is that of an archeological excavation. Just as the archeologist "unearths" both the precious and the dross, and a farmer like Harv plows the dead earth in order to revitalize it, so too the narrator-artist must mine his memory (memory of a Woman) in order to effect a re-creation by re-imagining, thus issuing in a "resurrection" of his very self at the story's end.

Like Updike's technique of dialectical movement, Stevens' poetry always proceeds in a series of antithetical terms, such as chaos and order, imagination and reality, stasis and change; these antitheses are rarely resolved in his poetry, and, if so, then briefly, only to return again. Like Updike, Stevens gropes for a final formulation about art and reality, but, also like him, he knows that it cannot be stated, for man is a temporal being and reality is in flux.[9]

But, in addition to this dialectical procedure, there is perhaps an even more significant "technical" affinity. For Wallace Stevens, poetry was "an act of the mind," and so art was itself the process whereby "the mind turns to its own creations and examines them."[10] By "creations" here he meant primarily *metaphor*, for he admitted in *The Necessary Angel* that

> Poetry is almost incredibly one of the effects of analogy . . . almost incredibly the outcome of figures of speech or, what is the same thing, the outcome of the operation of one imagination on another through the instrumentality of the figures. To identify poetry and metaphor or metamorphosis is merely to abbreviate the last remark. There is always an analogy between nature and the imagination, and possibly poetry is merely the strange rhetoric of that parallel. . . .[11]

For Stevens, the artist's imaginative alertness regarding the manifold potential of the metaphor allows him to shape reality in new ways since the metaphor is his instrument for exploring unsuspected resemblances between things, thereby bringing reality's hidden secrets to the surface. It is *through* the metaphor that reality and imagination meet. The metaphor itself, then, becomes for Stevens a vehicle of discovery, a method of movement, and, finally, an instrument for the integration of experience.[12]

The narrator of Updike's story "The Sea's Green Sameness" wrestles with the problematic relationship between Art and Nature; years later, Updike commented on this story by saying:

> I believe that narratives should not be *primarily* packages for psychological insight, though they can contain them, like raisins in buns. But the substance is the dough, which feeds the story-telling appetite, the appetite for motion, for suspense, for resolution. The author's deepest pride, as I have experienced it, is not in his incidential wisdom but in his ability to keep an organized mass of images moving forward, to feel life engendering itself under his hands. . . .[13]

When we reflect on these comments in the light of Stevens, we realize that in Updike too the "dough" that feeds the "story-telling appetite" and "keeps a mass of images moving" throughout his fiction is mainly metaphor. Plot is generally of secondary interest in his fiction; a plot outline of any of his novels always sounds shapeless and random. So too, seldom are his characters dramatic in themselves; rather, it is their recorded perceptions, rather than their human idiosyncrasies, that engage our attention. "Life is engendered" in his fiction most successfully *through* metaphor. For example, a characteristic hitherto overlooked is that *each* of Updike's novels is metaphor-centered (of course, usually in multiple fashion), and the title itself often signals the controlling metaphor. This is more obvious in *Rabbit, Run* where the metaphor of movement is ironically aimless, or in *Rabbit Redux* where "returns" are explored in manifold modes, or in *Of the Farm* where each of the characters "becomes" the farm-metaphor from various perspectives, or in *Couples* where "coupling" is not only the recurrent activity but where so many events are seen in double-focus and so many characters seem duplicates of each other, or in *The Centaur* where, by drawing upon the Chiron myth (a universalized metaphor), he broadens, deepens, and twists the divine/human analogies throughout. At first glance, this is less apparent in his first and most recent novels—until we note that in *The Poorhouse Fair* the fair itself, so central to the novel's structure, is actually the prime analogate for the joyous celebration of life amid apparent decay examined in each dialogue and dramatized in each event. More recently, in *A Month of Sundays*, one of the narrator, Marshfield's, last journal entries is that "the day after tomorrow, my month may seem a metaphor," which alerts us to the metaphoric implications of the novel's title, for the novel's "action" takes place in an unrealistic "no time" and "never-never land."[14] Updike's *Marry Me* finds its inspiration in Herrick's poem to his Mistress: not only is "marriage" its theme, but corresponding metaphors of linkage, separation, union, and desertion shape the novel. Finally, the title *The Coup* captures the range of violent social displacements that novel dramatizes.

Updike is sometimes castigated for over-writing, for "forever moving from event to embroidery, from drama to coy detail," in Richard Gilman's phrase,[15] but it is this Stevens-like probing of the manifold potential of metaphor that provides a likely explanation for this characteristic and not perverse artiness. J. Hillis Miller reminds us that this was an intentional strategy for Stevens, that the "Most salient quality of *Harmonium* is the elegance, the finicky fastidiousness, even sometimes the ornate foppishness, of the language. . . . These words cooperate with the words around them to create an atmosphere as rich and strange as that of a painting by Matisse or Dufy, and as much a new revelation of reality."[16]

One might object at this point that such an Updike-Stevens "connection" seems tenuous since many artists besides Stevens have used metaphor as an instrument for discovering and shaping their view of reality. What makes Stevens' aesthetic somewhat distinctive, of course, is his additional conviction that metaphor is a vehicle for *self*-discovery, the means whereby the self, estranged from a world external to it, is capable of bridging this divide and achieving, however briefly, an integration.[17]

It is precisely this conviction that many stories in Updike's *The Music School* address; or, more accurately, it is *in and through* the fiction that we find Updike the artist consciously wrestling with the reality/imagination dichotomy and its relation to the self. *The Music School* stories are not only special in Updike's *corpus* but create, in a sense, a new genre in the American short story tradition. For a good many of these stories are not narratives at all, but are *lyric meditations* in prose, more closely akin to the poetry of Stevens than our more usual categories. As in Stevens' poetry, many of these stories are structured as inquiries wherein the central character, often a first-person narrator, is being compelled to pursue the implications of real or imagined events from the past in an attempt to find some "connective" resolution. Updike himself has characterized "this mode of mine" as the "abstract-personal"—which has a Stevensian ring—and is well aware that some critics have "expressed impatience with my lace-making, so called." But, as with Stevens, here such "lace-making" is all.

A more detailed investigation of these parallel heuristic movements in all the major stories found in *The Music School* would demand a book-length study itself. For our purposes it is sufficient to concentrate on one dense and difficult story entitled "Leaves," which critics have overlooked, and offer it as a paradigm for such an investigation. Coincidentally, Updike selected "Leaves" as his *best* story upon being asked to contribute to Rust Hills' anthology called *Writer's Choice*. His comments about it are worth noting and enlighten our argument thus far.

> ["Leaves"] is in a mode of mine, the abstract-personal, not a favorite with my critics. One of them, reviewing *The Music School*, expressed impatience with my lace-making, so-called. Well, if "Leaves" is lace, it is taut and symmetrical lace, with scarce a loose thread. It was written after long silence, swiftly, unerringly as a sleepwalker walks. No memory of any revision mars my backwards impression of it. The

way the leaves become the pages, the way the bird becomes his description, the way the bright and multiform world of nature is felt
rubbing against the dark world of the trapped ego—all strike me as
beautiful, and of the order of artistic "happiness" that is given rather
than attained. The last image, the final knot of lace, is an assertion
of transcendental faith scaled, it seems to me, nicely to the mundane. [18]

"Leaves" is a very brief story, only nine paragraphs long, but in its
integration of imagery and subtlety of structure it represents well Updike's
successful effort to engage the Reality-Art-Imagination relationships, and
as a prose-poem it exemplifies the Stevens epigraph. [19]

The title "Leaves" itself suggests multiple meanings, each warranted
in the story, for the word "leaves" can connote the product of Nature (as
in grape leaves), and, as a verb, can indicate departure, loss, and time.
Significantly, it can also suggest a book's "leaves," its pages, which are
the outcome of art. The story is ostensibly a confession-meditation in that
the narrator, now isolated in a forest retreat, is essaying to recover from
the emotional disaster of imminent divorce by "sorting out the events" of
his predicament. The story's framework is both heuristic and cruciform.
The crux or X pattern is manifest in the sequence of reflections as the
narrator pursues the "connections" among them.

The opening paragraph is reminiscent of the Stevens epigraph, for in
it the narrator realizes that his previous self-absorption has blinded him
to the paradoxical discovery that, on the one hand, although he and
Nature are independent, his "curiosity" or attention now unites them and,
on the other hand, although physically part of Nature, his spiritual consciousness—now ironically the source of his guilt—also separates him
from it.

The grape leaves outside my window are curiously beautiful. "Curiously" because it comes upon me as strange, after the long darkness of
self-absorption and fear and shame in which I have been living, that
things are beautiful, that independent of our catastrophes they continue to maintain the "effect," which is the hallmark and specialty of
Nature. Nature: this morning it seems to me very clear that Nature
may be defined as that which exists without guilt. Our bodies are in
Nature; our shoes, their laces, the little plastic tips of the laces—
everything around us and about us is in Nature, and yet something
holds us away from it, like the upward push of water which keeps us
from touching the sandy bottom. . . . (p. 44)

This discernment about Nature and yet "that something that holds

us back" from it, in turn, issues in another realization: man's limited power
to make contact with and arrest Nature through language. Here the elusive natural object is a blue jay. The bird itself might "leave," but a
book's "leaves" might capture it—another "curious" relationship for
reflection.

> A blue jay lights on a twig outside my window. Momentarily sturdy,
> he stands astraddle, his dingy rump toward me, his head alertly frozen
> in silhouette. . . . See him? I do, and, snapping the chain of my
> thought, I have reached through glass and seized him and stamped him
> on this page. Now he is gone. And yet, there, a few lines above, he
> still is, "astraddle," rump "dingy," his head "alertly frozen." A curious
> trick, possibly useless, but mine. (p. 44)

The third paragraph then merges these self-nature, art-nature contrasts and congruities and develops them by introducing the story's controlling images. These images will be re-"connected" and transformed in
the story's final paragraph.

> The grape leaves where they are not in each other's shadow are golden.
> Flat leaves, they take the sun flatly, and turn the absolute light, sum
> of the spectrum and source of all life, into the crayon yellow with
> which children render it. Here and there, wilt transmutes this lent
> radiance into a glowing orange, and the green of the still tender leaves—
> for green persists long into autumn, if we look—strains from the sun-
> light a fine-veined chartreuse. The shadows these leaves cast upon
> each other, though vagrant and nervous in the wind that sends friendly
> scavenging rattles scurrying across the roof, are yet quite various and
> definite, containing innumerable barbaric suggestions of scimitars,
> flanged spears, prongs, and menacing helmets. The net effect, how-
> ever, is innocent of menace. On the contrary, its intricate simulta-
> neous suggestion of shelter and openness, warmth and breeze, invites
> me outward; my eyes venture into the leaves beyond. I am surrounded
> by leaves. The oak's are tenacious claws of purplish rust; the elm's,
> scant feathers of a feminine yellow; the sumac's, a savage, toothed
> blush. I am upheld in a serene and burning universe of leaves. Yet
> something plucks me back, returns me to that inner darkness where
> guilt is the sun. (pp. 44-45)

Reality and imagination conjoin by contrast. The shadowless "flat
leaves" of Nature, by taking the sunlight "flatly," spontaneously transmute
the sun's real shape and color the way a child's crayon would. A parallel
transmutation takes place as well. The "shadows these leaves cast" take

on a human coloration and suggest to the narrator's imagination a simultaneity of opposites, for they are at once barbaric and menacing, yet open
and inviting. Invited outward, only his eyes can venture *into* the leaves;
once there, he perceives, amid other ferocious shapes, that the elm leaves
are "feminine yellow." Yet "something plucks him back," his realization
of his ironic contrast with Nature. Whereas Nature's leaves, in receiving
the sun flatly, had transmuted it, his guilt-consciousness which is *his* sun
finally transmutes the "serene and burning universe of leaves" and returns
him to the darkness of self-isolation.

The apprehension of his private predicament leads him to reflect upon
its "connective" implications. Leaf-related imagery is introduced once
more, but here its use dramatizes the ironic contrast between Nature and
the human spirit. The implication is clear: despite the union of descriptive
"images," *actual* union between spirit and Nature *seems* impossible; only
a sharpening of one's awareness of our dialectical predicament seems
possible.

> . . . And once the events are sorted out—the actions given motiva-
> tions, the actors assigned psychologies, the miscalculations tabulated,
> the abnormalities named, the whole furious and careless growth pruned
> by explanation and rooted in history and returned, as it were, to Na-
> ture—what then? Is such a return serious? Can our spirits really enter
> Time's haven of mortality and sink composedly among the mulching
> leaves? No: we stand at the intersection of two kingdoms, and there
> is no advance and no retreat, only a sharpening of the edge where we
> stand. (p. 45)

The fifth paragraph, and hence "middle" section of this nine-para-
graph story, concerns the "sharpening edge" of memory, for the narrator
remembers "most sharply" the black of his wife's V-shaped dress as she
"leaves" to get her divorce.

> I remember most sharply the black of my wife's dress as she left our
> house to get her divorce. The dress was a soft black sheath, with a
> V neckline, and Helen always looked handsome in it; it flattered her
> pallor. This morning she looked especially handsome, her face utterly
> white with fatigue. Yet her body, that natural thing, ignored our ca-
> tastrophe, and her shape and gestures were incongruously usual. She
> kissed me lightly in leaving. . . . And I, satisfied at last, divorced,
> studied my children with the eyes of one who had left them, examined
> my house as one does a set of snapshots from an irrevocable time,
> drove through the turning landscape as a man in asbestos cuts through

a fire, met my wife-to-be—weeping yet smiling, stunned yet brave—
and felt, unstoppably, to my horror, the inner darkness burst my skin
and engulf us both and drown our love. The natural world, where our
love had existed, ceased to exist. My heart shied back; it shies back
still. I retreated. As I drove back, the leaves of the trees along the road
stated their shapes to me. There is no more story to tell. By telephone
I plucked my wife back; I clasped the black of her dress to me, and
braced for the pain. (pp. 45-46)

This paragraph recapitulates and broadens the color and fire imagery
noted above, and the remembered "leaving" introduces a new "natural"
association, for as his wife "leaves," her body, "that natural thing," appears
unconscious of the catastrophe of their divorce. Here Updike returns to
a frequent association in his fiction—that between women and Nature.
This association provides the central symbolic thread uniting the novel
Of the Farm, where the wife, Peggy, is allied throughout with "stupid
Nature."[20] In *Rabbit Redux* Rabbit, not unlike the narrator here, reflects
that he alone experiences guilt because "women and nature forget." A
rather subtle explanation for this association is offered in the story "The
Bulgarian Poetess" from *The Music School* collection. There the novelist,
Henry Bech, observes that sexual love is "a form of nostalgia. We fall in
love . . . with women who remind us of our first landscapes." (p. 169)
Bech is, of course, a fictional creation; however, two years before, in a
review of De Rougemont's *Love Declared* Updike expressed remarkably
similar sentiments by observing that a "woman loved, momentarily eases
the pain of time by localizing nostalgia, the vague and irrecoverable objects of nostalgic longing are assimilated . . . the images we hoard in wait
for the woman who will seem to body them forth include the inhuman—
a certain slant of sunshine, a delicate flavor of dust. . . ."[21] In short,
contemplation of the beloved Woman simultaneously returns the lover to
remembered natural landscapes, "images" he hoards, and to his very self.
This paragraph recounts this process artfully, for the narrator gradually
realizes that his imminent divorce from "that natural thing" (his wife) has
thus divorced him from "the natural world" (the leaves) and from his very
self; only upon returning to his wife do the leaves again state "their shapes"
to him.

This "middle" memory-interlude is brief, and the next paragraph returns us to the present time and his painful dread of what the future might
bring. He fears his wife's rejection, for, with that rejection, "the curious
beauty of the leaves will be eclipsed again." (p. 46) Earlier, the blue jay

had spurred on his imagination; his writing about him "had seized and stamped him on the page" and made him "mine." Now, however, a spider is sighted, hanging "like a white asterisk," and, unlike the earlier blue jay, it "feels a huge alien presence."

> I catch myself in the quaint and antique pose of the fabulist seeking to draw a lesson from a spider, and become self-conscious. I dismiss self-consciousness and do earnestly attend to this minute articulated star hung so pointedly before my face; and am unable to read the lesson. The spider and I inhabit contiguous but incompatible cosmoses. Across the gulf we feel only fear. The telephone remains silent. The spider reconsiders its spinning. The wind continues to stir the sunlight. (p. 46)

Their "natural" alienation is his major realization: man's "self-consciousness" inevitably places him in tension with Nature, and yet he continually seeks "fables" there. The depiction of the spider, seen as an "articulated star," seems a deliberate pun to imply this "fabulist" power in man, a power both re-active and creative. What, then, of art, of man's endeavor to bridge this gulf through language? This key question returns us to the story's central image of "leaves."

> In walking in and out of this cottage, I have tracked the floor with a few dead leaves, pressed flat like scraps of dark paper. And what are these pages but leaves? Why do I produce them but to thrust, by some subjective photosynthesis, my guilt into Nature, where there is no guilt? (p. 46)

At this point of apparent impasse, suddenly the narrator notices the vital green amid the shades of brown and that beyond the evergreens "there is a low, blue hill. . . . I see it, for the first time in months I see it. I see it as a child, fingers gripping and neck straining, glimpses the roof of a house over a cruelly high wall." (pp. 46-47) Just as in the third paragraph where a child's vision transmuted sunlight, here his child-like vision alters everything. This experience triggers a recent memory.

> Under my window, the lawn is lank and green and mixed with leaves shed from a small elm, and I remember how, the first night I came to this cottage, thinking I was leaving my wife behind me, I went to bed alone and read, in the way one reads stray books in a borrowed house, a few pages of an old edition of *Leaves of Grass*. And my sleep was a loop, so that in awaking I seemed still in the book, and the light-struck sky quivering through the stripped branches of the young elm

seemed another page of Whitman, and I was entirely open, and lost, like a woman in passion, and free, and in love, without a shadow in any corner of by being. It was a beautiful awakening, but by the next night I had returned to my house. (p. 47)

The memory of this all-too-brief but "beautiful awakening"—its significant associations, the unexpected short-lived union of both Nature and Art in his imagination wherein the branches of the elm and the page-leaves of Whitman unite to make him feel "like a woman in passion"— all these not only once brought him awake but do so again in recollection. The story ends with appropriate images of illumination, for no longer is Nature wholly "barbaric" and alien; the remembered union of Art and Nature alters everything, and, just as the "flat leaves" transmuted the sunlight, imagination can so transmute guiltless Nature that "sunlight falls flat at my feet like a penitent."

> The precise barbaric shadows on the grape leaves have shifted. The angle of illumination has altered. I imagine warmth leaning against the door, and open the door to let it in; sunlight falls flat at my feet like a penitent. (p. 47)

In both technique and theme we recognize similarities here between Updike and Wallace Stevens. Like so many of Stevens' poems, this story develops through an imaginative exploration of the potential implications of the central metaphor.[22] The plurisignificant metaphor becomes an instrument for discovery, therefore, the vehicle for grappling with the mysterious relationship between natural reality and man's imaginative consciousness. The poem, or the story here, not only records this process of discovery and the problems engaged, but is the process.

Furthermore, not only does this story proceed like a Stevens "meditation," but it deals specifically with the Stevens problematic and, in a sense, reads like a commentary on the Stevens epigraph. In "Leaves," the "real" autumn leaves at the story's start are both inviting and repulsive, and make the narrator aware that he is "at the intersection of two kingdoms"; these real leaves then merge with a memory of his wife's "leaving" so that once again "real nature" (symbolized by the spider) seems alien, for they "inhabit . . . incompatible cosmoses." These memories and thoughts then conjoin with his recollection of the imaginative *Leaves of Grass* which, in its turn, once had united with the elm tree "leaves" in his own imaginative "awakening," so that, finally, memory of this previous union of "leaves" brings a "new angle of illumination" to the real autumn leaves which he now imagines falling "flat at my feet like a penitent." The story's structure, then, records the central theme in Stevens: that, despite the apparent dichotomy between the realms of imagination and reality, a reciprocal interpenetration is possible, and the "leaves" of an artist's book can capture it briefly—"it" being a merger of reality, memory, and imagination. Nature informs the artistic imagination, and, in turn or reciprocally, his imagination *trans*forms Nature and the art-work is born.

In closing we should observe further, however, that the story's last lines ("The angle of illumination has altered. I imagine warmth leaning against the door, and open the door to let it in; the sunlight falls flat at my feet like a penitent.") also introduce a religious perspective to the scene that is non-Stevensian. As we heard Updike himself express it, these lines betray the further recognition "of the order of artistic 'happiness' that is given rather than attained. The last image, the final knot of lace, is an assertion of transcendental faith scaled, it seems to me, nicely to the mundane."

We have noted at length—especially in the first chapter—that Updike's perception of the opposition between Creation and Nothingness induces moral as well as ontological questions. Man's self-consciousness, his sense of ontological alienation from Nature and Creation that "Leaves" explores, can inspire the Stevensian impulse to bridge the conflict via the imagination. Their brief union is achieved through metaphor, as this story demonstrates.

However, this dialectical opposition prompts other questions as well and addresses other chambers deeper than the imagination. For, as Auden emphasized in *The Dyer's Hand*, the imagination of the artist is itself "a natural human faculty and therefore retains the same character whatever a man believes. The only difference can be in the way he interprets the data." (p. 459) Unlike the imagination, then, that other aspect of consciousness we call conscience is rooted in specifically moral, not aesthetic, instincts and its promptings issue from a wholly different wellspring of beliefs about one's alienation from Creation.

Auden's "data" are common; interpretation is all. "Leaves" records *both* the transcendental movement outward of the trapped ego understood in aesthetic terms, and the equally transcendental movement in faith of the morally trapped ego as it seeks a different kind of "reconciliation," i.e. forgiveness, a realization that can only be "given rather than attained"—in short, a grace.

5: *Couples* and *Marry Me*

The publication of *Couples* in 1968 brought Updike notoriety and solvency. *Time* did a cover story on him and his work. *Life* did a special feature; and the best-seller list was engraced by having *Couples* join its usual second-rate items for several months. The reason for the popular success of *Couples* is easy to detect: it was about sex, even better, about suburban sex. One of Updike's Great Secret Things—apparently the one most interesting to readers—was now out of the closet, not only exposed but dissected and lovingly described. Furthermore, it was a serious treatment of sex, in spots almost avuncularly narrated; thus *Couples*, though more explicit than the soft-core fumblings of a Harold Robbins or Irving Wallace, could be read without a brown paper cover and with head held high. Moralists might cluck, and critics might cavil, but here was an old-fashioned novel about the new-fashioned subject.

At first blush, *Couples* appears to be a radical departure for Updike in that explicitness has replaced the delicacy of metaphor and allusion so characteristic of his work. Not so. It is true that, at times, the novel indulges in the excessive precision of the biologist or in the grand sweep of the social historian, but it is an artist's sensibility that sculpts it and rescues the work from its potential drowning in detail or its evaporating in the broad view. Ironically, Updike himself has protested that the "book is, of course, not about sex as such: It's about sex as the emergent religion, as the only thing left."[1] In *The Music School* collection Updike, in Stevens-like fashion, had sought out metaphors as the mode for exploring the mystery of sexuality. In *Couples* he reverses the process; sex now becomes the metaphor and symbol for the exploration of human meaning in a world that seems devoid of meaning. Sex "as the emergent religion" will parody those spiritual instincts and efforts at communal groupings

117

that religion once energized and channelled. Sex "as the only thing left" becomes the only viable metaphor for man's search for personal and communal meaning. Adultery in such circumstances thus becomes the only modern equivalent for romantic adventure and spiritual aspiration, and it will further take on the qualities of an imaginative quest and become, in its way, a quasi-artistic pursuit. The Three Great Secret Things— Religion, Sex, and Art—are meant to inform each other and interact as metaphors for the mind and its complex yearnings. The folly, as Updike's fiction implies, is to make one an exclusive substitute *in fact* for either of the others. All three secrets engage the mysteries of Time and Creativity from different perspectives, for all three address man's elemental impulse for immortality and his desire somehow to conquer personal death; but woe to man if he forgets the tenor of his metaphor, those other referents toward which his soul and language grope.

There are several obvious reasons why the novel *Couples* and the Romance *Marry Me* should be treated in tandem and discussed in a single chapter. Even though *Couples* was published eight years earlier in 1968, that novel and *Marry Me* deal with the same cultural milieu (the New England middle class), the same brief time-period (the era of the Kennedy presidency), that unique historical moment which, in retrospect, emerges as a dramatic transitional period between a more tradition-oriented Cold War era and the consciousness-raising changes of the late 1960's. As Jerry, the hero of *Marry Me*, expresses it, this is "the twilight of the old morality, and there's just enough to torment us, and not enough to hold us in." Furthermore, the long second chapter of *Marry Me* entitled "The Wait" was published (later slightly modified) on February 17, 1968 in *The New Yorker*, a few weeks before the appearance of *Couples*—evidence, perhaps, that both works germinated in the same imaginative season.

Those major themes which we noted in *The Music School* collection are again apparent: the mystery of woman's sexuality, the joys and guilts of adultery, and America's new pilgrims "faltering toward divorce." Yet, where these stories were meditative and heuristic and tentative in tone, these works are dramatically recounted, multiple in narrative perspective, and generally dialogic in development. The "voice" that unites much of *The Music School* is a singular one, partial to a masculine perspective. By contrast, these works also enter the mystery of woman's sexuality, but from the inside, and also engage the mystery of man's sexuality from her perspective. In fact, the women characters in both *Couples* and *Marry Me* are the most keenly drawn, the most interesting and sympathetic; the men are often obtusely insensitive or crude or egoistic.

The clue to the thematic, even archetypal, bond that unites *Couples* with *Marry Me* and connects them with Updike's previous novel *Of the Farm* can be discovered on the dust-jackets to their hard-bound editions. There Sex, Religion, and Art join hands once more. Updike takes great pains in selecting the appropriate cover for his books when it is possible for him to do so. The dust-jacket for *Couples* is that of a William Blake water-color depicting Adam and Eve sleeping. In the water-color two angels, one with mournful expression, hover over the sleepers while, beside them, an ugly toad, his head tilted upward with both dark eyes bulging, looks up at the sleepers. The cover for *Marry Me* is also of Adam and Eve, a photo of a sarcophagus of Valerius Adelphia from the fourth century entitled "The Garden of Eden." Where the Blake water-color captured the pre-lapsarian scene, this photo is obviously post-lapsarian. In it we see Adam and Eve covering their genitals with leaves as they eat from the Tree of Knowledge around which a serpent coils.

Earlier in discussing *Of the Farm* we examined the pivotal importance of the minister's Barthian sermon on the creation of Man and Woman. That sermon concerned the pre-lapsarian account in Genesis and described the ideal Man-Woman relationship as established by the Creator in His order of Creation. *Couples* and *Marry Me* explore that order's disruption, the subsequent moral and psychological "divorce" between Man and Woman, and their desperate efforts at recovering that lost order by fashioning a new one in its place, one achieved by clinging to each other to keep out the cold and the darkness.

As the many comprehensive readings of *Couples* demonstrate (*Marry Me* so far has been ignored by scholars), there are many points of entry and several layers of interpretation that these works invite. However, I suggest that we begin with those dust-jacket clues. By probing the Adam and Eve symbolism in these fictions, I feel that one can better unite the thematic strands found not only here but elsewhere in Updike's *corpus*. I will argue that this Adam and Eve motif illuminates Updike's preoccupation with the relationship between sexuality and the experience of dread and the fear of death, and provides symbolic insight into his characters and their complex relationships. Finally, I will argue that Updike's employment of the Adam myth draws upon a traditional Adamic image of America itself, an image that was itself steeped in controversy a century ago, and that these fictions—when seen as social criticism—ought to be read in that tradition's light.

A. A PSYCHOLOGY OF SEXUALITY: GUILT, DREAD, AND ORIGINAL SIN

A discussion of the sexual tensions found in Updike's novels can be approached in any number of ways. A Freudian interpretation, which most critics favor, is one legitimate avenue; others, as we have seen, can be that of Jung's psychology or that of Barth's theology. Each approach sheds light on this shadowy world and highlights certain aspects of that Great Secret Thing. However, each fails to some degree, for none of these approaches is inclusive enough to render intelligible the specialized range of vocabulary and complex emotional response that Updike associates with sexuality. In describing sexual encounters, Updike will continually employ the words "guilt," "dread," and "sin"; and, as we have noted in *The Centaur* especially, sexual promptings will inevitably engender thoughts about death. My contention is that these words and associations enjoy the same precision that one expects and discovers in every attempt at "accuracy" of description and designation found throughout Updike's writing.

Earlier we reviewed Updike's artistic adaption of certain themes found in Kierkegaard's writing. The Adam and Eve motif present in *Couples* and *Marry Me* inspires a further consideration of Kierkegaard's thought, precisely his analysis of the psychology of human sexuality. It was Kierkegaard who first explicitly associated the terms "guilt," "sin," "dread," and man's fear of death with the sexual impulse. To appreciate the complexity of Updike's vocabulary and the ambivalent character of sexuality in his fiction, one is hard put to find a better guide than Kierkegaard. Unlike Freud or Jung or Barth, Kierkegaard continually unites psychology with theology; consequently, his thought provides the best entry into these fictions that themselves unite the two Great Secrets: Sex and Religion.

For Kierkegaard "guilt" is the inevitable result of the disruption of the ordered relationship between man and God. Guilt and "sin" are related but not identical; "sin" is a theological category, whereas "guilt," which ought to be theological also, can remain a "mere" psychological category. The reason is that sin is a category that requires a revelation, i.e. one has to be told why he feels guilty, for he cannot discover the reason by himself.

Sin, therefore, is a specification of guilt, a clarification of it. Scriptural revelation reveals to man the reason for his vague feelings of guilt, specifies and gives a precise name "sin" to man's experience. Hence, Kierkegaard will define sin as "guilt before God," and the "before God" marks the crucial distinction, a new perspective on guilt.

Consequently, guilt will be a more universal experience; it is the universal given of unease and restlessness that all men share. One senses a disruption, a disorder in his world for which he senses a responsibility (guilt), but often he does know its true cause or name (sin). The category "sin" alerts the person to the realization that the disorder and its effect, guilt, has an infinite dimension to it, that it results from a breach between man and God. Without this realization, guilt will either estrange the person in private self-torment without outlet, or else one's guilty feelings will push outward and become fixed on finite relationships. Since such relationships are manifold, guilt grows and metastasizes within a realm of ignorance, confusion, and recrimination. Guilt then becomes, in a sense, infinite in its possible multiplicity, touching upon all human relationships although it ironically lacks the one infinite dimension that would make it intelligible.

Kierkegaard was quite harsh in condemning those who would airily equate guilt with unhappiness. In his Journal he wrote, "Human sympathy defends itself against the unhappy man by explaining his unhappiness as guilt: thus one is rid of him."[2] Unhappiness is a human evaluation and one associates it with any number of factors like physical debility, economic disappointment, social evils, and so on. Here the criterion of happiness is implicitly quantitative; we want more and have less and so we are unhappy and regret it. But regret and guilt are hardly the same thing for Kierkegaard. For him guilt is obviously a spiritual quality (impervious to quantitative standards), indicative of an absolute and infinite relationship that is awry; hence, it is not a temporal category but partakes of and points to an eternal, timeless aspect of the human personality. As a result, no outsider can appreciate another's guilt, for he will erroneously transpose it into quantitative terms; being a spiritual condition, guilt is always a private affair. As Kierkegaard put it, "In paganism one saw the furies pursue the guilty, saw their hideous forms—but the gnawing of remorse cannot be seen; it is hidden, a hidden pregnancy fathered by a bad conscience."[3]

Kierkegaard's genius led him toward an investigation of guilt in terms of its psychological manifestation as dread, and this exploration, in turn, led him to reconsider that primal guilt theologians have called original sin. These psychological explorations meet in his early work *The Concept of Dread*, a work so often opaque and dense in language that it would try Penelope's patience.[4]

Nonetheless, the thrust of Kierkegaard's argument is quite clear and especially telling when Updike's fiction is examined in its light. For Kierkegaard's concern is with the transition from innocence to knowledge that is dramatized in the Genesis myth of the fall of Adam and Eve. To him, Adam's original innocence was rooted in ignorance, an ignorance he shared with the rest of Nature. Like Nature itself, Adam's world-view was limited to immediate concerns and the present time; as a result, he was oblivious of the distinctions between good and evil—which are reflective categories he knew not of. Kierkegaard says that Adam at this stage was in a state of "dreaming innocence," like that depicted in Blake's water-color. However, this Adam was also a dreaming "spirit," and it is spirit that distinguishes him from the rest of Nature. Adam's dreaming spirit inevitably led him to enter imaginatively the realm of "possibility," i.e. a realm that drew his dreams beyond the immediate present and thus intimated to him that a different kind of future was possible. This new realm of possibility awakened in Adam the realization of a new power, the power of freedom, for, amid his dreaming, he became aware that *he* could determine his future, choose among the variables that those dreamy "possibles" offered. This heart-quickening experience issued in dread. For Kierkegaard, dread is the most ambiguous of human experiences and he called it "sympathetic antipathy and antipathetic sympathy," a somewhat awkward definition but one that captures dread's radical ambivalence.

Dread is related to the emotion of fear, but is fear of a special kind. Unlike other fears, dread has no specific object to fear; in fact, dread is a fear of nothing. In other words, because dread concerns the realm of possible choices and not actual facts, it is a fear of the unknown, of the not yet, but still of an unknown one realizes is possible. Kierkegaard's definition points up the fact that such possibilities are simultaneously *both* attractive and repugnant when contemplated, that dread induces the "dizziness of freedom," a sensation that is both delightful and terrifying.

At this stage, however, Adam's dread is still innocent, and it is here that Kierkegaard offers an observation about children and their innocent dread that is pertinent for an appreciation of the experiences of the many children found throughout Updike's fiction.

If we observe children, we find this dread as more definitely indicated as a seeking after adventure, a thirst for the prodigious, the mysterious. . . . This dread belongs to the child so essentially that he cannot do without it; even though it alarms him, it captivates him nevertheless by its sweet feeling of apprehension.[5]

A child's dread, like that of the dreaming Adam, is innocent; dread becomes true guilt only after a choice is made. Nonetheless, a child's dread is portentous, for it exposes that very quality of "spirit" or potential freedom that makes the human race unique in all of Nature. Throughout Updike's fiction, especially in the two books under consideration, the innocent dread that the children manifest will be a counterpoint to the dread the adults experience. In both *Couples* and *Marry Me* the children are rarely center-stage; rather, they drift on like a Greek chorus offering an ironic commentary on the adults' dread-ful dialogues. Not only do their imagined hurts, suspicions, recriminations, and impulsive adventures parallel the ever-shifting emotions and impulsive actions of their parents; but, more significantly, it is precisely their dread of the unknown and of the possible (death, loss, secrets, the future) that makes them counterparts of their parents. The innocent and the guilty are united, willy-nilly, because both share in the same humanity and a similar spirit.

Kierkegaard addressed this perplexing truth about such human sharing between the innocent and the guilty in *The Concept of Dread* and related it to "sin." His starting point was Christian Dogmatic Theology's assertion that Original Sin entered the world through Adam's fall and that, subsequently, everyone in the human race inherits it. Kierkegaard accepted the dogma's assertion, but he wondered how it was possible to inherit a "sin" since sin is an act of personal freedom, the result of a choice one makes before God. If this goes unexplained, how can one honestly feel guilty about a sin he himself did not commit? Why feel guilty about another's sin? The theological dogma does not explain how this original sin, universally shared, comes into one's individual existence; however, the dogma does presuppose that there is something in human nature itself that makes sin not only possible but likely. Consequently, Kierkegaard addressed himself to this question: what is there about man that makes sin *universal* and at the same time does not make sin *necessary* since to be "sin" at all it must be the free act of the individual? In other words, what quality or qualities do we all share with Adam that make us all potential Adams? His answer: Dread.

In the Eden story Adam hears God's prohibition "Only of the

tree of the knowledge of good and evil thou shalt not eat" and the judgment "Else thou shalt die." Both the prohibition and the judgment alarm Adam and induce a state of dread within him because they confront him with two new, very real, possibilities. As yet, both the knowledge of good and evil and the experience of death are inconceivable to him; both are unknown, but now unknown possibles, and so the prohibition and the judgment awaken in Adam imaginable opportunities for new experiences. At this point Adam's dread is a fear of nothing—in the strict sense of not yet being actual or realized—and yet, in another sense, it has become a dread of "something," a possibility that he realizes he has the power to make actual.

It is important to note, in order to appreciate both Kierkegaard and Updike, that Adam here is not tempted by God or by the world or by the serpent; instead, he is tempted by his very self, by the fascination of his own dreams of the future, attracted and frightened by the possibles that he alone can make real.

The words "his very self" are crucial here. Kierkegaard's tripartite notion of the "Self" is, perhaps, not too congenial for the modern mind nourished by the mother's milk of Freud's terminology; and yet, Kierkegaard's description of the constitution of the self highlights better than more reductionist theories do those aspects of irremedial tension proper to human psychology. For Kierkegaard, the human self is composed of three factors: 1) the *body*, that component which he shares with all of material creation and is the temporal constituent; 2) the *soul*, that component which draws man beyond Nature, beyond the finite toward the infinite, and is the eternal constituent; 3) the *spirit*, which is his designation for the synthesizing power between soul and body, between the eternal and the temporal. For Kierkegaard, man is "spirit," he is a synthesis. Soul and body are polarized powers or dynamic drives which are ever in strife; as such, they are existential opposites, contradictory impulses that must be held together in synthesis by spirit. The self, then, is a battleground of warring dynamisms and always finds itself in a state of disequilibrium. True, soul and body are dynamically related to each other; yet, each can operate in quasi-independent fashion unless spirit, the synthesizing factor, keeps them inter-related. Kierkegaard in *Sickness Unto Death* describes the results that occur when this dialectical balance of the components body and soul are fragmented.[6] When fragmentation occurs, i.e. when spirit is not performing its synthesizing job, man's activity spins off in unbridled pursuit of those possibilities energized by just one of these polar components. For example, a non-dialectical pursuit of "eternal" or "infinite" possibilities that soul engenders will lead man toward absolutizing himself, his goals, and his world-view; spurred on by the body element, pursuit of temporal and finite possibilities will issue in man's immersion in the ephemeral, the materialistic, the animalistic. Reminiscent of Plato's image for man, spirit's task is to rein in and keep in tandem the on-rushing horses of body and soul, for only spirit is truly free. Little wonder, then, as we have seen, that an "awakening spirit" is imbued with dread.

Spirit, however, is not only the synthesizing constituent of the self, but it is also the focal point, on the one hand, for the love of this world and the temporal (the body dynamic) and, on the other, for aspirations toward God and the eternal (the soul dynamic). Thus when Adam's "spirit" emerges because awakened by dread, he finds himself stretched between infinite (God) and finite (the world) possibilities. After Adam chooses and falls, even fallen Adam retains his spirit and remains stretched, desirous of the earth and dreaming of God, dreading both his desires and his dreams. Kierkegaard will argue that everything both good and evil follows from this spiritual ambivalence of fallen man: moral consciousness, spiritual yearning, guilt, fear of death, sexuality, all the things associated with the "humanity" of the race. All of these emerge together and are simultaneously tainted and/or ennobled by the subsequent conflicts of spirit. Consequently, what is "inherited" from Adam is not sin—sin is voluntary—but dread, spirit, sexuality, knowledge of good and evil, and oneness with the human race. Every individual, endowed with such a mixed heritage, will himself reenact Adam's primal transition and sin will come to be. It is in this sense that sin is original, i.e. the same psychological and physical factors we all share are such that each individual "originates" Adam's sin once again.

Many of Updike's short stories dramatize these ambivalent tensions and some characters reenact that primal transition. Also, every major character in his novels embodies and often consciously engages those very tensions that Kierkegaard describes. Most readers are aware of this, and it is usually those readers given to religious commitment who are most responsive to it. However, as we observed in the Introduction, it is precisely this group that is most often dismayed by Updike's explicit treatment of sex. To them, such explicitness runs counter to the religious and spiritual sensibility so evident elsewhere in his fiction. It appears to them that his usual sensitivity is abandoned where sex is concerned.

I have no intention here of either defending or deploring Updike's explicit rendering of sexual relationships. That is primarily an aesthetic judgment, I believe, and the quality and accuracy of such judgments depend upon other than religious factors, such as: individual taste, one's range of reading experience, familiarity with what "explicit" might mean in contemporary fiction, and, finally, a certain sureness and inclusiveness of perception that forestalls one's condemning particular episodes until the fiction as a unit is appraised.

Intelligent people, of course, will disagree and, one hopes, in intelligent ways. Nevertheless, no reader of Updike's fiction can deny that he treats sexuality with the seriousness it deserves. (When at times it deserves otherwise, he will treat it as such.) In a recent interview he defended the explicitness of *Couples* by asserting that he wished to render the "truth about sex." He admitted that *Couples* was "written on a kind of cusp provided by Henry Miller and others" and that now, older, he would "probably de-emphasize it since [sex] is no longer a frontier."[7] At any rate, sex in these works is meant to be treated truthfully and the truth at issue is very much a Kierkegaardian truth.

In an interview in 1968, the year it was published, Updike was asked about the ending to *Couples* and he replied:

> I guess I'm saying that there's a fierce God above the kind God and he's the one Piet believes in. At any rate, when the Church is burned, Piet is relieved of morality, and can choose Foxy . . . can move out of the paralysis of guilt into what is a kind of freedom. He divorces the supernatural to marry the natural. . . . So that the book does have a happy ending. There's also a way, though, I should say (speaking of "yes, but") in which, with the destruction of the church, with the removal of the guilt, he becomes insignificant. He becomes merely a name in the last paragraph; he becomes a satisfied person and in a sense dies. In other words, a person who has what he wants, is a satisfied person, a content person, ceases to be a person. Unfallen Adam is an ape. Yes, I do feel that to be a person is to be in a situation of tension, is to be in a dialectical situation.[8]

Unfallen Adam is an ape, at best asleep as in Blake's water-color. Updike's conviction is like that of Kierkegaard: unfallen Adam possesses an unawakened "spirit," and yet, paradoxically, it is spirit that constitutes the fully human, it is spirit that places a person in a dialectical situation, between the competing dynamisms of body and soul. Thus Piet can enter "a kind of" freedom by embracing one phase of the dialectic, Foxy's body, and renounce the searches of soul, represented by Angela. He becomes satisfied, contented, asleep as if retreating to a stage before the fall. This makes for a "happy" ending in that a resolution has been made in freedom; but, as Kierkegaard reminds us, unhappiness and guilt and dread are not identical.

Contemporary exegetes of the book of Genesis have suggested that it is indeed possible to interpret the whole story of Eden and man's fall as a transgression that is sexual in nature.[9] Here the presence of the serpent as tempter is pivotal since this figure was borrowed from a central symbol of the Canaanite fertility cults that the Hebrews despised. Consequently, Eve's and then Adam's temptation is of a sexual order and Adam's desire for immortality reflects man's desire for the quasi-immortality that he achieves through his offspring in the sexual act. Adam is tempted "to be like God," to be not only immortal but to acquire the knowledge of good and evil with which he associates this power. After the fall, God's condemnation describes the actual good and evil that will ever issue as the result of sexual intercourse. (Gen. 3:15-16) Adam and Eve will acquire such knowledge through experience.

Of course, three centuries ago, without the scholarly blessings of modern exegesis, Milton's *Paradise Lost* became the *locus classicus* for such a sexual interpretation of the fall. As we shall see, Milton, with his Calvinistic perspective, is a more likely inspiration for Updike.

> She gave him of that fair enticing fruit
> With liberal hand; he scrupled not to eat,
> Against his better knowledge, not deceived,
> But fondly overcome with female charm.
>
> . . . .
>
> As with new wine intoxicated both,
> They swim in mirth, and fancy that they feel
> Divinity within them breeding wings
> Wherewith to scorn the Earth. But that false fruit
> Far other operation first displayed
> Carnal desire inflaming; he on Eve
> Began to cast lascivious eyes, she him
> As wantonly repaid; in lust they burn. (*Paradise Lost*, Bk. IX,
> ll. 996-999; 1008-1015)

Both Updike and Kierkegaard attend to the sexual consequences of the fall, Updike in dramatic, Kierkegaard in analytic terms. Kierkegaard's analysis of sexuality clarifies the moral as well as the psychological tensions that sexuality engenders. Other considerations regarding sexuality such as the strictly psychological (i.e. *sans* the moral dimension) can be approached through Freud or Jung, and an idealistic theology of sexuality can be glimpsed through Karl Barth, but in Updike's fiction sex is not only psychologically complex but also morally and religiously ambivalent; as I said earlier, Kierkegaard's thought is a better guide.

Kierkegaard's ideas concerning the effect of Adam's fall on sexuality are necessarily linked with his description of the Self. The self is a synthesis of the soul and body via the spirit; as a consequence, the self is not three kinds of "things" bundled together in one package—that is, a biological thing, a rational thing, plus a third thing that accounts for man's ideas of transcendence. One should hesitate to assign distinctive functions to the soul, the body, and the spirit, as if they were separate entities operating independently, for the self is the synthesis of these factors. As a result, Kierkegaard will argue that even the bodily functions of man are qualitatively different from those of other biological beings since the body of man is always qualified by his spirit and dynamically polarized by his soul. Man's sexuality does not differ from that of animals because of a different bodily apparatus, nor because his reason (soul) allows him to choose time, place, and partner; instead, the distinctive feature of human sexuality is that the sex act, being qualified by spirit, alters one's very character. In other words, even the automatic operations of sexuality necessarily will become for man occasions for self-questioning, self-realization, or self-destruction; his spirit, his self-consciousness emerges and, since spirit *is* freedom for Kierkegaard, sexuality dramatically makes man aware of new possibilities for growth and destruction. It is at this point that he experiences dread; inevitably, then, every sexual experience will usher in dread-ful symptoms.

> He who becomes guilty in dread becomes as ambiguously guilty as it is possible to be. Dread is a womanish debility in which freedom swoons. Psychologically speaking, the fall into sin always occurs in impotence. But dread is at the same time the most egoistic thing, and no concrete expression of freedom is so egoistic as is the possibility of every concretion. . . . In dread there is the egoistic infinity of possibility, which does not tempt like a definite choice, but alarms and fascinates with its sweet anxiety. [10]

The sexual experience, then, is a dramatic moment arousing the latent possibilities which make up the human self, and, since dread betokens the reality of human freedom, it is part and parcel of human experience. Kierkegaard says that the first reaction of the spirit to the sexual is modesty or bashfulness because the "real significance of bashfulness is that spirit, so to speak, cannot recognize itself at the extreme point of synthesis,"[11] i.e. at the "body" polarity. The sexual impulse reaches its climax when it is united with the "erotic" as in love between a man and a woman. The "erotic" is not spiritual as yet nor is it base; rather, the erotic is "the union of the psychical and the physical," i.e. soul and body. The erotic is one of the noblest manifestations of the sexual impulse; even so, the erotic still is fraught inevitably with dread.

> As dread is posited in bashfulness, so it is present in all erotic enjoyment (not by any means because it is sinful) and this is so even though the priest were to bless the couple ten times. Even when the erotic expresses itself as beautifully and purely and morally as possible, without being disturbed in its joy by any wanton reflection, dread is nevertheless present, not as a disturbing element, however, but as a concordant factor.
> . . . One thing, however, is sure, that in describing love, pure and innocent as they may represent it, all poets associate with it an element of dread.[12]

Kierkegaard's observation that "all poets associate with [the erotic] an element of dread" is an apt description of Updike's work. Throughout his fiction the characteristics described by Kierkegaard—egoism, fear of loss and nothingness, "spiritual" emptiness, and even modesty—are dramatized in the sexual encounter.

Furthermore, God's dread-inducing judgment "Or else thou shalt die" is inevitably linked with sexuality. Even after the Fall and with the dead and dying all around him, the import of that judgment still remains a dread-ful mystery, an unknown possible. On the one hand, the sex act betokens a conquest of death in that it confers a quasi-immortality realizable through offspring. On the other hand, that "quasi" restriction is the kicker and the short-lived intensity of the sex act itself evokes fears of death. In *Bech: A Book*, Bech's recorded reflection captures this insight succinctly from a male's perspective.

> His phallus, a counterfeit bone, a phantasmal creature, like Man, on the borderline of substance and illusion, of death and life.[13]

Almost every "hero" in Updike's fiction—Rabbit, Joey Robinson,

Peter Caldwell, Bech, Piet Hanema, Jerry Conant, Rev. Marshfield, Ellellou—associates sexuality with death. Often their experience is described in images of falling, dizziness, and weightlessness. What might
appear to be exclusively a metaphor for sexual sensation is also a rendering
of the psychological reactions of dread that sex initiates. Kierkegaard
described dread in these terms:

> One may liken dread to dizziness. He whose eye chances to look down
> into the yawning abyss becomes dizzy. But the reason for it is just as
> much his eye as it is the precipice. For suppose he had not looked
> down.
>
> Thus dread is the dizziness of freedom which occurs when the spirit
> would posit the synthesis, and freedom then gazes down into its own
> possibility, grasping at finiteness to sustain itself. In this dizziness free-
> dom succumbs. Further than this psychology cannot go and will not.
> That very instant everything is changed, and when freedom rises again,
> it sees that it is guilty.[14]

It is not so surprising, then, that all the major characters in Updike's
fiction will be ridden with some kind of guilt. Those among them who
are religious believers will sometimes attribute this guilt to sin (recall that
sin, unlike guilt, is a revelatory category and that one must first believe
in order to understand it). Each is preoccupied with the natural, the
bodily, most keenly heightened in the sexual encounter, but all such
meetings will reflect the attraction and repugnance proper to dread. Furthermore, each is often inspired by otherworldly intimations as well, and
these often occur in dreams (vide Kierkegaard); such visitations, though,
will also be dread-ful.

Updike, in many ways unique among his contemporaries, attempts to
capture these multi-faceted ambivalences in his fiction. It is erroneous to
characterize such fiction as gloomy, for Updike's goal is not sadness, but
truth and accuracy. If, as some exegetes and Milton and others suggest,
Adam's temptation was sexually based, then his subsequent Fall resulted
in ambiguous effects upon man's sexuality. The Fall brought death into
the world, and yet sex continues to usher life into it. The Fall brought
the knowledge of good and evil, and yet sexual "knowing" can either
debase or be the most dramatic avenue for man's self-knowledge and the
promptings of the spirit. Yeats' phrase, "Love has pitched his mansion in
the place of excrement," admits of many reflections both sour and sweet.
Updike's fiction is meant to invite the same.

B. Adam and Eve in Tarbox

The plot to *Couples* is fairly easy to summarize, at least in outline. In the first chapter we are welcomed to Tarbox, Massachusetts, "the post-pill paradise" as one character calls it, a former fishing town now inhabited and socially swayed by an upwardly mobile, affluent, educated middle class, most of whom commute to work in Boston. Tarbox is what suburbia meant during the Kennedy era. The old town is a place, the new town is a state of mind. Physically, though not spiritually, Tarbox is still dominated by the old Congregational Church at its center. Above its cupola a golden weathercock with a copper English penny as its eye provides Tarbox with its most obvious link with its colonial and religious past. We are told that "Children in the town grew up with the sense that the bird was God. That is, if God were physically present in Tarbox, it was in the form of this unreachable weathercock visible from everywhere."[14] The sexual symbolism of the weathercock as simultaneously a precarious and vestigial and dominant appendage to this remnant of traditional religion introduces one of the novel's major metaphors.

The action of *Couples* recounts the activities of ten Tarbox married couples. Several of the couples seem interchangeable, duplicates of each other and without distinctive personalities, and so the reader is hard put to tell them apart. This blurring is deliberate, for we readers are visitors in town. As they would be to visitors, the couples are introduced casually by the omniscient narrator; only gradually do we begin to differentiate who's who and, more importantly in the circumstances, who's with whom. We soon discover that these couples are drawn to each other in an unconscious effort to find substitutes for that sense of "congregation" that the old church once provided. As a result, the couples' gatherings take on cultic and quasi-religious alignments. Their get-togethers are punctuated by celebratory feast-days (secularly inspired) and are replete with repetitive rituals like Sunday basketball games, party games that demand self-sacrifice and confession, ceremonies of induction, and so on. The "priest" who presides at these rituals—the dentist, Freddy Thorne—is not only celebrant and father confessor, but also possesses powers of exorcism and excommunication. It is Freddy, a figure both sacerdotal and satanic, who observes that "we have made a church of each other," and he is correct.

Gradually, the personalities of the central characters begin to emerge. Besides Freddy Thorne, they are Piet Hanema and his wife Angela and

Foxy Whitman and her husband Ken. A good deal of the novel's action early on is an account of Piet's sexual conquests among the couples, but later its main attention is devoted to Piet's relationship with Angela and Foxy.

Almost every serious critical investigation of *Couples*—and it is the most heavily researched and exhaustively analyzed of all of Updike's novels—has addressed the Tristan and Iseult and/or Don Juan theme in its exposition of Piet's adventures.[15] Commentators use as their starting point and touchstone Updike's extensive review of Denis De Rougemont's *Love in the Western World* and *Love Regained* that is reprinted in his collection *Assorted Prose*.[16] (I might add that a similar investigation of *Marry Me*, in the light of the Tristan story particularly, would be equally fruitful, although no critic has tackled that project as yet.)

Although I agree with such extensive explorations of the Tristan and Don Juan motifs and have profited from the critical insights they offer, I believe that this approach, no doubt because of its very success and pertinence, has become scorched earth by now. For this reason I submit another perspective, that of the Ur-theme of Adam and Eve which I feel buttresses the Tristan/Don Juan, Love-Death themes without distorting them, and still offers new insights and illuminates further complexities. For example, while the Tristan theme points up the complications of Piet's character and his women-relationships, this Ur-theme better engages the malevolent honesty of the novel's most interesting and lively character, Freddy Thorne. I also feel that Kierkegaard's psychology of sexuality serves as well, if not better, as a framework for understanding the complex emotions that the sexual encounters described in *Couples* generate.

The story's "hero" Piet is both an innocent and a fallen Adam. His last name itself is symbolic when we recall that the name Adam is the Hebrew word for man. He himself reflects, "HANEMA, his name, himself, restraining in its letters all his fate, *me, a man, amen, ah.*" (p. 13) Throughout the novel he is a man caught between two worlds: prelapsarian memories of his parents' greenhouse world with its lush vegetation and congenial warmth and this new world of Tarbox which, as its name implies, is a receptacle of sorts wherein people cling together out of sexual passion and yet remain struck in their attempts at sublimating their fear of death. The novel records his transition from such dreaming innocence toward new knowledge, a "new kind of freedom," and his subsequent estrangement and expulsion from the post-pill paradise.

For Piet-Adam there are several variations on the Eve-figure which he encounters. He discovers in Georgene Thorne a "guiltlessness," an expression on her face "of peace deeper than an infant's sleep" that he does not find in his wife Angela. And yet, Angela, as her name implies, does offer other facets of the pre-lapsarian Eve. Throughout, her sexuality evokes in men heavenly metaphors, even when crudely put, appropriate for a woman who is transported by her love for the stars. Even the odious Freddy Thorne observes that "she's my ideal. I idolize her. I look at that ass and I think Heaven." (p. 148) Piet says to her, "Your cunt is heavenly," and he has noticed that when "his hand discovered hers mons Veneris swollen high, her whole fair floating flesh dilated outward toward a deity, an anyoneness, it was Piet's fortune to have localized, to have seized captive in his own dark form." (p. 194) When Piet's affair with Foxy grows more serious and binding for him, Angela "seemed to Piet to be growing even more beautiful, to be receding from him into abstract realms of beauty," (p. 215) and he will acknowledge to her that "Being with you is Heaven."

In Kierkegaard's sexual dialectic, Angela represents the "soulful" component of the self, that impulse toward the ethereal and the eternal which the sex encounter evokes. By contrast, Foxy represents the "body" component and so, as her name suggests, the corresponding animalistic impulse that is generated by the same encounter. Piet, whose name suggests the "spirit" element in man, thus becomes the focal point for these contending impulses, for he is drawn to both Angela and Foxy in almost equal measure.

Unlike Angela, Foxy is unethereal and earthly, the figure of Eve as temptress; also like Eve, she is both an individual and a universal woman. "Her face so close to his seemed a paradigm, a pattern of all the female faces that had ever been close to him. Her blank brow, her breathing might have belonged to Angela; then Foxy turned her head . . . and was clearly not Angela, was the Whitman woman, the young adulteress." (pp. 203-4)

The sexual encounters between Piet and Foxy in this "post-pill paradise" tend to accent the gymnastic pleasures of fellatio and cunnilingus rather than those of intercourse. It is significant, then, that the only new life conceived will be ended through Foxy's deliberate abortion. When Updike was asked in a 1968 interview about this emphasis on fellatio, he replied in Edenesque metaphors:

> It's a way of eating, eating the apple of knowing. It's nostalgic for them, for Piet of Annabelle Vojt and for Foxy of the Jew. In De Rougemont's book on Tristan and Iseult he speaks of the sterility of the lovers vis-a-vis each other and Piet and Foxy are sterile vis-a-vis each other.[17]

As the Piet-Foxy affair develops (symbolically during the sterility of winter), the allusions to Eden begin to predominate. Piet observes, almost in parody of an Adamic complaint, that "The fact is, all fall I've been frightened of everything. Death, my work, Gallagher, my children, the stars. . . . My whole life seems just a long falling." (p. 312) He soon realizes "that for them to keep seeing each other now would be evil, all the more in that it had been good. They had been let into God's playroom, and been happy together on the floor all afternoon, but the time had come to return the toys to their boxes, and put the chairs back against the wall." (p. 323)

When Foxy complains that adultery is so silly because it causes so much trouble, Piet responds, "It's a way of giving yourself adventures. Of getting out in the world and seeking knowledge." To which Foxy asks, "What do we know now, Piet?," and he answers, "We know that God is not to be mocked." (p. 343) This response, without the Adam theme, would sound inflated or worse.

Piet is the only character in the novel who still clings to the strict Calvinism of his ancestors. His brand of Calvinism is an odd mix of fatalism and freedom, covenant and estrangement; in a way he is Milton's Calvinistic Adam *redux*. When Piet learns of Foxy's pregnancy, his prayers conjoin egoism with determinism and he prays for the death of the fetus. One prayer is especially Adam-like and laden with Edenesque imagery.

> His being expanded upward in the shape of a cone tapering toward prayer. Undo it. Rid me of her and her of it and us of Freddy. Give me back my quiet place. At an oblique angle she had intersected the plane of his life where daily routines accumulated like dust. . . . He had been innocent amid trees. She had demanded that he know. Straight String of his life, knotted. The knot surely was sin. Piet prayed for it to be undone. (p. 376; also cf. p. 346)

The images of falling, slipping, abysses, and pits, so reminiscent of Kierkegaard's imagery for Adam's dread, accumulate and dramatically build in this chapter which is ironically entitled "Breakthrough." Once Foxy's pregnancy is confirmed and an abortion is decided upon, he and

Foxy must turn for help to Angela and Freddy Thorne. It is at this point that Piet realizes his dependence on Angela and her role in supporting his Calvinistic beliefs.

> . . . he believed that there was, behind the screen of couples and houses and days, a Calvinist God Who lifts us up and casts us down in utter freedom, without recourse to our prayers or consultation with our wills. Angela had been the messenger of this God. (p. 415)

And so, no longer a believer in freedom but in fate, Piet must submit and engage Freddy Thorne as intermediary to secure an abortion. To do so he must elicit Angela's cooperation; without her intervention Freddy's wily powers will be inoperative. For Freddy desires not only Angela but *through* her Piet as well, i.e. his submission to and admission of the kind of knowledge Freddy has broadcast. The fruit in Foxy's womb, ready to be plucked, is the occasion for their confrontation.

To equate Freddy's with the serpent's role in the paradise of Tarbox seems excessive at first because a fairly rigid, traditional expectation has been assigned to the serpent over the centuries in that it has become associated with demonic, preternatural powers. But the serpent in the Genesis story represents many things other than the extraordinary, and so too does Freddy. He is the priest at the revels, and if not diabolically clever, certainly a "thorn in the flesh," but just as often he is the buffoon as was the Devil in medieval mystery plays. Freddy is the most outspoken truth-teller at the revels and, as he acknowledges, also its most subtle liar. He, more than any other man among the couples, is desirous of Angela (the image of soul) and also the one most intuitive regarding Foxy's predicament (the image of body). It is unsurprising that he and Piet should confront each other early on as rivals, for Piet admits "he threatens my primitive faith." (p. 304)

Throughout the novel Freddy's physical characteristics are described in animalistic or shape-shifting imagery proper to Satan. Besides having an icy hand, there is "a fishy inward motion of his lips": as "a mouth, it was neither male nor female, and not quite infantile . . . his eyes were lost behind concave spectacle lenses that brimmed with tremulous candlelight," "his hair . . . a colorless fuzz, an encircling shadow above his ears." (p. 26) When Freddy puts on his skin-diving suit, we are told:

> His appearance in the tight shiny skin of black rubber was disturbingly androgynous; he was revealed to have hips soft as a woman's and with the obscene delicacy of hydra's predatory petals his long hands flitted

> bare from his sleeve's flexible carapace. This curvaceous rubbery man
> had arisen from another element. (p. 226)

> In the slots of his flippers his toenails were hideous; ingrown, gan-
> grenous, twisted toward each other. . . . (p. 241)

We are told that Freddy "was used to rejection; he savored it, as if a
dark diagnosis had been confirmed. Further, he sensed that his being
despised served a unifying purpose for the others, gave them a common
identity, as the couples who tolerated Freddy Thorne." (p. 26) Foxy, at
their first meeting, "felt in him, and then dreaded, a desire to intrude
upon, to figure in her fate." (p. 36) Later, after making a shrewd analysis
of Angela's plight in a conversation with Piet, "Freddy's smile implied he
enjoyed access to mines of wisdom, to the secret stream running beneath
reality." (p. 356)

Freddy appears to "know" everything and at the parties he is king,
"the king of chaos" (p. 71); being a dentist, he is also the most brutal
realist and gives voice to their common fear of death.

> People hate love. It threatens them. It's like tooth decay, it smells and
> it hurts. I'm the only man alive it doesn't threaten, I wade right in
> with pick and mirror. I love you, all of you, men, women, neurotic
> children, crippled dogs, mangy cats, cockroaches. People are the only
> thing left since God packed up. By people I mean sex. Fucking. Hip,
> hip, hooray.
> . . . OK, what's not tragic? In the western world there are only
> two comical things: the Christian Church and naked women. . . .
> Everything else tells us we're dead. (pp. 145-46)

At one of the parties Freddy organizes the "Wonderful" game wherein
each person must name the most wonderful thing he can think of. (cf.
pp. 237-44) When asked what the point of the game is, Freddy answers
that the point is that "at the end of the game we'll all know each other
better," for we have been told that "Exposure was, in the games Freddy
invented, the danger and the fruit." As the game develops the players'
answers subtly correspond with the Eden motifs we have noted. The first
response addresses the wonder of Creation itself, for Carol Constantine
explains why she selected "a baby's fingernails" as her choice by saying,
"the way it produces out of nothing, no matter almost what we do . . .
what a lot of *work* somehow, ingenuity, *love* even, goes into making each
one of us, no matter what a lousy job we make of it afterwards." Piet's,
the second answer, reminds us of the Blake water-color when he chooses

"a sleeping woman" because "when she is sleeping, she becomes all woman." When Terry Gallagher next selects the works of Bach because "he didn't know how great he was," Piet corrects her and says, "Don't you believe it. He wanted to be great. He was mad to be immortal." No one probes Foxy's choice which is "the Eucharist," a sacramental sacred eating long symbolized as the antidote to the death-bringing fruit of the Tree of Knowledge. But it is Freddy's choice that follows which elicits objections and stirs ethereal Angela to make her choice.

> (Freddy) "The most wonderful thing I know is the human capacity for self-deception. It keeps everything else going."
> "Only in the human world," Carol interjected. "Which is just a conceited little crust on the real world. Animals don't deceive themselves. Stones don't."
> Angela sat up: "Oh! You mean the world is *everything*? Then I say the stars. Of course the stars."

The choices offered in this game artfully capsulate the novel's major themes and dramatic tensions and insinuate the myth of Creation and Fall. Piet's rather naive objection to Freddy's choice of self-deception is pertinent at this point in the novel, for he argues, "What impresses me isn't so much human self-deception as human ingenuity in creating unhappiness. We believe in it. Unhappiness is us. From Eden on, we've voted for it. We manufacture misery, and feed ourselves on poison. That doesn't mean that the world isn't wonderful."

After Piet's decision to have Foxy's fetus aborted and personally confront death as its instrument, he begins to see Freddy in another light. He exonerates Freddy's complicity in the abortion by transposing it into an act of love for his friends and, as soon as he does so, Piet realizes that it was as though "he and Freddy, the partition between them destroyed, at last comprehended each other with the fullness long desired. . . . Hate and love both seek to know." (p. 398)

Once the abortion has taken place and his divorce is imminent, Piet naively senses exhilaration that Freddy's influence upon him is over. "[He] was pleased to feel that at last he had been redeemed from Freddy Thorne's spell; the old loathing and fascination were gone." However, like all such redemptions, Piet's is paid for. By the novel's end he doubts whether he is still a Christian and the ambivalent feelings he once felt for Freddy are now transferred, ironically, to Foxy. He grows gradually aware of her slyness, her pretense at resistance in sex, her egoism, and the potential destructive power that he now senses in their sex together. (pp. 434ff.) He acknowledges with a touch of irony that Freddy has become "his mentor and savior," for which remark Foxy hushes him and says, "Let's pretend there's only us. Don't we make a world?" (p. 437) They do and have.

Foxy's letters near the end of the novel reveal a like realization of Piet's new Adam status. She writes to Piet that "I have felt in you, I have loved in you, a genius for loneliness, for seeing yourself apart from the world. When you desire to be the world's husband, what right do I have to make you my own?" (p. 450) And in a postscript to that letter she adds: "After weeks of chastity I remember lovemaking as an exploration of a sadness so deep people must go in pairs, one cannot go alone." (p. 451) With these lines, the novel's title of *Couples* takes on its final irony.

Foxy and Piet must leave Tarbox, and Piet is, in Updike's words, "Lot, the man with two virgin daughters, who flees Sodom, and leaves his wife behind."[19] But he is also Adam as well, forced to move to Lexington now that Tarbox has cast him out and is guarded by the cherubim of the remaining couples. The flaming sword of Genesis was seen in the lightning that destroyed the Church, a signal of Piet's disbarment. At first, Piet takes on a symbolic status: "The couples, though they had quickly sealed themselves off from Piet's company, from contamination by his failure, were yet haunted and chastened, as if his fall had been sacrificial." (p. 456) Soon though "the town scarcely remembers Piet . . . with his red hair . . . his quick eyes looking as if they had been rubbed too hard the night before, the skin beneath them pouched in a little tucked fold, as if his maker in the last instant had pinched the clay." (p. 458) Even Adam's faintly heroic symbolic status is forgotten and his face is beyond recall. The novel's unheroic, ironic close reminds us of the final lines to Milton's more noble exit.

> Some natural tears they dropped; but wiped them soon;
> The world was all before them, where to choose
> Their place of rest, and Providence their guide:
> They hand in hand, with wandering steps and slow,
> Through Eden took their solitary way.

"The Hanemas live in Lexington, where, gradually, among people like themselves, they have been accepted, as another couple." (p. 458)

C. ADAM AND EVE IN GREENWOOD

As an undergraduate at Harvard, Updike majored in English poetry of the seventeenth century, a century much concerned with images of Eden. If *Couples* betrays Updike's collegiate interest in Milton's *Paradise Lost*, it is even more obvious that *Marry Me*, with its epigraph taken from Robert Herrick, renews a passion for Milton's contemporary that dates from student days. Updike did his Senior thesis at Harvard on Herrick's poetry and it was entitled "Non-Horatian Elements in Herrick's Echoes of Horace." In that thesis Updike argued that Herrick's Christian ethical sensibility radically transformed the images and phrases that he borrowed from the Stoical Horace. For example, "In many poems, e.g. 'Corinna's gone a-Maying,' an implicit Christian awareness of sin undercuts an explicit pagan sensuality. . . ." (p. 29) This thesis is fascinating to read— going beyond the antiquarian impulse of the scholar—because it reveals *in embryo* Updike's later interest in joining Classical and Christian themes in his fiction, and is an excellent introduction to those qualities that characterize a good deal of Updike's own light verse.

> The inference is that Herrick is able to conceive of himself as a sinner; Horace, even for artistic purposes, can not. But this is only one manifestation of a general characteristic of Herrick's work— its humility. . . . In a larger sense, his humility is the Christian awareness of the smallness of earthly things. His poems are short, his subjects are trivial, his effects are delicate. Yet at the same time he is willing to describe tiny phenomena with the full attention and sympathy due to a "major" theme. . . . In proportion to God's infinity, all things are infinitesimal; yet God's infinite love makes each important. "Are not two sparrows sold for a farthing? and one of them shall not fall on the ground without your Father" (Matt. 10:29). Certainly, Herrick's poetry deserves to be cherished not because it is adroit or roguish, but for the sake of its distinguishing quality, an unaffecting and Christ-like tenderness. (p. 40)

The thesis closes with this eloquent assessment: "Compared with Catullus and Donne, Horace and Herrick do not feel deeply. Compared with Vergil and Milton, they possess little dramatic power. But by writing with care and by writing about things, however trivial or fanciful, which excited their imaginations, Horace and Herrick have created some of the world's most graceful poetry." (p. 43)

Although one hesitates to label *Couples* Miltonic and *Marry Me* Her-

rickean, some features of the tone and style—as well as some imagery—
proper to these vastly different poets are present in these two diversely
shaped novels. Some narrative sections in *Couples*, though hardly written
in blank verse, are composed in a style that is stately, ornate, detached,
given to the long lyric line and the accumulation of image and allusion.
Here the narrative vantage point is a global one, moral in emphasis, and
concerned with history and fate; in short, that vantage point proper to
Milton's God of Calvinism. By contrast, in *Marry Me* the sentences are
generally short, simple, and direct in description, the narrative voice is
unobtrusive, so that the story moves quickly through a series of episodes,
almost impressionistically noted. As in Herrick's poetry, the Christian
and moral sensibility is disguised beneath the almost brightly lyric celebration of a pagan Eden where, alas, weeds grow along with daffodils and
snakes often look like toys.

Herrick's subjects ("I write of Youth, of Love, and have access/ By
these to sing of cleanly Wantonness./ I sing of Times trans-shifting.") are
the themes of *Marry Me*. The action is set between March and November
of 1962 (*Couples* extends from Spring 1963 to Spring 1964), and Herrick's
own recurrent image of the rising and setting sun that punctuates love's
progress, enlivens its urgency, and dramatizes its eclipse, continually ac-
companies the behavior of the two couples from March to November.

Updike explained why he categorized *Marry Me* as a Romance in a
brief interview.

> It's a story that could only have happened in John Kennedy's
> reign. He infused all of us with a romantic sense of ourselves that's
> gone. Anything that happened before 1965 seems kind of innocent to
> me. It's my last romance—about romantic love. A romance operates
> on a slightly different principle from a novel. Instead of muscles, it has
> springs and trap doors. It's something of a valentine. It's meant to have
> the texture of the fabulous.[20]

The Kennedy era was the age of Camelot in America and, in retrospect, it appears as remote as the age of the Round Table. That particular
sense of a distant and irretrievable past is characteristic of Romance.
Couples, even though it deals with the same period and with similar
characters, is quite clearly a novel in that it re-creates the inter-actions
of the whole society of Tarbox; its concerns are with the accuracy of social
and psychological detail; and its characters are closer to "real people" who
resist stylization.[21] The distinction between the novel and romance is a
slippery one and is in need of endless qualifications. Nonetheless, the ten

couples in *Couples* are evidently immersed in a mini-society that is part of a wider society, and the events of history (e.g. John F. Kennedy's death) impinge upon their consciousness. In *Marry Me* the four major characters appear detached from any broader world, as if they are floating free and inhabiting a private one, a never-never land that they alone populate.

This is evident in the very simplicity of the plot, so unlike the sprawl of relationships and events in *Couples*. *Marry Me* concerns only two couples: Jerry and Ruth Conant and Richard and Sally Mathias—a pair quite reminiscent of Piet and Angela Hanema and Ken and Foxy Whitman. All four are articulate, intelligent members of the middle class (Jerry is a designer and animator of television commercials and Richard inherited a chain of liquor stores), and they are spiritually akin to the Tarbox residents, except that they live farther south in Greenwood, Connecticut, near Long Island Sound. The story starts with the idyllic adulterous tryst between Jerry and Sally on a Long Island beach in March, a tryst that Herrick-like renews both their Springish adolescent fancies and their fantasies. These, in turn, lead them to a furtive meeting in Washington, D.C. and, later, a prolonged wait at the airport there, made frantic by their fear of discovery. Neither their lies nor their love protects them for long, however, and the bulk of the novel is devoted to the reactions of their spouses. Ironically, unbeknownst to Sally or Jerry, Richard and Ruth a year before had enjoyed their own adulterous relationship, but Ruth broke it off for reasons as complex as those now offered by Jerry and Sally for staying together.

Complication, then, comes not through plot but through character. Jerry is thirty years old and, like Piet, is ridden with fears of death, religiously and morally haunted, so indecisive that he wants Ruth to resolve the issue. But Ruth, pragmatic, earthbound, and unhaunted, refuses to do so. Her counterpart Richard seems not that reluctant to see Sally go, but her decision waits on Jerry's—and so this romance becomes a roundelay of competing voices and repetitive refrains. As in Herrick's poetry, *Marry Me* is narrowly focused; its effects are achieved through understatement, through a highlighting of the apparently trivial, through the observed detail and its psychological referent. The key to the novel's frame and thematic shape is found in Ruth's unconscious doodling while on the telephone. ". . . her right hand had been doodling, on the back of a windowed envelope, squares interlocking with squares. Their areas of overlap were shaded; light and dark were balanced, confused though she had been."[22] The novel concludes with three different endings. These represent Jerry's possible choices. Through such a device, Updike seems to be inviting his readers to make their own choice or else continue the doodling of Ruth.

Earlier I mentioned that critical interpretations of *Couples* in the light of the Tristan and Iseult story would serve equally well in interpreting *Marry Me*. In fact, the Tristan saga finds a richer lode in this Romance because, throughout, especially in Jerry's voice-over reminiscences, Updike explicitly employs the romantic, medieval imagery typical of the courtly love tradition. (cf. pp. 33, 46, 69, 284, 299-300) Furthermore, unlike the more pragmatic, unliterary Piet, Jerry, the failed artist, often seems aware that he is parodying De Rougemont's argument regarding the Tristan story. E.g. "What we have, sweet Sally, is an ideal love. It's ideal because it can't be realized. . . . Any attempt to start existing, to move out of this pain will kill us." (p. 46) "As an actual wife or whatever, she stopped being an *idea*, and for the first time, I *saw* her." (p. 284)

Yet I believe the even more ancient motif of Eden and the Fall will serve as well, if not better. The story's setting is in Greenwood, a symbolic name no doubt, and we are told that it is a place where its inhabitants ever kept trying "to render Greenwood even more of a Paradise." (p. 125)

The story begins with that idyllic tryst of Jerry and Sally who meet on a remote beach that, labyrinth-like, can only be approached by a road "full of unexplained forks and windings and turnings-off" and "ambiguous turns." Ray Charles' song "Born to Lose" is heard over the radio and its lyric ("Every dream/ Has brought me pain . . .") immediately establishes a thematic contrast with the idyllic setting. It is evident that nostalgia already grips the lives of these lovers, for "Each time, they were unable to find the exact place, the perfect place, where they have been before." (p. 4) The dunes wear the look of "clean-swept Nature, never tasted" and, in our first glimpse of Sally, "she seemed, blonde and freckled and clean-swept, a shy creature of the sand." (p. 5) The couple walk down the beach "looking for the ideal spot" for their love-making. Once it is found, they begin without hurry, a proof, it seems, that they were "the original man and woman—that they felt no hurry, that they did not so much excite each other as put the man and the woman in each other to rest." (p. 7) Afterwards, in a symbolic action, both drink from the shattered bottle of warm wine. (Recall Milton's postlapsarian description: "As with new wine intoxicated both. . . .") Sally drinks first and "His heart tripped as if at some danger but when she lowered the bottle her face was pleased and unharmed." When Jerry follows, he cuts the bridge of his nose on the bottle and Sally shows him "a pink blot of blood on her white finger-tip" and remarks that now they both share a secret about the origin of his cut that no one else can share. Sally later will think of the broken bottle as emblematic of herself, but it is emblematic now of Jerry as well.

A conversation follows concerning the book Sally is reading, a novel by Alberto Moravia. (Later, as their affair becomes more complicated and a drift begins, Sally will take up Camus' *The Stranger* where the image of the sun is quite different in accent from Herrick's.) Sally gives the opinion that Moravia is "good," a rather imprecise critical assessment that Jerry pounces upon. This casual conversation introduces a theme that will re-appear and take on different connotations as the story develops. Through-out *Marry Me* conversations about "good" and "right" versus their oppo-sites characterize much of the dialogue. But the words "good" and "right" have multiple meanings and Updike exploits each one. "Good," for ex-ample, can enjoy a moral or sexual or aesthetic signification (the Three Great Secrets again), and each of their possible meanings is defended and dramatized in this Romance. (cf. pp. 11, 47, 119, 150, 207, 249, 257, 276-77) Subtly at issue is the question of the knowledge of good and evil and its exploration. It is significant, then, that this idyllic opening chapter should end with Jerry's admission that he can't go on with the affair. " 'Baby, I can't swing it,' he said, and the flutter of her nodding made their bodies vibrate together. *I know. I know.*" (p. 13)

In the next chapter, "The Wait," the lovers meet in Washington, D.C., and Sally recalls the awkwardness of their first and second experiences of love-making. But she also remembers that, finally, on their third night together, "Jerry and Sally made love lucidly, like Adam and Eve when the human world was of two halves purely"; and yet, afterwards, she "involuntarily cried out, pierced by the discovery, 'Jerry, your eyes are so sad!' " (p. 33) Later, "it haunted her and she wondered if that was why Jerry had taken her into his life, to be taught about suffering." (p. 42)

Jerry, whom other characters label as an "innocent" or as one unac-quainted with suffering, is in fact both a moral malingerer and spiritually sensitive. We are told that "Jerry believed in choices, in mistakes, in damnation, in the avoidance of suffering. [Sally] and Richard believed simply that things happened." (p. 45) Despite several unattractive char-acteristics like childish indecisiveness and egoism, Jerry still remains the most articulate explicator of the novel's central themes. One conversation is pivotal where he remarks to Sally:

"What we have is love. But love must become fruitful, or it loses itself. I don't mean having babies—God, we've all had too many of those—I mean just being relaxed, and right, and, you know, with a blessing. Does 'blessing' seem silly to you?"

"Can't we give each other the blessing?"

"No. For some reason it must come from above."

Above them, in a sky still bright though the earth was ripening into shadow, an airplane hung cruciform, silver, soundless. . . .

(Jerry) ". . . Maybe our trouble is that we live in the twilight of the old morality, and there's just enough to torment us, and not enough to hold us in." (p. 53)

But this second idyllic tryst ends, another airplane brings them home, and, instead of blessings, they meet curses once their secret is out. Sally's husband Richard seems to be a cousin to both Ken Whitman and Freddy Thorne in *Couples*. Cold and methodical like Ken, he is profane and serpentine like Freddy. Richard has only one eye; the other, blinded in a childhood accident, "wore a kind of cap of frost."

Jerry wondered what it would be like to see with only one eye. He closed one of his and looked at the room—the chairs, the women, the glasses invisibly shed a dimension. Things were just so, flat, with nothing further to be said about them; it was the world, he realized, as seen without the idea of God lending each thing a roundness of significance. (p. 225)

Richard is unique in that he is that rarity, a professed atheist who delights in what others see as blasphemy. When Ruth's affair of a year ago with Richard is recounted, we grow aware that Richard is a figure both attractive and menacing, even to Ruth. Their erotic encounters are generally described with Edenesque overtones.

(The Demonic) "Richard became an incubus upon her. She felt him fumbling and butting his way toward a secret that ached to be discovered. The unpleasant frost in his eye, where other people had a black point feeding on the light, chilled her. . . ." (p. 85)

(Imagery of the Fall) "It was all matter-of-fact controlled, satisfactory: under this alien man there was a time, time in which to make the trip to the edge and fall, fall and arrive where she had begun, pressed to the earth as if safe." (p. 96)

(Imagery of Eden's Tree) "His bulk above her felt like some strange warm tree she was hugging because she was 'it' at hide-and-seek. Out of doors, in nature, the queerness of being kissed was clarified. . . .

(Later) She judged herself improved and deepened in about the normal
amount—she had dared danger and carried wisdom away. . . ."
(pp. 94-95)

The Richard-Ruth affair counterpoints that of Jerry and Sally. For
both pairs sexual "knowing" brings a special wisdom. In both cases it is
a Mathias who is the aggressive enticer in this Eden world of Greenwood.
Sea and sun imagery predominate in the Jerry-Sally relationship; the forest
setting and its imagery characterize Ruth and Richard's relationship.

Despite the fact that Ruth is nominally a Unitarian and pragmatically
an atheist, Updike cleverly associates, by way of the tree and forest symbolism, her religious impulses with that of her own fall and acquisition of
knowledge. Ruth is fascinated by the great elm situated outside their
bedroom window, pointedly "one of the few surviving in Greenwood."

> Of all things accessible to Ruth's vision the elm most nearly per-
> suaded her of a cosmic benevolence. If asked to picture God, she would
> have pictured this tree. (p. 98)
> Her elm, her sacred elm, was flooding the road in golden leaves
> and resuming the nakedness in which its arabesques and tracery were
> all revealed, leading her eye upward and upward, homeward to some
> undivided principle of aspiration. (pp. 197-98)

Ruth's climactic car accident re-establishes this motif from another
perspective and her reaction to it is replete with allusions to an ambivalent
Eden. In one of Updike's most kinesthetically moving passages, Ruth's
car plunges off the road into a "sunken strand of trees, elm and red maple
and swamp oak"; and "when the number of trees seemed to multiply
hopelessly, she lay down on the front seat and shut her eyes." (p. 160)
The car nuzzles to a stop and Ruth, rather composed, "deduced that this
was not Paradise and she was not dead. . . . She was trespassing, she
perceived; she should get off van Huyten's precious land. She had hurt
his wall and his trees." (p. 161)[23]

After leaving the scene of the accident, Ruth becomes aware that a
policeman is listening to her, and yet she is careless "as if, in breaking
through van Huyten's wall, she had come into a green freedom." (p. 164)
Later, when she and Jerry return to the scene of the accident, she recounts
once more "the skid the other way, the wall, the calm trees, the Edenesque beauty and intensity of the dripping woods when she got out of the
halted, smoldering car." (p. 169) Jerry sees in the accident a divine omen
and remarks, "I've been waiting, I suppose, for God to do something, and

this was it. His way of saying that nothing is going to happen. Unless you and I make it happen." (p. 171)

After this climactic, symbolic accident—a collision in Eden—the themes of knowledge, freedom, sexual dread, the need for decision, and the terrible consequences of every choice begin to predominate. But these themes are artfully planted, almost concealed, within the series of conversations that make up the last half of Marry Me. At this point Jerry becomes the focal point of these contending thematic forces and becomes, as it were, a Kierkegaard exhibit-specimen of ambivalent dread personified. Even though each of the other characters will be inevitably affected by the choice Adam-Jerry makes, each remains something of an outsider, not really sympathetic with his existential dilemma. For example, "Ruth disliked, religiously, the satisfaction he took in being divided, confirming thereby the split between body and soul that alone can save man from extinction. It was all too religious, phantasmal." (p. 186)

Those reviewers who applauded Marry Me quite evidently shared imaginatively in Jerry's moral and psychological labors; those who did not, evidently did not.[24] However, those who did imaginatively partake in Jerry's Kierkegaardian angst and its stark presentation of ambivalent impulses no doubt appreciated best the story's rather startling ending.

As the story proper closes (i.e. before the tripartite ending is appended), Jerry and Richard confront each other over the telephone. Throughout, they have been mismatched counterparts: Richard, the smug, quasi-demonic agent of decisiveness who is "in Hell" over the situation versus Jerry, a vacillating Adam, spiritually stretched between the polar promptings of body and soul, a man haunted by indecision. So far each has lived in a different moral world. Finally, the counterparts meet and their fate is joined. The resolution of the "situation" depends on Jerry's decision to stay married or divorce and re-marry. This situation endows Jerry with a previously unknown power, the opportunity to introduce Richard into a new mode of knowledge, that of helplessness that can be resolved only by another's choice. All four, including Richard the atheist who once blasphemously used a crucifix as a nailpicker, are plunged into the drama of Eden once again. The Romance proper ends with Jerry gazing out toward Ruth's sacred elm tree where "the arms of the elm crawled and rotted in a godless element that was his enemy's essence. Richard was the world." (pp. 286-87) This image reminds us of the dust-jacket photo of the sarcophagus of the Garden scene where the serpent coils about the tree and appears to climb from its roots. Suddenly, Jerry "knows" hatred and understands that hatred "knows" him as well. The words "good" and "evil" are now somewhat clarified for Richard and himself. For both it is a hard-won knowledge; the difference lies in its possibilities for a redemption. The story ends with these poignant lines which are simultaneously ironic and telling:

> Look, Sally-O, doesn't Christ make a good fingernail-picker?
> Gazing through the half-mirroring black glass, glass that seemed the cold skin of his mind, Jerry rejoiced that he had given his enemy the darkness an eternal wound. With the sword of his flesh he had put the mockers to rout. Christ was revenged. (p. 287)

D. THE AMERICAN ADAM AND THE PARTY OF IRONY

Perhaps it might smack of special pleading or, worse, of silliness to suggest that *Couples* and *Marry Me* are best read in the light of America's literary tradition in the nineteenth century, specifically that tradition of romance associated with Nathaniel Hawthorne. Elsewhere, I rather ungraciously described *Couples* "as an old-fashioned novel, often being more stuffy than sensational, so Victorian that at times it reads like an oversexed opus by George Eliot—in short, this is Updike's *Middlemarch* about those in the coach class of the jet set."[25]

Older and wiser perhaps, I now realize that, despite such eminent Victorian similarities which are possibly worth pursuing, Updike's sensibility—religious, moral, and aesthetic—is far closer to Hawthorne's than to that of George Eliot. Updike, like Hawthorne, is one of the most difficult authors to situate among his contemporaries and their fashionable ideologies, no doubt for the same reason. Both resolutely make their imaginative residence in America and devote all their attention to an America that they see in moral transition. When they move off their imaginative turf, as Hawthorne did in *The Marble Faun* and Updike does in parts of *Bech: A Book* and in *The Coup*, they do so with more than a backward glance; instead, the foreign setting itself becomes a metaphor for a peculiarly American experience, namely: that related to the Adam myth.

R. W. B. Lewis, in his excellent study *The American Adam*, demonstrates that the age of Hawthorne was characterized by an ongoing debate between two opposing points of views, each of which was caused by the invigorating feeling that a new culture was in the making, and that this debate touched upon the moral, intellectual, and artistic resources of man in this new society. One might say that the Three Great Secret Things were being probed even then. Lewis makes clear that, as this dialogue developed, an underlying myth—that of Adam—permeated the major terms of the debate and, in fact, the myth provided imaginative direction and emotional energy to the more obviously rational arguments proposed. He employs Emerson's own distinction between the "Parties of Memory and of Hope" to clarify this opposition.[26]

For the party of Hope—represented by Emerson, Thoreau, and Whitman—the key word was "innocence," and their image was that of a sinless Adam, a radically new personality, emancipated from history and ancestry, an archetypal man whose moral stance was prior to experience and whose radical newness meant a radical innocence. In opposition was the party of Memory, nostalgic for America's Puritan and Calvinistic heritage, whose image was that of "Adam fallen," a sinner badly in need of redemption, whose condition was obviously manifest in the light of contemporary corruption.

Between these two opposing parties, Lewis finds a third which he calls "the Party of Irony," and he places Nathaniel Hawthorne firmly within it. Lewis does so because "it was Hawthorne who saw in the American experience the re-creation of the story of Adam and who, more than any other contemporary, exploited the active metaphor of the American as Adam—before and during and after the Fall."[27]

Unlike his contemporaries, Hawthorne was ambivalent about the Adamic image not only because of ideological misgivings but also by reason of his artistic instincts; again and again his narratives will attempt to dramatize *all* the conflicting myths of Adam. Lewis observes:

> But Hawthorne was neither Emersonian nor Edwardsean [Calvinistic]; or rather he was both. The characteristic situation in his fiction is that of the Emersonian figure, the man of hope, who by some frightful mischance has stumbled into the time-burdened world of Jonathan Edwards. . . . The situation, in the form which Hawthorne's ambivalence gave it, regularly led in his fiction to a moment of crucial choice: an invitation to the lost Emersonian, the thunder-struck Adam to make up his mind—whether to accept the world he had fallen into, or whether to flee it. . . . It is a decision about ethical reality, and most of Hawthorne's heroes and heroines eventually have to confront it.[28]

That paragraph, with a few minor adjustments, would serve as a description of *Couples* and *Marry Me* and of the ethical dilemmas faced by Updike's two Adams, Piet and Jerry. It is important to recall that both *Couples* and *Marry Me* were written during a similar period of debate in American history—from 1967 to 1974. As de Tocqueville remarked, "among democratic nations each generation is a new people," and seldom was this truth ever more apparent. Once again there was a conflict between the party of Hope and the party of Memory. Although a non-Bible-reading public did not enunciate the debate in the terms of the Adam myth, the myth did its subliminal work. The new party of Hope had in its membership flower children, feminists, clergymen, all those desirous of emancipation—whether from the old sexual mores, or from traditional family or ecclesiastical structures or from foreign entanglements or from whatever—with the result that a radical newness was not only desired but deemed possible. The slogan "Make love not war" was a disguised invitation for a pre-lapsarian start; a renewed innocence could turn aside evil; the Fall could be undone. Consciousness-raising, of course without its post-lapsarian consequences, would be the midwife for this new birth and deliverance.

The party of Memory in the 1960's and early 1970's was hardly composed of members who were strict Calvinists but, dogma aside, they did embrace Calvinism's fundamental suspicions about the race and subscribed to a vision of the world as a fallen one wherein justice and peace and freedom, though ideals, could actually be realized only through a balance of power, i.e. through a recognition of ever-competing evils. Their image of Adam also made them wary of all calls for emancipation. For they instinctively knew that it was not the innocent Adam but the fallen Adam who was truly human; that it had been this tragic Adam who, by trickling increment, had shaped society's sexual mores, established family ties as protective, constructed churches to remind man of his limitations. This view of Adam was not innocent at all, but at least he seemed wiser if sadder. Coincident with these suspicions, though, was a genuine nostalgia for a "lost America" that had suddenly vanished, an America that they sensed was oddly more truly "innocent" than the present one a-borning, an innocence that was rooted in striving, sacrifice, solidarity, and perhaps even Swing music.

In a source I cannot find, W. H. Auden once said that one can distinguish a liberal from a conservative by asking him where his ideal of paradise can be found. If he answers by describing a Golden Age in the past, a lost Garden of Eden, then he is a conservative; if he offers a Utopia in the distant future, then he is a liberal. Auden felt that only Christianity demands both perspectives. When asked, though, what happens when such differing conceptions come into conflict, Auden answered, "murder."

Fortunately, there were few incidents of actual murder between these parties in the 1960's and early 1970's, but the point of the debate did concern one's fundamental image of America and where a Paradise could be found. On this point nostalgia and an untheological millenarianism clashed. That an outsider, perhaps a philosopher or the like, dispassionate and detached, might notice that these ideals of Adamic innocence occasionally overlapped, meant nothing—America was once again at war with itself and its image of itself.

It is not surprising, then, that an artist as sensitive to social forces and as informed about American history as Updike is, will imaginatively engage this debate. However, he will not do so as an advocate but will proceed as did Hawthorne, his ancestor in the party of Irony. Like Hawthorne, Updike *qua* artist (his own personal political leanings are another question) is sympathetic to both parties and his fiction will be a product of this controlled division of sympathies.[29] *Couples* and *Marry Me* will pose questions to both sides in the debate.

Where Hawthorne might place the setting for his questions to the debate in a Salem of long ago as he did in *The Scarlet Letter*, Updike will place his in the New England of the Kennedy era which immediately preceded the decade, that era of a supposedly New Frontier and Great Society, of a romantic Camelot. Then he will ironically punctuate his story with grim bulletins about death (the *Thresher* drowning, Kennedy's baby, Kennedy himself) and upheaval (the Cuban missile crisis, the conflicts in Laos and Vietnam).

The setting and the social interaction of *Couples* and *Marry Me* are decidedly more reminiscent of Hawthorne's *The Blithedale Romance* than of *The Scarlet Letter*. (As we shall see, the latter will figure prominently in *A Month of Sundays*.) In *The Blithedale Romance* Hawthorne focused on a dead society of the very recent past, the Brook Farm experiment that was conceived, built, and ruined within less than a decade, much like Kennedy's Camelot. The denizens of Brook Farm were energized by the optimism of Emerson's Transcendentalism; consequently they turned their backs on a corrupt world and banded together to form "a socialistic colony in which the conditions that had prevailed since the Fall should prevail no more. . . . The law of love will be put into effect in a practical way for perhaps the first time in human history. Man will no longer be shut up in the prison of the self."[30]

Tarbox is a Blithedale resurrected, a place, as Freddy Thorne observes, devoted to "humanizing each other." This is Updike's description of the distress at the past and the utopian visions of a new society that these couples will embrace:

> Having suffered under their parents' rigid marriages and formalized evasions, they sought to substitute an essential fidelity set in a matrix of easy and open companionship among the couples. . . . They put behind them the stratified summer towns of their upbringings, with their restrictive distinctions, their tedious rounds of politeness, and settled the year round in unthought-of places, in pastoral mill towns like Tarbox, and tried to improvise here a new way of life. Duty and work yielded as ideals to truth and fun. Virtue was no longer sought in temple or market place but in the home—one's own home, and then the homes of one's friends. (p. 106)

Unfortunately, both Tarbox and Blithedale are destroyed from within. The words "love" and "humanizing each other" admit of many meanings; their realization in action can bring either destruction or cohesion. To deny Adam's fall is precisely to misunderstand that these meanings are potentially multiple and that the lessons in learning the vocabulary are hard won.

The Blithedale experiment failed because the ideal of brotherhood was replaced by selfhood, faith was replaced by skepticism, and the roseate visions of community darkened into hostility and antagonism. Suspicion not love eventually reigned, for, as Hawthorne implies, that promised bond within the community—a man-made substitute for the old Puritan Covenant—was incapable of communal cohesion. Yet, an ironic aping continued. When Coverdale returns to Blithedale at the end of the romance, it has become a battlefield of fresh antagonisms and mutual suspicions, with Hollingshead resembling a Puritan magistrate. Similarly, at the end of *Couples*, the members of Freddy's "church" are either lapsed or scattered, and yet he functions, as did Hollingshead, like a Puritan magistrate *manque*, ostracizing sinners like Piet.[31]

In *Couples* and *Marry Me* it is Updike's two Calvinistic heroes, Piet and Jerry, who, though plunged into this Blithedale, still retain a vaguely pledged membership in the party of Memory. And yet, since both wish to be free as well, freed from their dread and their fears, both become the focal center of the Adamic debate. The fact that both novels end with a good deal of ambiguity and that the reader himself is left to wrestle with the terms of the debate is what one would expect from a writer whose membership is in the party of Irony.

In closing I would like to quote from Paul Elmer More's eloquent statement on Hawthorne found in his 1904 *Shelburne Essays*. I include it here because, if one substitutes Updike's name for Hawthorne's, it elegantly summarizes Updike's efforts and success in the composition of both *Couples* and *Marry Me*.

> . . . to us of the western world, over whom has passed centuries of human brooding, and who find ourselves suddenly cut loose from the consolation of Christian faith, his voice may well seem the utterance of universal experience, and we may be even justified in assuming that his words have at last expressed what has long slumbered in the human consciousness. . . . Not with impunity had the human race for ages dwelt on the eternal welfare of the soul; for from such meditation the sense of personal importance had become exacerbated to an extraordinary degree. What could result from such teaching as that of Jonathan Edwards but an extravagant sense of individual existence, as if the moral governance of the world revolved about the action of each individual soul? And when the alluring faith attendant on this form of introspection paled, as it did during the so-called transcendental movement into which Hawthorne was born, there resulted necessarily a feeling of anguish and bereavement more tragic than any previous moral stage through which the world had passed. The loneliness of the individual, which had been vaguely felt and lamented by poets and philosophers of the past, took on a poignancy altogether unexampled. It needed but an artist with the vision of Hawthorne to represent this feeling as the one tragic calamity of mortal life, as the great primeval curse of sin. What lay dormant in the teaching of Christianity became the universal protest of the human heart.[32]

6: *Bech: A Book*

One striking characteristic of the Updike novels that we have examined is that so often the central character is an unsuccessful or failed artist. Peter Caldwell is "a second-rate abstract expressionist" at best; Joey Robinson is a failed poet; Piet Hanema desires to make his restorations artistic but is frustrated by modern tastes; Jerry Conant is an animator of television commercials and not the artist he hoped to be. We discover in all these characters and their circumstances the clash between the innocently optimistic ideal of the creative artist (like Whitman's or Emerson's Adam) and the complex reality encountered by man as moral agent (that is, fallen Adam impregnated with dread)—in short, caught between aesthetic and moral ideals.

A similar kind of character and a similar kind of tension are found throughout Hawthorne's fiction a century ago. R. W. B. Lewis argues that such characters and tensions betray Hawthorne's anxieties about an American culture that had not come apart, but inversely had not yet come together. Consequently, Hawthorne's fiction reveals multiple anxieties, often at cross-purposes, regarding the place of the artist in America, and Lewis summarizes Hawthorne's dilemma by saying:

> Hawthorne exhibited an uneasy awareness of the almost willful contemporary impoverishment of artistic resources; perhaps this accounts for the proportion of artists he invented—or at least for the proportion of frustrated artists. . . . Hawthorne's anxiety was increased by the conviction that creativity was an analogous, possibly an even alternate, route to salvation. For Hawthorne could neither share the belief of his Puritan ancestors that the artistic enterprise was at best a mere trope for the really impressive work of the rescue of the human soul; nor could he arrive at the later romantic avowal that what had formerly

153

been described as the rescue of the soul was in reality a concealed metaphor for the greatest human accomplishment—that is, for art.[1]

Repeatedly, especially in our consideration of *The Centaur* and *Couples*, we have noted a like ambiguity, a similar division of sympathy in Updike's work. The important difference is that for Hawthorne America as an imaginative ideal had not yet come together because of the warring parties of Hope and Memory; for Updike, any accepted image of "America" seemed, at best, to be falling apart since neither the Whitmanesque nor the Puritan ideal was feasible any longer for the serious artist.

What, then, was a writer to do? In the light of Hawthorne's dilemma, Lewis reviews the two most popular contemporary choices our writers make in seeking a way out of this impasse. On the one hand, with Joyce as his inspiration, the writer can make the artist *the* representative figure in the modern world, make his explorations indicative of the modern mind and its quest, make the artist Man writ large. Or, on the other hand, he can despair of mimesis and retreat from attempting to probe and capture the realistic vitality and moral ambivalence of the world around him and, instead, with Gide as his guide, concentrate on the artist's alienation, on the trials themselves of writing, on the rather specialized problems of the artistic vocation.[2]

It is important, I think, to emphasize that neither Hawthorne nor Updike makes either of these radical choices, although it might seem so in *Bech: A Book*. Instead, sympathetic to both impulses, they attempt to combine them. Consequently, an atypical union of mimetic intent and intense artistic self-preoccupation will characterize their fiction and ever issue in that distinctive sort of ambiguity and ambivalence proper to those who are members of the party of Irony.

Bech: A Book, published in 1970, must be read in the light of these ambivalent artistic concerns, for this collection addresses the more specialized problems an artist faces, as well as those more generally shared anxieties experienced on the American scene. The ever-shifting point of view, the multi-leveled irony, the varying psychic stimuli the different settings evoke, the doubling back in time-focus, the inclusion of comments on "classical" American authors, the scheme of question and answer interviews that subtly both unite and disrupt the on-going "story," all of these devices contribute to the realization that Bech is definitely Bech, a writer by instinct and profession, and yet Bech is us as well, an American us in the post-Kennedy 1960's. To consign *Bech: A Book* to the category "comic satire" about writer's block is to misread its other, more universal intent.

Bech is called A Book rather than a novel, not because it lacks imaginative unity, but, no doubt, because it was conceived and architected in piecemeal fashion. Updike has admitted that when he returned in 1964 from Russia and Eastern Europe as a representative in a writers' exchange, he had collected some impressions peculiar to a writer. To convey these he invented the Jewish writer Henry Bech as a vehicle for those impressions and wrote "The Bulgarian Poetess." That story, which also appears in The Music School collection, went on to win the O. Henry award for the finest short story that year. Spurred on by this success, he then wrote "Bech in Rumania" and "Rich in Russia," after an abortive try at a long Russian Journal, the remains of which are now included as an appendix to Bech: A Book. Domestic inspirations from America's changing scene in the 1960's led him to compose "Bech Takes Pot Luck" in an American setting; then a London story "Bech Swings?" made a Bech collection feasible. To complete it and unify loose strands, Updike wrote "Bech Panics" as a bridge chapter and "Bech Enters Heaven" to give it a final shape.[3] Since the publication of this collection Updike has written three more Bech stories, and so a sequel can be expected. Like Rabbit, Bech lives on, ever ready to return.

In an interview in 1970, the year Bech was published, Updike, in a quote worth repeating, addressed the more specialized aspects of the collection.

> Now as for the Bech stories. . . . For a writer, life becomes overmuch a writer's life. Things happen to you that wouldn't happen to anybody else, and the way of using this to good advantage, of course, is to invent another writer. At first, he is very much an alter ego, but then, in the end, not so. At any rate, I have used the writer in Bech as a subject in order to confess sterility in a truthful way. . . . In my book I tried to—and I believe I did—package and dispose of a certain set of tensions which I have as a practicing writer. . . . Mine is merely a kind of complaint about the curious position the American writer now finds himself in; he is semi-obsolete, a curious fellow without any distinct sense of himself as a sensible professional.[4]

These lines on many points read like a restatement of Lewis' assessment of Hawthorne's dilemma and, just as Hawthorne created a rather prim and myopic Coverdale to establish artistic distance from himself, so Updike invented Bech. Bech in many ways is everything that Updike is not: he is a blocked writer, a bachelor, a Jewish celebrity whose emotional and imaginative roots are urban, a World War II veteran whose initial successes were published in the now defunct *Liberty* and *Collier's* magazines. To further that distance, Updike provides Bech with an extensive bibliography of primary and secondary sources, itself an hilarious gem, wherein we find a list of popular and scholarly dissections of Bech's work, the titles of which betray the scholars' mounting frustration with Bech's *oeuvre*. Updike apparently experienced as much delight in composing this bibliography as the reader receives. But, besides the artistic reasons, Updike admitted that the "bibliography was also a matter of working off various grudges, a way of purging my spleen. I've never been warmly treated by the *Commentary* crowd—insofar as it is a crowd—and so I made Bech its darling."[5]

To compound the fun Updike has Bech write the foreword to the collection (an enterprise that takes him eight days), and Bech gives a rather restrained and quizzical blessing to its contents. The foreword is addressed to the author John and, should we mistake who that John might be, Bech subtly informs us that the "Bech" one discovers within these pages is not necessarily all Henry but a literary gumbo concocted and flavored by "John."

> . . . in Bulgaria (eclectic sexuality, bravura narcissism, thinning curly hair), I sound like a gentlemanly Norman Mailer; then that London glimpse of *silver* hair glints more of the gallant, glamorous Bellow. . . . I got a whiff of Malamud in your city breezes, and I am paranoid to feel my "block" an ignoble version of the more or less noble renunciations of H. Roth, D. Fuchs, and J. Salinger? Withal, something Waspish, theological, scared, and insulatingly ironical that derives, my wild surmise is, from you.[6]

That last sentence alerts us to the fact that, when we discover satiric nudges in *Bech: A Book*, the object of the jab is more often Updike himself, his own prose style, and familiar fictive *angsts* than Henry Bech. In fact, Updike considers *Bech* not "satirical, really; it was never really a concern of mine to poke fun at the Jewish writer, or the New York-Jewish literary establishment in this country. I hope I always gave Bech my full sympathy, my full empathy."[7]

At the risk of dampening the rich fun in the book, it is important to emphasize that the figure of Bech himself and his Jewish background are introduced not in order to exploit ethnic particularities but to provide

Updike with a symbolic figure whose problems and fears are able to represent both the literary situation and the ambivalent moral and cultural status of contemporary America in the 1960's. Here Bech's Jewishness is emblematic in multiple ways. First of all, when one thinks of a literary establishment since World War II, i.e. those writers who have repeatedly met with artistic success and have eloquently given a distinctive pattern of insight to American literature, it is quite evident that a sizeable number come from Jewish backgrounds. To be an important writer in the 1960's and to be Jewish were hardly synonymous, of course, but the expectation was keen enough not to seem far-fetched, although likely. Who, then, better than a Bech could embody those strains and anxieties proper to an American writer? Furthermore, once Bech was chosen, who better could exemplify the gradual and yet seemingly abrupt transition that had taken place within the American conscience and consciousness since World War II? In that 1970 interview Updike offered a telling observation on this very point by saying:

> All the graces we think of as Jewish reflect a totality of embrace of the world. It's something you feel in the Jewish sensibility that isn't elsewhere—although you do find something like it in Southern writing. Conceivably, the war ruined our sense of the world being divided and charged in every particle, a sense of the world that I think various Protestant writers have tended to view as part demonic. But it seems to me that the Jewish Americans kept up the belief a little longer—it is implied, at least, in their mental activities of all sorts. They arrived at the written page equipped with the belief in the instinctual importance of human events. . . .
>
> However, I'm not sure there are going to be increasing waves of such writing from those with a Jewish background.[8]

Bech's sterility and dread, therefore, are not restricted to a professional writer's "block" alone but are symptomatic of the immobility, futility, and desperation perceived by sensitive souls throughout American culture. That sanguine resourcefulness, once so characteristic of the American temperament and personified in its image of itself as the American Adam, was renewed for a time, in transformed fashion, by the energy and distinctive optimism of Jewish writers after World War II. As Updike himself observed, even the familiar Jewish "victim" figure was of a special sort in that "along with this sense of being a victim is an underlying tone that the world is somehow getting better under these awful conditions . . .

there's always available some other kind of triumph, or the thought that what happens is in some way good for them, or, at least, the balm that is inevitable."[9] One might add, then, that the post-War Jewish victim was not so unlike Billy Budd or Hester Prynne after all, and that the Jewish writer sincerely expected his own "barbaric yawp" to be heard, for he presumed the ears to hear were out there, anxious to hear his "song" and travel the open road with him as guide.

But by the mid-60's with his Whitmanesque *Travel Light* behind him, Bech finds himself at an impasse; both the old frontier and the New Frontier are gone, and he dwells in an America that is emotionally un-recognizable. Perhaps the finest parallel text to use in appreciating *Bech* and its themes is to be found in a speech Updike gave at the American Enterprise Institute in 1976 entitled "The Plight of the American Writer." In this address Updike relates the financial, political, and linguistic ad-vantages American writers enjoy vis-à-vis their foreign confreres, but then adds that, despite these assets, "the profession of the writer in the United States has been sharply devalued in the last thirty years and has suffered loss both in the dignity assigned to it and the sense of purpose that shapes a profession from within."[10] Unlike his foreign counterparts, the Ameri-can writer lacks a "cohesive and tangible audience." Ironically, the very absence of artistic restrictions—not only political but also sexual—inhibits the writer in a sense, cutting him off from "the vocabulary of gesture and innuendo that society invents to circumvent its taboos [which] are so precious to art; one thinks of the moment when Hester Prynne in *The Scarlet Letter* takes off her cap and lets her hair fall down in the forest. . . ."[11] Those very restrictions under which pre-1955 writers labored were challenges to their imaginations and elicited from them the "ingenuities of correlative symbolism, euphemism, and telling omission."

However, in an era where everything is permitted, explicitness is all and yet, imaginatively, not enough; when everything can be said, one wonders whether anything in particular is worth saying or saying in a special way. Bech's writing block is thus not a private affair, for Bech is the quintessential post-War adult: granted unlimited freedom of speech but without anything to say. Like his country, his own past success has inhibited him and, seemingly, rendered him speechless. Unsurprisingly, Bech will find imaginative refreshment only during the travel chapters; at least abroad he will be inspired to think big (and that only) about his next novel *Think Big*. By contrast, on the homefront he will be continually terrified by visions of decay and death and impotence. Impotence is a key metaphor here. In that Washington address Updike observed:

> If any law at all can be proposed, it is that art flourishes *before* a national potency has been fulfilled; Elizabethan poetry has more patriotic energy than Victorian; the Americans of the 1850's wrote with a confidence impossible to those of the 1950's. Not now could Melville write, "The world is as young today as when it was created; and this Vermont morning dew is as wet to my feet, as Eden's dew to Adam's."[12]

This image of the American Adam amid freshness flourished in an era of pre-potency. Yet, we ought not forget that Nature herself continually presented a Janus-face even in this idyllic Eden. For those members of the party of Hope, the American wilderness was seen as wild but wonderful, meant to be tamped by Adam's feet and floriate through his sweat: Nature was his given, the New World was his oyster. On the other hand, as Hawthorne's ambiguous use of forest imagery and Melville's of the sea suggest, thoughts of an intractable Nature generated terrors as well, evoking sensations of hostility, brutality, and loneliness. Indeed, Nature and the land were part of the American promise; but that promise, reflecting the Old Testament covenant, guaranteed both life and death, vitality and decay.

The excellent chapter "Bech Panics" reenacts this primordial American ambivalence and updates it. Earlier in "The Bulgarian Poetess" chapter, we had been told that, upon arriving in Sofia, Bech stayed in his hotel room all night, behind a locked door, reading Hawthorne (namely, "Roger Malvin's Burial"). "The image of Roger Malvin lying alone, dying, in the forest—'Death would come like the slow approach of a corpse, stealing gradually towards him through the forest, and showing its ghostly and motionless features from behind a nearer and yet a nearer tree'— frightened him. Bech fell asleep early and suffered from swollen, homesick dreams." (p. 51) For Bech, a man professionally prone toward creating images, this image of Roger Malvin will be re-created within him, just as Hawthorne the artist's personal dilemma is his.

In "Bech Panics" Bech is invited to give a series of lectures at a girl's school in Virginia at the beginning of Spring. The earth-smells of the countryside coming to life oddly fill him with dread and a fear of dying. His anguish is compounded by his contact with the virginal vitality and sexual innocence of these girls whose "limbs [were] still ripening toward the wicked seductiveness Nature intended."

> Their massed fertility was overwhelming; their bodies were being
> broadened and readied to generate from their own cells a new body to
> be pushed from the old, and in time to push bodies from itself, and so
> on into eternity, an ocean of doubling and redoubling cells within
> which his own conscious moment was soon to wink out. (p. 112)

Confronted by Nature's twin powers of creative newness and foresee-
able decay, Bech enters upon an existential crisis in these Edenesque
surroundings, a crisis that reads like a parallel text to Kierkegaard's description of it in *The Concept of Dread*. He begins to wonder: "Who was
he? A Jew, a modern man, a writer, a bachelor, a lover, a loss. . . . A
fleck of dust condemned to know it is a fleck of dust." (p. 124) This
identity crisis reaches its climax (as does the recurring imagery) while
Bech walks alone in a wooded area on the outskirts of the campus.

> . . . the grandeur of the theatre in which Nature stages its imbecile
> cycle struck him afresh and enlarged the sore accretion of fear he
> carried inside him as unlodgeable as an elastic young wife carries within
> her womb her first fruit. . . . He felt increasingly hopeless; he could
> never be delivered of this. In a secluded, sloping patch of oaks, he
> threw himself down with a grunt of decision onto the damp earth, and
> begged Someone, Something, for mercy. He had created God. And
> now the silence of the created universe acquired for Bech a miraculous
> quality of willed reserve, of divine tact that would let him abjectly
> pray on a patch of mud and make no answer. . . . (p. 125)

Bech thus becomes a new species of the American Adam, one un-
foreseen by the optimists of a century ago. In his essay "The Plight of the
American Writer," Updike outlines the unique development in American
history that culminates in Bech's peculiar crisis. He argues that the very
abundance of riches available in our virgin wilderness, combined with our
rapid success in taming and exploiting it, made a new sort of individualism
possible. Updike states that this individualism was further abetted by the
ethos of Protestantism, an ethos that still characterized America right up
to its expansionism via the moonshots.

> The communal theocracy of the Puritan settlements, and the solidarity
> of the pioneers in the face of danger, are makeshift fabrics compared
> to the ecclesiastical and feudal interdependence of the Old World; by
> rejecting the mediating institutions of Catholicism, Luther and Calvin
> freed men to be independent, competitive, and lonely; and so Amer-
> icans are. Also, by giving to the individual conscience full responsi-

bility for relations with God, Protestantism, with its Puritan shading, conjured up a new virtue: *sincerity*. . . .

The same passion for sincerity, however, tends to bind the writer to confessional honesty and to an intensity which cannot be consistently willed.[13]

This paragraph reads like a profile of Henry Bech, for Bech is no longer, strictly speaking, a Jew except racially; the American ethos has done its work too well for that. Bech, instead, is now Everyamerican and those visions of abundance and vitality, which a century ago sparked exhilaration, now generate nightmares. Furthermore, to be both an individual and sincere—those virtues demanded especially of the American writer—inevitably issues in loneliness and the dread of the self-lie. The fears of Hawthorne and others have come true, for America and Bech embody them. After he recovers from this incident in the woods, Bech becomes embarrassed and angry that he cried to Someone, Something for mercy; as we learn in the comic final chapter, Bech's idea of "Heaven" and the "God he created" have been elsewhere for too long. His Heaven is the image of success, of making it, a distinctively American view of Heaven. Unfortunately, such a Heaven, being self-created and empty of mediation, inevitably is divorced from real Earth and its teeming vitality. Words like "immortality" and "eternity" have lost their spiritual connotation of permanence; now these words enjoy only an earthly meaning, that of endless multiplication, of a "massed fertility that is overwhelming," of teeming propagation without end or purpose.

Bech is childless, artistically sterile, and frightened at Nature's manic potency; nonetheless, he, like so many other Updike heroes, instinctively and yet almost by default (i.e. *faute de mieux*), adopts the contemporary identification of genital success with other more truly generative achievements. The post-pill paradise, rather than any other image of Eden, captivates the mind, and sex seems the only viable entry into recovering the deeper yearnings of the race and of the self. Sex is the emergent religion and the emergent Aesthetic as well, for the former Religious Quest for a Heavenly Paradise now is transposed into a Sexual and Artistic Quest. As a result, "Immortality" is no longer to be sought in union with God but is sought in a woman's arms or in the Nobel Prize.

Bech's writing block thus becomes symbolic of more than a literary crisis, for he unites these two emerging views of Heaven, identifying the sexual with the aesthetic. Unfortunately, as usual though, man must always die in order to get to Heaven. Throughout *A Book*, Bech is ever in quest for an Eve-like figure; for him women are "supernatural creatures," vessels of special powers, alien forms as elusive as fictional inspirations have been for him. We are told that his "transactions with these supernatural creatures imbued him, more keenly each time, with his own mortality. His life seemed increasingly like that sinister fairy story in which each granted wish diminishes a magic pelt that is in fact the wisher's life. But perhaps, Bech thought, one more woman, one more leap would bring him safe into that high calm pool of immortality where Proust and Hawthorne and Catullus float, glassy-eyed and belly up." (p. 135)

When he meets the Bulgarian poetess, Bech feels that he might have finally discovered that prototype of Woman he had been seeking, that ideal to which De Rougemont refers. He and the poetess engage in a conversation about the Art of Fiction; but inevitably in Updike, this one Great Secret is allied with the other two. Here the religious referent is not explicit, but the conversation implicitly touches upon those postlapsarian Adam and Eve realizations that each person reenacts in solitude.

> Vera calmly intruded. "Your personae are not moved by love?"
>
> "Yes, very much. But as a form of nostalgia. We fall in love, I tried to say in the book, with women who remind us of our first landscape. A silly idea. I used to be interested in love. I once wrote an essay on the orgasm—you know the word?—"
>
> She shook her head. He remembered that it meant Yes. "— on the orgasm as perfect memory. The one mystery is, what are we remembering?" (p. 68)

But Bech and the poetess must part. His nostalgia, his quest for immortality, his efforts at retrieving memory and mystery will be directed elsewhere. This is what makes the book's final chapter, "Bech Enters Heaven," at once so poignant and comic. Bech's memory and nostalgia, frustrated in the areas of Sex and Religion, have too long concentrated on their possible redemption through Art. His Eden has become a reminiscence of that grey building in northwest Manhattan to which his mother dragged him as a boy. Now no longer a boy and so with Eden behind him, he must face forward: what was Paradise past, an Eden, has become Paradise future, a Heaven.

However, Memory and Hope must always meet in Irony, and in irony the book ends with Bech being inducted into this literary Olympus of his and his mother's dreams; at last he has won immortality amid the mummies of the literary establishment.

The light in his eyes turned to warm water. His applause ebbed away. He sat down. Mildred nudged him. Josh Glazer shook his hand, too violently. Bech tried to clear his vision by contemplating the backs of the heads. They were blank: blank shabby backs of a cardboard tableau lent substance only by the credulous, by old women and children. His knees trembled, as if after an arduous climb. He had made it, he was here, in Heaven. Now what? (p. 186)

7: *Rabbit Redux*

In the late fall of 1971, Updike published *Rabbit Redux* (led back), his sequel to *Rabbit, Run*. Although the characters are familiar, this novel is less a sequel to the earlier *Rabbit* than a development of the historical and sociological concerns apparent in Updike's writings from *Couples* on. This older Rabbit is, in many ways, a WASP version of Bech, a man displaced by cultural change and made passive and inarticulate by on-rushing political and social currents.

Updike had said that he decided to write the sequel "when I couldn't get started on another book I was trying to write and the Sixties pressed heavily upon me. And I got sick of people talking about Rabbit, sick of them asking me what happened to him. So I decided to revisit my old friend. . . ."[1] If *Rabbit, Run* was Updike's quintessential novel of the 1950's, *Rabbit Redux* is such for the 1960's. If in the first novel we found a Rabbit who was a frustrated American Adam anxious to discover new frontiers, in the sequel we find him not only an American Adam fallen and unredeemed but immobilized. Moreover, his Edenesque Garden has now been invaded by blacks. "It's as if . . . seeds of some tropical plant sneaked in by the birds were taking over the garden. His garden. Rabbit knows it's his garden and that's why he put a flag decal on the back window of the Falcon. . . ."[2] The American Adam's dream is now localized and transformed into Pizza Paradises and Bliss Burger shops or synthetic evocations of the original frontier, such as the Phoenix bar in which the story opens.

The action of the novel takes place between July and October 1969, ten years after the events of *Rabbit, Run*. Harry Angstrom (few call him Rabbit any longer) is now thirty-six years old, politically conservative and clearly domesticated. The sequel is divided into four chapters. In the first chapter, we see a mirror reversal of *Rabbit, Run*. Harry has long since "returned" after running away and lives in a housing development called

165

Penn Villas with his wife Janice and thirteen-year-old son Nelson. In *Rabbit, Run* it was Harry who did the philandering and sought freedom; *Rabbit Redux* opens with his discovery that the once mousey, diffident Janice is now seeking liberation (sexual and otherwise) and is having an affair with Charlie Stavros, a salesman of Greek descent who works at his father's Toyota lot. Eventually Janice moves in with Stavros, leaving Harry to care for Nelson. This first chapter ends with Harry visiting his sixty-five-year-old mother who is gradually wasting away with Parkinson's disease. While there, he witnesses the American moon shot of Armstrong, Collins, and Aldrin.

In the second chapter Harry meets Jill, a rich eighteen-year-old runaway and political idealist, in an all-night bar catering to blacks. He takes her to his home where she remains with him and Nelson, becoming both his lover and surrogate daughter (reminding us of his drowned daughter Rebecca in *Rabbit, Run*). The third chapter centers on Skeeter (Hubert Johnson) who is a young black militant and Vietnam veteran. Harry, like both a "Good Samaritan" and the "Statue of Liberty," (p. 358) also takes Skeeter into his home to protect him. This chapter is divided into evening "seminars" at which Skeeter presides, seminars that review from a black perspective American history, the Vietnam war, and America's future. To his neighbors' displeasure, Harry takes up the anti-establishment life-style of his two guests. One evening a peeping Tom sees Jill and Skeeter in sexual congress and later, while Harry is away, the house is burned, Jill is killed, and Skeeter escapes. *Rabbit, Run* ended with a daughter drowning; here a surrogate daughter is burned alive—also through neglect. The Biblical water and fire are the instruments of destruction.

The final chapter is devoted to the agency of Mim, Harry's younger sister who is now a Las Vegas call girl. Mim returns to her parents' home where Harry and Nelson now live and, like a *deus ex machina*, begins to straighten out the tangled relationships. In order to expedite Harry's reunion with Janice, Mim in an act of supererogation (?) sleeps with Stavros. When Stavros subsequently suffers a heart seizure, Janice brings him back to life (reflecting inversely the drowning of Rebecca in the first novel). Fearful that their affair will kill him, Janice in a gesture of self-sacrifice leaves Stavros and returns to Harry. The novel closes with Harry and Janice going to the Safe Haven Motel where they sleep in apparent contentment. Both are now *redux*, although the final lines end their story on a note of ambiguity. "He. She. Sleeps. OK?" (p. 407)

Rabbit Redux met with a mixed critical reception when it appeared.

The most notable positive reading was that offered by Richard Locke in *The New York Times Book Review,* who pronounced that "*Rabbit Redux* is a great achievement, by far the most audacious and successful book Updike has written."[3] Locke went on to apply to *Redux* Thomas Mann's rhapsodic response to his brother Heinrich's new novel: "great in love, in art, in boldness, freedom, wisdom, kindness, exceedingly rich in intelligence, wit, imagination, and feeling—a great and beautiful thing, synthesis and resume of your life and your personality."

A good number of other reviewers showed much greater restraint. Paul Theroux's reaction, that *Rabbit Redux* is "a tedious album of the most futile monochromes of Sixties America,"[4] seemed the opinion more generally shared among these critics, though theirs was less harshly stated. It is important, however, to recall in the light of such criticism that the arrival of *Rabbit Redux* followed upon a period of excessive soul-searching in American culture. No other era in American history was so self-consciously examined in the media and in scholarly circles as was the period of the late Sixties. Furthermore, Norman Mailer's success in *Armies of the Night* and *Miami and the Siege of Chicago* (1968), with a narrative mode that joined journalism with novelistic techniques, had created different expectations on the part of readers, expectations for a more evidently personal voice, for immediacy and true-life drama, especially for authorial advocacy of issues, so that the delicate restraints and subleties proper to fiction seemed rather square by comparison. To compound Updike's difficulties and thus affect this novel's reception, shortly before *Rabbit Redux* appeared, Saul Bellow in *Mr. Sammler's Planet* had successfully used the motif of space exploration for his exposition of contemporary America; and Bernard Malamud had vividly dramatized black/white racial tensions in *The Tenants.*

And yet, even after placing this novel's arrival in context, I must admit that I find *Rabbit Redux* Updike's weakest novel. (*Marry Me* is redeemed by its first and third chapters.) This novel is not a book-length howler like Hemingway's *Across the River and into the Trees,* Fitzgerald's *This Side of Paradise,* Mailer's *Barbary Shore,* in that one does not shield one's eyes out of that mixture of embarrassment and courtesy one feels in happening upon the naked corpse. *Rabbit Redux* is more disappointing than bad; its parts simply cannot redeem the whole. Yet it ought not to be dismissed since the reasons for its weakness demand examination and, by contrast, point up the strength of Updike's successes. As with people, the vices proper to a novel can often be the result of an excess of some previously manifest virtue or of its quite unexpected absence. In this instance the critical question becomes a comparative one.

When one recalls Updike's earlier novels *The Poorhouse Fair, Rabbit, Run, The Centaur, Of the Farm*, he notes that these are in the main novels of psychological realism, dramatizing the moods and aspirations of his central characters. The emphasis is on their subjectivity, and so Updike's fictive achievement can be measured by the accuracy of his rendering their innermost thoughts, their distinctive voices that ring with a personal register, their inevitably ambiguous humanity. This fictive world eventually became recognizably an Updikean one: sensitive characters, their sensations described sympathetically and with precision, who live in a world where "small" truths still stand revealed as truths. Throughout there is a sureness of tone, an imaginative compassion, an intelligence that probes closely but never distorts, a narrative voice that is democratic in that it gives each character his due. Critics like Alfred Kazan and John Aldridge might carp because Updike in these works apparently avoided "big" themes (whatever they might be) and ignored major cultural and historical issues which, they felt, are the novelist's proper province.

Whether or not this critical prejudice merits serious attention is a moot point. (I personally feel it is what a Wittgensteinean would call a category mistake, confusing aesthetic criteria with moral or ideological biases.) The fact is that, with the publication of *Couples* and especially so with *Rabbit Redux*, we do find Updike's fiction more explicitly engaging wider, more historically grounded, cultural issues. In *Bech*, we heard Henry Bech continually renouncing the mantle of the sociologist; in *Rabbit Redux* to our surprise we find Updike himself wearing it. By this I mean there is a decided shift in perspective and in narrative stance, with the result that the novel's tone is altered, becoming overly discursive instead of descriptive, unified more often by argument than by sensibility.

At the risk of offending sociologists whose work is far too complex for facile summary, it can be said that the sociologist's stance is necessarily objective, that the truth he seeks is a general truth not a particular one, a general truth garnered from data accumulated from one segment or cross-section of a society. His is a knowing and perceptive eye, but that eye discriminates in a specialized way since the validity of his argument relies on the quantitative, on the classification and organization of data. A novelist must do something quite different. He seeks instead the universal, not the statistically general; he engages feelings, not facts; he elicits our imaginative response and not our intellectual agreement. Most important, the findings of the social sciences are, almost by definition, statable. The results of art elude such definition since the art of fiction, at its best, engages mystery, the mystery of the human and, its corollary, the mystery of language. These twin mysteries have always been Updike's proper province.

In Updike's more successful fiction, his formidable descriptive powers are revelatory of character, and the many lush descriptive passages are either invested with feeling or indicative of it. In *Rabbit Redux*, though, itemizing often takes the place of description, and unselected detail crowds out character. As a result, the novel's resolute facticity almost resists transformation: nothing is left out, so nothing is left over to challenge our imaginations. For the sociologist, more is more; for the artist, less is more. Years ago Norman Mailer criticized (unfairly, I think) Updike's early novels by saying the "trouble is that young John, like many a good young writer before him, does not know exactly what to do when action lapses, and so he cultivates his private vice, he *writes*."[5] Perhaps this criticism is appropriate to *Rabbit Redux*. It is one of Updike's novels (*Couples* is another) that needed editing, for where one hopes for imagination and insight, he finds more often an undiscriminating camera and tape recorder instead. As Pope said, "Words are like leaves; and where they most abound/Much fruit of sense beneath is rarely found."

The difficulty is that *Rabbit Redux* is so obviously a thesis novel. The effectiveness of a thesis novel lies in the unity and pertinence of its theme and in its ability to convince. Here Updike's theme—the decline and disruption of America's old image of itself—is both evident and inarguable. Ironically Updike said it best when he observed that the "novelist is of interest only for what he does through empathy and image-producing and image-arranging; the more consciously a theorist he is the more apt he is to become impotent or cranky or both."[6] This says it well. For sad to say, one hears too often in *Rabbit Redux* the crank's voice, a raspy quality uncharacteristic of his other novels. As Gene Lyons points out, "Image follows predictable image of ugliness, sterility, decay, hostility, and betrayal,"[7] with the result the reader protests that a lie or at least a dubious half truth is being urged. The Sixties were dreary perhaps . . . but that dreary? That exclusively dreary?

This is the novel's major defect, and one can say simply that Updike's sense of humor apparently abandoned him during its composition. As we have argued at length, recurring characteristics of Updike's fiction are its ambiguity, its concern with middleness, its gentle, thoughtful irony; and all these qualities issue from his keen humorous sensibility. After *Redux*, Updike will recover his sense of humor in *A Month of Sundays* and *The Coup*, and that characteristic tension, with humor as its imaginative instrument, will make a bright return.

Humor, of course, also generates the artistic distance that is so often lacking in this novel. One might say that forensic ruminations rush in where humor normally fears to tread. Coincidentally, Updike once expressed reservations about certain aspects of Saul Bellow's work by remarking: "There is in Bellow a kind of little professor, a professor-elf, who keeps fluttering around the characters, and I'm not sure he's my favorite Bellow character, this voice. He's almost always there, putting exclamatory marks after sentences, making little utterances, and in general inviting us to participate in moral decisions."[8] *Rabbit Redux* avoids exclamations and moral suasions, but a similar professor-elf is there, peeping out or with tiny fingers orchestrating events.

For clarity's sake, a comparison is in order. Both *Rabbit, Run* and *Rabbit Redux* are written in the third person historical present. In *Rabbit, Run* this technique was most effective in capturing the ambivalent immediacy of Rabbit's many runnings, the emotional chaos of events (as in the drowning scene), the dramatic unity of action and dialogue. It also provided Updike with a narrative angle that allowed him to describe vividly the inner thoughts of his characters. In *Rabbit Redux* the same narrative angle is maintained, but here the authorial voice continually intrudes: philosophic *mots* more appropriate to the professor than to blue collar types are sprinkled about, trivial incidents elicit Schopenhauer-like reflections, an air of *Weltschmerz* pokes through and deflates almost every vivid experience. This gives the novel a double-layered quality that is often disconcerting, a structure that too often substitutes telling for showing. The result is that *Redux* seems like two separate novels: the first and the fourth chapters make one, the second and third chapters another.

Perhaps a related problem is that Updike was separated for too long from Rabbit and Rabbit's world—except in memory—with the result that his realistic ear betrayed him. There are scenes in the novel that work wonderfully: Harry's exchanges with his father and with his wife—vintage Updike—and Harry's first encounter with blacks in Jumbo's Friendly Lounge at the beginning of the second chapter. Here Updike's ear captures the distinctive rhythms, allusive vocabulary, stop-start evasions, all those tricks of speech distinctive to both the white and black lower classes. However, once Jill and Skeeter enter the novel, realistic speech departs.

At times Updike does catch their cadences but misses any consistency of expression. Skeeter, especially, is less a character than an amalgam, for he speaks in multiple voices, some beyond his education. In the novel we are told that "He has many voices, Rabbit remembers, and some of them not exactly his." (p. 206) What sounds like a pertinent observation is actually an artistic problem. Jill's voice, by contrast, is a monotone, quite unexpected of a girl from her background and given her radical idealism. One senses that typology has replaced character here. Even Rabbit in his scenes with Skeeter and Jill is not his recognizable self.

In Updike's fiction voice reveals character and *vice versa*; this is the reason why his dialogues are so artistically effective. In *Rabbit Redux*, though, the voices of Jill and Skeeter (and in scenes with them Harry as well) are fragmented because as characters they are unrealized. One might argue that such multiple voices are legitimate when the characters are complex or ambiguous or when the narrative frame supports and abets ambivalence (as in *The Coup*, for example), but this is not the case here.

Upon reading my criticism of Jill and Skeeter as believable characters, Updike expressed his disagreement by writing to me and observing that "This was an era when we lived by television, and those two just came in off the set into Rabbit's lap." (personal letter of July 9, 1979) I feel that Updike's remark does not necessarily contradict my own reading, but it definitely does qualify my criticism of the "shadowy" personalities of Jill and Skeeter and induces further reflection.

Television effectively dominates the novel's action: just as Harry's interior world is divided into black and white categories that now are merging beyond his control, so too the black and white images on his TV screen provide his only entry into the world of changing external reality. The news on television "which is all about space, all about emptiness" (p. 22) thus becomes the objective correlative for the news of Harry's soul; ironically, he "lives by television."

But in the novel that external "reality" offered by television is itself continually called into question. When the event of the moon landing occurs, we hear that "At last it happens. The real event. Or is it? A television camera on the leg of the module comes on: an abstraction appears on the screen." (p. 99) When the moon-children Jill and Skeeter enter the action, they are similarly abstract: shadowy figures like ghosts on a screen, disembodied models of a generation as "far out" to Harry as are the astronauts, so that their reality is also suspect. Thus far Harry has delighted in the "shadowless" world of his linotype office (p. 30) when news was recognized as linear and patterned and expressible in language. Suddenly these two visitors, narrowing the conventional dimensions of space and time, as Updike aptly puts it, "just come in off the set into Rabbit's lap."

In the late 1960's "abstract models" like Jill and Skeeter were the almost mechanized offspring of television; they impinged on our consciousness and inhabited our dreams over and above any exercise of our volition. They were *there*, uninvited yet fascinating; like the televised war that generated them, they just happened, they fell into our laps and made us stir. Curiously, television also gave these abstract models an unreal immediacy; we interacted with these recognizable strangers, shadowy figures usually glimpsed only in a moment, but because of our passivity our interaction was unfree and so impersonal. Updike has captured this odd ambiguity well; to use the grand cliché, by doing so he has taken a bold artistic risk. Nonetheless, although my admiration is keener, I still feel that the risk-taking does not quite come off because our engagement with Jill and Skeeter as fictional characters is, unfortunately, too like our experience in watching television, namely: a sense of vicarious presence is attained but the experience remains essentially ephemeral, distanced, and so ultimately undeserving of our genuine imaginative empathy and emotional involvement.

All negative criticism aside, however, there is much to admire in *Rabbit Redux,* and an examination of its techniques and themes is important for any consideration of the development of Updike's *oeuvre.* In our analysis of *The Music School* collection, we noted that many of Updike's later short stories, though artistically realistic, were in fact "lyric meditations," edging closer to poetry than conventional fiction. The artistic effort in these stories lay in the probing for an adequate metaphor in order to explore the unexpected resemblances between things. Metaphor and symbol became the vehicles of exploration, methods for movement, instruments for integration, with the result that the story was less a conventional short story than a prose-poem. In *Rabbit Redux*, however, Updike has employed this same technique in order to integrate a lengthy novel. In the stories we considered Updike used Nature as the analogy to unite reality and imagination; in *Rabbit Redux* the analogy will be an historical event (the moon exploration in space) that itself is already replete with symbolic associations. The voice in *The Music School* stories was "abstract-personal"; in *Rabbit Redux* we hear a similar voice (perhaps unfortunately, as my previous criticism suggests). But as in Stevens' poetry, it is the technical virtuosity and linguistic allusiveness that is of primary interest rather than thematic concerns. As in Stevens, a single theme or image is approached through varying perspectives, reiterated by voices in opposition, and exhaustively explored.

The novel's central themes are indicated on the dust jacket to the hard-back edition. There we see a series of stripes (red, white, and grey) with the grey, pitted moon up in the right corner and in the center another globe separated by off-center stripes and containing the novel's title and the author's name. The colors chosen, red, white, and grey, suggest the tarnishing into off-white of the American dream, and the grey also suggests the simultaneous merger and contention of black and white races in contemporary America. The remote moon, also grey, recalls the moon exploration of 1969, that quest for a new frontier where the American flag could once again be planted. The central globe is more ambiguous; separated from the moon and imposed upon the flag-like stripes, its lines are in disharmony with its surrounding stripes, no doubt suggestive of Rabbit's alienated world, his private America.

Updike has said that he also chose the cover motifs to link the novel with its predecessor, *Rabbit, Run*. "There is a lot of moon, of course, in *Rabbit, Run*, sun and moon (beginning of the second section) and the theme, and the jacket of the book was meant to show the two circles lunar and solar, of his dream late in the book."[9] In the earlier novel, Rabbit dreamt that he saw the sun eclipsed by the moon and found there an explanation of death, that "lovely life [is] eclipsed by lovely death." This inspires him to go forth to found a new religion, but he soon "realizes it was a dream, that he has nothing to tell the world." When we meet Rabbit ten years later, he is visited by more prosaic dreams, his evangelistic impulses are dormant, and the moon itself has become an accessible planet, romantic only in a patriotic sense.

The moon exploration in July 1969 becomes the controlling metaphor of the novel, the occasion for planting the American flag's stripes found on the jacket cover. Other historically centered events will also work as metaphors but will be subordinate to this trope.[10] For example the incident at Chappaquiddick Island and the drowning of Mary Jo Kopechne will find its metaphoric counterpart in Harry's sexual encounters with Jill where underwater images arise (pp. 157, 201, 285) and in associations between Mrs. Angstrom's deteriorating condition and drowning. (pp. 73, 194) Furthermore the drowning image is reminiscent of the infant Becky's drowning in *Rabbit, Run* and will characterize both Rabbit's and Nelson's reactions to Jill's death. (p. 323) Jackie Kennedy's marriage to the Greek tycoon Aristotle Onassis will have its counter-part in Janice's liaison with the Greek Stavros. The racial riots in York, Pennsylvania, will foreshadow Skeeter's appearance and a rape in Brewer will counterpoint his "rape" of Jill and Rabbit. A Norwegian sailor's efforts to cross the Atlantic to America in a paper boat (p. 58) takes on ironic overtones in the light of America's present turmoil and of the complex technology of the moon exploration. The television news coverage of the Vietnam War with its imagery of bombardment and burning will become a major motif in sexual descriptions, (pp. 70, 157, 346) while the language of the Vietnam peace negotiations will adumbrate Rabbit's sexual politicking with Stavros (p. 181). The Vietnam Moratorium day will coincide with Harry's loss of his job and will presage the reunion of Janice and Harry—and so on. In addition, historical personages will be the occasion for inside jokes: Skeeter's name is discovered to be Hubert Johnson, a name that unites the twin architects of the Great Society; and Rabbit has a dream that President Johnson wants Stavros to be Vice President because he needs a Greek (by 1969 Nixon had one in Agnew). (pp. 70, 71) The world of public history thus joins hands with the world of private history by way of analogy.

Rabbit's job as a linotype operator for the Brewer *Vat* will also be a contact point for integrating the thematic and historical developments of the novel. Rabbit's occupation is passé and, like himself, a victim of technological change. A linotypist's concern rests entirely with space and with the contrast between black and white, as well as with language—thus Rabbit's labors subtly and ironically point up the novel's central themes. We are told that "All around him, Rabbit hears language collapsing"; (p. 150) the other aspects of his job (space and black/white contrasts) are collapsing as well. Throughout, the novel will be punctuated by Rabbit's type-setting local stories that link Brewer with the wider world. Headlines will relate to the story's development: Brewer's Factory Tools Components are Headed Toward the Moon, (p. 27) A Widow is Raped and Beaten by Blacks, (pp. 153-54) Local Excavations Unearth Antiquities (the remains of speakeasy as well as arrowheads), (pp. 184ff.) the Arrest of Blacks in Jimbo's Lounge, (pp. 215ff.) the Arson Blaze that gutted his own home. (pp. 339ff.) Through this device Updike is able to make Brewer a microcosm of America and unite past action with the present.

But, as we have said, the controlling metaphor is that of America's

voyage out into space, its landing on the moon, and its return to earth.
The plot structure reflects this movement: as the story opens, Rabbit is
earth-bound and unadventuresome; once Janice leaves, he ventures into
the void; in the middle section, like the astronauts, part of him travels
in orbit to the dark side of the moon (Skeeter), while another part begins
a free fall, eventually stepping onto a new planet (Jill); the novel ends
with his return to earth (Janice) and an ambiguous usage of the astronaut's
confirmation (OK?). Each chapter opens with an epigraph taken from an
astronaut conversation and is indicative of that chapter's thematic development and dramatic action.

The imagery from space exploration is exploited on many levels. Reminiscent of a major motif in *Rabbit, Run*, space is associated with nothingness and emptiness of spirit. Here Rabbit's home in Penn Villas represents
his own isolation and suspension in a void. We are told that "everything
is warm, wet, still coming to birth but himself and his home, which
remains a strange dry place, dry and cold and emptily spinning in the
void of Penn Villas like a cast-off space capsule." (p. 132; cf. also pp. 60,
76, 84, 99, 332, 406) In *Rabbit, Run*, nothingness takes on a theological
dimension; here that dimension is absent. Nothingness, instead, is descriptive of political, moral, and social realities. Jill's summary criticism
of Rabbit is an accurate one when she says to him, "You carry an old God
with you, and an angry old patriotism. And now an old wife. . . . You
raced to the conclusion that everything is nothing, that zero is the real
answer." (p. 228) In *Rabbit, Run* nothingness was a symbolic force, a
negative power which Rabbit confronts; in *Rabbit Redux*, nothingness is
merely etiolation, absence, or emptiness.

The space-moon exploration metaphor also figures prominently in
those scenes that describe sexual activity. Although *Couples* enjoys a more
erotic reputation, *Rabbit Redux* contains the most frequent and the most
explicit depictions of sex found in any of Updike's novels. Sex in *Couples*
was lyrically described, tapping the lush tradition of Romance; in *Rabbit
Redux* the lyricism of sex is absent. Here, in line with the novel's central
metaphor, sex is portrayed as mechanical, an interlocking of objects in
space, or as a plunge into a void, so that the exoticism of outer space
replaces the eroticism of earth found in *Couples*.

As far back as Classical mythology, the moon has enjoyed sexual
associations, and Updike exploits and updates them. When the novel
opens, Rabbit's sexuality is dormant. He and his wife have been sexual
strangers apparently since their daughter's death. "It had all seemed like

a pit to him then, her womb and the grave, sex and death, he had fled
her cunt as a tiger's mouth." (pp. 27, 36) Once Janice leaves him and he
enters the new black environment of Jimbo's Lounge, he becomes conscious of the moons on his fingernails; and Babe, by embracing his thumb
with "its colorless moon nail," tells him his sexual good fortune, but
remains troubled by the bad shadows on his knuckle. (cf. pp. 89, 113,
117, 123) There he meets Jill, a moon-child, who has been and will be
again "spaced out" by drugs. When they achieve sexual union, it occurs
"on a scratchy carpet, the television screen a mother planet above them
. . . they are crying over secrets far at their backs, in opposite direction,
moonchild and earthman." (p. 202) Like the Eagle space capsule of Apollo
IX, Rabbit will first near Jill's gravitational influence and eventually land
on a "different but pretty" planet as the epigraph to the chapter suggests.
(p. 101) Unfortunately, the predicted bad shadows enter with Skeeter's
appearance. Jill herself will depart by entering the more distant void of
death and Rabbit will make his return to earth, as one *redux* to Janice.
True to the space exploration metaphor, Rabbit, in order to return, must
first "link up" with Janice before their terrestrial descent. This takes place
in the pointedly named *Safe Haven* motel where they repair for rest, not
sexual refreshment. In bed Rabbit "feels that they are still adjusting in
space, slowly twirling in some gorgeous ink that filters through his lids as
red. In a space of silence, he can't gauge how much, he feels them drift
along sideways deeper into being married. . . ." (p. 405) Eventually, the
necessary "docking" operation takes place. "He lets her breasts go, lets
them float away, radiant debris, the motel room, long and secret as a
burrow, becomes all interior space. He slides down an inch on the cool
sheet and fits his microcosmic self limp into the curved crevice between
the polleny offered nestling orbs of her ass. . . ." (pp. 406-07) Rabbit,
returned to his burrow, is on his way back to earth.

Despite, or perhaps because of, this controlling metaphor, there is a
good deal of artistic inconsistency in this novel's treatment of sex. The
Great Secret of Sex is out, but one wonders in the circumstances whether
it was ever worth keeping in the first place. Led on by the moon exploration metaphor, the reader expects that Rabbit will have sexually "ar-
rived" or "landed" when he meets the moonchild (Jill), especially after
his long voyage of denial. At the beginning of the novel we are told that
Rabbit "hates" sex (pp. 59, 69); and yet, since his is the primary narrative
focus, we need not be told. We hear Rabbit reflect that "Sex ages us.
Priests are boyish, spinsters stay blackhaired until fifty. We others, the

demon rots us out." (p. 71) Consequently, we expect a change when Rabbit revives sexually in uniting with Jill, but this is not so. Both during and after the Jill-moon experience, Rabbit remains essentially unchanged by sexual activity and still views sex as a grim business. Near the novel's end he tells Janice, "But all this fucking, everybody fucking, I don't know, it just makes me sad. It's what makes everything so hard to run. . . . There must be something else." (pp. 397-98) Given the elaborate moon exploration metaphor, the reader expects some more pertinent and dramatic "discovery" than that.

There is a similar inconsistency, I think, in the novel's treatment of another of the Great Secrets: Religion. Unlike the Rabbit of *Rabbit, Run*, Rabbit in *Rabbit Redux* is no longer religious save in the loosest and most nostalgic sense. Now he only prays on buses, recalling the traveling motif of the first novel and yet without furthering it in the light of this novel's metaphor (pp. 12, 199). Rabbit feels "No belief in an afterlife, no hope for it, too much of the same thing, already it seems he's lived twice." (p. 104) When Peggy asks, "Don't you think God is people?" Rabbit answers, "No. I think God is everything that isn't people. I guess I think that. I don't think enough to know what I think." (p. 110)

Since Rabbit is evidently so passive and unreflective (so unlike himself in *Rabbit, Run*), religious issues will come into focus only during the "learning seminars" conducted by Jill and Skeeter. These seminars are much like the endless "rap sessions" so popular in the Sixties where the "rap" designation was generally a misnomer, since monologue, not dialogue, more often characterized them. Perhaps the popularity of such rap sessions can be partly explained by the fact that the Sixties was an era given not only to pacifist and political passions but also to mystery cults and to renewed interest in various aspects of Eastern philosophy and to eccentric versions of Christianity. In many ways these new enthusiasms were quaintly medieval, an odd reminder of the pious zealotry and fervor and the inevitable sectarianisms found in much of Western Europe after the Crusades and its subsequent contact with and absorption of Oriental philosophy. The year 1969 in some respects was not so different from the year 1169, after all: both were periods of an abortive Crusade and its aftermath. Both Jill and Skeeter represent differing versions of what Ronald Knox analyzed so brilliantly as "Enthusiasm" in his study of the Manichean revival in the twelfth and thirteenth centuries. Knox notes that two contrasting but concomitant symptoms of the enthusiastic revival are a preoccupation with "ecstasy" and a conviction that the Second Coming is imminent.[11]

Jill is the ecstatic; in previous drug trips she claims to have seen God; on one occasion He appeared "like the inside of a big lily, only magnified a thousand times, a sort of glossy shining funnel that went down and down." (p. 146) Jill's "theology" is strongly reminiscent of the tenets of the Manichean Cathari sect in the Middle Ages. [12] She will indulge freely in promiscuous sex but still consider herself oddly virginal, arguing that "I don't think it counts when you let somebody do it to you and don't do anything back . . . it just happens on the surface, a million miles away." (p. 213) This unique defense is characteristic of the Manichean's sharp moral division between matter and spirit. To hold that all matter is evil may lead either to a severe repression of carnal instincts (somewhat indicative of Rabbit early in the novel), or it may lead to a contempt of these very instincts as belonging to matter, and so possessing only a material significance, as in Jill's case. Jill's Manicheanism is not logically neat, to say the least, but like its original adherents she embraces a radical dualism between spirit and matter and a suspicion about human freedom and individuality.

> (Jill) "Man is a mechanism for turning things into spirit and turning spirit into things."
> "What's the point?" Nelson asks.
> "The point is ecstasy," she says. "Energy. Anything that is good is in ecstasy. . . . Our egos make us blind. Whenever we think about ourselves, it's like putting a piece of dirt in our eye."
> "There's that thing in the Bible."
> "That's what He meant. Without our egos the universe would be absolutely clean. . . . The only consciousness would be God's. Think of it, Nelson, like that: matter is the mirror of spirit. But it's three-dimensional, like an enormous room, a ballroom. And inside there are these tiny *other* mirrors tilted this way and that and throwing the light back the wrong way. Because to the big face looking in, these little mirrors are just dark spots where He can't see Himself." (p. 159)

As is so often the case in the history of Enthusiasm, an "ecstatic" distortion of Christianity inevitably issues in a curious kind of Pantheism, here a hip panpsychism. By contrast, Skeeter's religious enthusiasm focuses on the Second Coming, its second symptom. Skeeter is a self-proclaimed Messianic and apocalyptic figure, the Black Jesus. In *Couples* Updike dramatized the entry of the "new emergent religion, sex." Here Skeeter is priest of that emergent religion of sex and drugs; his "revival" meetings will be historical seminars; his sermons unwittingly will bring about fire and damnation. In his tirades Skeeter will draw upon the language of Christianity and in shocking fashion will reinterpret its familiar theology with lewd imagery. (p. 210) Richard Locke sees Skeeter as the Anti-Christ. Updike, though, has said he has been surprised that "among the critics no one's given serious consideration to the idea that Skeeter, the angry black, might *be* Jesus. He *says* he is. I think probably he might be. And if that's so, then people *ought* to be very nice to him."[13]

Such opposite conjectures about Skeeter's character point up the artistic inconsistency in the novel. It is indeed difficult in the light of Skeeter's behavior to take Updike's remarks about him seriously. Skeeter is never revealed as other than a despicable character. Given the novel's realistic framework, the reader is entitled to expect of a "Black Jesus" character traits other than irresponsibility, cruelty, moral weakness, schizophrenia, and cowardice.

True, Skeeter throughout the novel does enjoy a *symbolic* identity with Christ: he sees himself pursued by Herod (Nixon) (p. 225), his obscene beatitudes are recorded (p. 264), and his departure (in Galilee yet) is replete with Christic associations, such as a promise to "return only in glory," a departing blessing, and the final sight of him "looking oddly right . . . hanging empty-handed between fields of stubble where crows settle and shift, gleaning." (pp. 336-37) But one feels the symbolism here is an overlay (quite unlike its legitimacy in *The Centaur*), that it is arbitrary and jarring, given the discrepancy between the dramatic character and the symbol. Skeeter might well win both Rabbit's and Jill's act of "faith" in him by way of moral coercion (pp. 276, 300); we readers, though, remain free to withhold our aesthetic act of "faith" in him despite any artistic coercion.

I feel that many of the defects found in *Rabbit Redux* are redeemed in Updike's next novel, *A Month of Sundays*. In it we meet a character who embodies *all* the distinctive quirks and odd passions found in Rabbit, Jill, and Skeeter respectively, but one who revitalizes them and gives them artistic order and a curious integrity that wins our smiling sympathy.

8: A Month of Sundays

Since the publication of *Couples*, Updike's subsequent novels have been greeted with relatively inattentive scholarly scrutiny.[1] This was especially unfortunate in the case of *A Month of Sundays*, published in 1975, for this novel demands greater scholarly attention not only because it capsulizes humorously so much thematic material found in Updike's previous fiction (the *what* of his vision, so to speak), but more significantly because its fictive and psychological structure (its *how*) is somewhat unique in Updike's corpus and well rewards close analysis.[2]

The thematic *what* of the novel is immediately evident from its opening page. We are greeted by the Rev. Thomas Marshfield, a Protestant minister and doubting Thomas, who, because of adulterous indiscretions amidst his congregation, has been exiled to a Western Desert resort established for such de-flocked clergymen. The regimen imposed for his recovery requires banishment of the Bible, daily rounds of golf and poker, and the insistence that he keep a daily diary and record "what interests me most," which in his case is sex and religion, the one his preoccupation, the other his occupation. These twin interests thus constitute the material for his daily jottings whereby he recounts his "downfall" and also become the subjects for the weekly sermons he composes—all written for the eye of an unseen reader who, he discovers eventually, is the manageress, Ms. Prynne.

This diary setting allows Updike free range to exhibit his stylistic gifts. At first Marshfield's writing is over-wrought and florid, redolent of the stained-glass prose of preachers, but subtly it becomes increasingly colloquial and its tone becomes more personal. The free association that the diary-therapy prescribes also provides Updike the chance to offer a comic resume of targets he has scolded in his fiction from *Couples* on:

181

liberal theology, the sexual revolution, women's liberation, the New Left, Watergate morality—all of which are reviewed in parody of the confused conservative.

Updike, of course, is already famous (some might say notorious) for the creation of such cock-eyed clergymen or clergymen *manque* like Marshfield and for the elaborate wedding of sex/religion themes. One hears in Marshfield's sermonizing echoes of both the Rev. Eccles and Kruppenbach in *Rabbit, Run*, of Rev. March in *The Centaur*, of the minister in *Of the Farm*, of Rev. Pedrick in *Couples*, as well as of such lay priest-characters as Hook in *The Poorhouse Fair* and Freddy Thorne in *Couples*. The vacillating Marshfield, the fallen-away Barthian whose faith is most evident in its absence, thus becomes a summary figure in Updike's work, including within himself, as it were, all of the previous ministerial manifestations found there. In retrospect they all seem but shards of Marshfield's variable personality. But more significantly, because Marshfield is the novel's center, the interweaving of sexual/religious imagery and theme, occasionally manifest in *Rabbit, Run*, *The Centaur*, and *Couples*, becomes the predominating pattern.

But *A Month of Sundays* is far more than a tired recapitulation of Updike material as some reviewers suggest. The clue that the novel contains added thematic material and a more subtle structure is found in the book's two epigraphs. The epigraphs provide the key to the novel's ambivalent structure and meaning, not in the mechanical sense of unlocking it automatically, but in a musical sense, in that the epigraphs become the "tonic center" of the composition to which all the parts are related.

The first epigraph is taken from Psalm 45: "My tongue is the pen of a ready writer."[3] The more familiar preceding lines are omitted but still implied: "My heart overflows with a goodly theme as I sing my ode to the King." Psalm 45 was originally a secular song celebrating the wedding of an Israelite king, but the Jewish and Christian traditions have appropriated it as celebrating the marriage of the Messianic king with Israel (prefiguring the Church). The Psalm's fusion of secular/sacral, marriage/fidelity, redeemer/community comprises the novel's central motifs.

The Psalmist's "tongue" takes on a further sexual connotation as well in the light of Marshfield's most competent sexual activity and is made explicit in his reflection upon Psalm 22:19 where "All they that go down to the dust shall bow before him." (p. 20)

More significantly, however, the tongue is "the pen of a ready writer";

thus a third major theme is interwoven with the sexual/religious: that of writing itself and of the relationship of the writer both to his reader and to his own writing. The outrageous Joycean puns and Nabokovian footnotes found throughout are not gratuitous purple patches but are integral to its thematic structure. For to exploit this third theme, Updike has deliberately entered what Robert Alter calls "the genre of the self-conscious novel." Alter defines the "self-conscious novel" as one that expresses its basic seriousness through playfulness, for it is

> a novel that systematically flaunts its own condition of artifice and that by doing so probes into the problematic relationship between real-seeming artifice and reality . . . in which from beginning to end, through the style, through the handling of narrative viewpoint, the names and words imposed on the characters, there is a consistent effort to convey to us a sense of the fictional world as an authorial construct set up against a background of literary tradition and convention.[4]

Certain aspects of Alter's definition have appeared in Updike's previous fiction, of course, most notably in The Centaur, but never has that definition characterized the *whole* of a novel and its shape. Updike, up to this novel, has seemed content with the conventional framework of psychological realism in his fiction and has been resistant to the "self-conscious" techniques employed by his contemporaries like Pynchon, Hawkes, and Barth. John Barth has called him "the Andrew Wyeth of our literature"; and, although Vermeer might be more accurate, his allusion is an apt description of one aspect of his work.[5]

Throughout A Month of Sundays, however, Updike continually signals to us that this is definitely not realistic story-telling in diary form. Various devices such as requests for the reader's imaginative cooperation, invitations to conjure up further detail on one's own, switches in tenses, the doubling-back and eccentric footnoting, combined with warnings about the credibility of the account suggest strongly that things are not what they seem. The style itself is deliberately inconsistent: ornate and baroque parodies of eighteenth-century narrative; stately and detached imitations of Liberal Protestant sermons; passionate, straightforward pleas; slangy humor and precious puns; a stagey parody of a soap-opera confrontation which ends with the inappropriate punch line "I think it is his duty to shit or get off the pot." Yet, despite these stop-start evasions and diversions, there remains a continual forward "tilt" to the novel, a unifying energy that propels it toward some truth-discovery.

This forward tilt is manifest on several levels, one of which fulfills a

crucial aspect of Alter's definition of the "self-conscious novel." The progress of Marshfield's entries in his diaries exhibits his deepening awareness
of himself *qua* writer and of the questionable nature of his effort. His first
entry exposes but does not engage these central issues by asking, "Who
are you, gentle reader? Who am I? I go to the mirror." (p. 6) With these
questions as background, the succeeding entries will manifest: a) the
emotional range of the writing experience along with b) the progressive
realization of *its* dubious ontological status, leading to c) a cross-question-
ing about the very reality of *both* the writer and reader as well. Pertinent
quotations from the text, taken sequentially as they appear, point up this
"self-conscious" development.

1) the initial playful power of the writing experience: "This is fun.
First you whittle the puppets, then you move them around." (p. 12)

2) its arbitrary nature: "These sentences have come in no special
order. Each of them has hurt. Each of them might have been different,
with the same net effect." (p. 19)

3) its temporal artificiality: "Why can't I keep this in the present
tense?" (p. 28)

4) the dubiety of invention: "Or perhaps these words were never
spoken, I made them up, to relieve and rebuke the silence of this offi-
ciously chaste room." (p. 33)

5) its complex relationship to "truth": "Worse, I must create: I must
from my lousy fantasies pick the nits of truth. What is truth? My fantasies
are what concern you?" (p. 91)

6) the resultant confusion between imagined and real existence: "It
occurs to me, remembering that fabled time when I lived in the world
and had my being there." (p. 117)

7) its illusory but intoxicating omnipotence: "They seem dolls I can
play with, putting them now in this, now in that obscene position."
(p. 178)

8) and yet, its problematical actuality: "Spent an hour now rereading
. . . the pages we (you and I, reader; without you there would be the
non-noise of a tree crashing in the inhuman forest) have accumulated."
(p. 202)

9) the awareness of differing "existences": "You are yet the end, the
intelligens entis, of my being, insofar as I exist on paper. Give me a body."
(p. 220)

10) the final ambiguity about fiction's ultimate source and meaning:

"Did I dream this? . . . The day after tomorrow, my month may seem a metaphor. . . ." (p. 226)

There is also a studied awareness, throughout, of the writer as addressing various traditions in implicit dialogue: not only the Christian theological tradition from the mystics Eckhart and Pascal to the dogmatic Karl Barth, but the literary tradition of the self-conscious novel. The Joycean and Nabokovian touches are a bow to its modern practitioners; explanatory footnotes like "I swear, Alicia's name is real, not contrived to fit Wonderland," (p. 97) call direct attention to another contrived fable of fall and discovery. The figures of Ms. Prynne and Chillingworth, Marshfield's rationalistic father-in-law, are introduced to confirm this connection. The character of Ms. Prynne functions on several levels, of course: like her namesake, Hester in *The Scarlet Letter*, she is an "ideal reader" of a tale about sacerdotal infidelity and alone can receive his repentance and dramatize forgiveness. Her intra-literary role also alerts us to the fact that Updike is turning Dimmesdale's Puritan dilemma upside down into that of Marshfield, a "poor Wasp stung by the new work-ethic of sufficient sex, sex as the exterior sign of interior grace." (p. 218)

Throughout this study we have repeatedly returned to Updike's childhood fascination with what he called in his boyhood memoir "The Three Great Secret Things" (Sex, Religion, and Art).[6] Few critics would deny that these three "secrets" continue to be his adult themes, and yet rarely has he integrated them so consistently as in *A Month of Sundays*. Throughout there is a triple-layered simultaneity of interaction; just as Marshfield's "month may seem a metaphor," so too explicit reference to one of the secrets implies a reciprocal reference to the other two. Some characters embody this triple reference, such as Ms. Prynne (to Sex as victim of American Puritanism, to Religion as ostracized Protestant, to Art as Hawthorne heroine), but there are also several triple-layered thematic movements and symbols that reinforce this multiple interaction.

The theme of Generation and Re-Birth. On the explicitly *religious* level, a Scriptural text quoted in both Marshfield's first and second sermon is that of Matthew 12:39 where Christ condemns "this wicked and adulterous generation that seeks for a sign." Omitted but implied are His following words: "but the only sign given it will be the sign of Jonah," referring to His Resurrection. Pointedly, the final sermon is an affirmation of St. Paul's emphasis on the corporeal nature of resurrection after death, i.e. the import of the sign of Jonah. Marshfield's own religious progress parallels these texts: a most worthy representative of this adulterous generation, by the story's close he experiences some "signs" and is "afraid, not afraid, afraid to be born again." (p. 226)

His *sexual* progress is parallel: at the story's start he is impotent and a masturbator, incapable of true generation, but the diary ends with intercourse and new life. And, on the artistic or *writing* level, Marshfield, after sterile efforts that are like his father's sermon-writing, i.e. "ejaculations of clatter after foreplays of agony," (p. 18) creates "at last, a sermon that could be preached." (p. 212)

The theme of Seduction. The diary consists of Marshfield's tales about the seduction of other women; yet, ironically, he intends *through* his writing about them to seduce his Ideal Reader. It is not surprising that he meets his initial seductive success through his most religious sermon about Christian corporeality.

The themes of Fidelity and Goodness. Marshfield is one whose vocation is "pledged to goodness and fidelity," but his is a wavering religious faith, his conduct is that of an unfaithful spouse, and, as writer, he continually warns us to question the fidelity of his account. Confused about true "faiths," he is even more puzzled about the nature of goodness and fulfilling its pledge. The rationalist Chillingworth's ethical question, "Is the pleasant the good or not quite?," becomes his triple-layered query. Basic to all his theological fulminating is his critique of all antinomianisms that would equate the good with the pleasant, but he is not so sure himself. He realizes his final sexual imprisonment when he discovers that his wife has become "good in bed," a frightening prospect. As a writer, his diary efforts are initially easy and his sermons pleasant; only after he encounters difficulties, do they truly become "good."[7]

There are several other central themes related to these, such as Transparency, Nothingness/Something, but of equal importance are the triple-layered symbols throughout. A central one is that of "bones," concretely inspired by the dinosaur bones in the desert. We find Marshfield self-consciously reconstructing the "bones of his narrative," commenting on his phallic "bone," as well as recalling Augustine's prayer, "Let my bones be bedewed with Thy love." This symbol becomes crucial in the final sermon on Resurrection where God's existence (*Qui m'y a mis*), as Marshfiled contends, "we already know in our marrow." (p. 212)

Exploration of other unifying images and symbols such as seed, palms, desert, dome reveals similar patterns. But, like the multi-layered themes, these cannot be examined in isolation. Furthermore, it is Updike's invention of the ever-shifting, humorous, often mocking voice of Marshfield that keeps these multiple referents in true tension. Updike's choice for his second epigraph, therefore, is another "key" reminder. It is a quote from theologian Paul Tillich that "This principle of soul, universally and individually, is the principle of ambiguity." It is precisely this principle that animates A Month of Sundays.

But this novel is doing other things as well and quite artfully. Beneath its often flippant playfulness it records a radical psychological and religious exploration that becomes more evident only when its pictorial shape emerges. Updike said of his work in a 1969 interview that "I really begin with some kind of solid, coherent image, some notion of the shape of the book and even of its texture. The Poorhouse Fair was meant to have a sort of Y shape. Rabbit, Run was a kind of zig-zag. The Centaur was sort of a sandwich. I can't begin until I know the beginning and have some sense of what's going to happen between."[8]

One discovers such an integrating image in A Month of Sundays in Marshfield's description of the novel's setting: "The motel—I resist calling it a sanatorium, or halfway house, or detention center has the shape of an O, or, more exactly, an omega." (p. 4) This omega-shaped dwelling— the center of which, significantly, is a pool reflecting the sky—itself reflects the novel's own shape. The omega mirrors the circuitous movement of the diary's development, its temporal duration following the four phases of the lunar cycle, and the shifting sensibilities of the diarist from the enclosed () to the more open omega.[9]

Furthermore, this omega-shape characterizes well Updike's handling of the interconnection among the "three great secret things." For example, if we visualize the Religious thematic concerns as situated upon one foot of the omega and the Sex themes as situated upon the opposite foot of the omega, one discovers that the "self-conscious" Artistic techniques act like a wedge, as it were, unifying as well as maintaining in polar tension these opposing themes. What Marshfield says of his interpretation of events—"[it] may be imposed in retrospect, a later loop of the film overlapping" (p. 30)—is an apt description of the many artistic "loops" which, omega-like, shape the novel by closure, disclosure, and connection.

In addition to structural shape, the omega-motif unites "the three secret things" on the symbolic level too. 1) Religion. In the Christian tradition Christ is described as the "Alpha and Omega" whose return is awaited in the last chapter of the Book of Revelation. Marshfield twice quotes the final words of that particular chapter ("Even so, come") and, although ostensibly written to Ms. Prynne as a sexual plea, it takes on an additional religious resonance in the context as we shall soon see. 2) *Sex*. The association of the letter "o" with a woman's pudendum is common throughout literature and found elsewhere in Updike's fiction where "o" reflects a woman's "receptive womb."[10] Specifically, this omega-shaped novel ends with Marshfield's "penis up into its ideal shape" entering Ms. Prynne's womb. 3) *Art*. Not only does the letter "omega," being the limit or end of the alphabet, suggest the perverse limitations of all letter-writing that Marshfield experiences; but Omega, being at the opposite end of A, reminds us of this novel's up-ending of *The Scarlet Letter*, the kind of joke in which Updike delights.

Finally and most importantly, the omega-shape is *the* fitting image for the triple-layered psychological exploration this novel develops. In Jungian psychology such a circular omega is the perfect ideograph for the unconscious Self toward which the Conscious Ego aspires.[11] Jung calls this circular ideograph a "mandala," and its shape reflects the harmony, order, and unity which is the ideal goal of the psyche. The Ego, for Jung, though only a small part of the Psyche, is a *centrum* of the field of consciousness; its function is to be a highly selective distillery of perceptions, memories, thoughts, and feelings. In short, its role is to act as the organizing principle of the *conscious* mind. The Self, however, is an *unconscious* archetype for Jung which is manifest through mandala-like images of harmony; although It is ultimately unknowable, still the mandala-image of the Self is a centering force and ideal that attracts the whole personality.

In *A Month of Sundays* Marshfield humorously, but explicitly, invites the reader to consider his personality in such mandala-like fashion but in excessively *Ego*-conscious terms:

> Imagine me as a circle divided in half, half white and half black. In the white side were such things as father's furniture, Karl Barth's prose, the fine-grained pliancy and gleeful dependence of my sons when they were babies, my own crisp hieratic place within the liturgy and sacraments. . . . This was the Good. I credited God with being on this side. On the other side, which might be labelled the Depressing rather than the Evil, lay Mankind . . . my own rank body, most institutional and political trends since 1965, the general decadent trend of the globe. . . . Alicia, by claiming a wedge of mankind for the Good and the Beautiful, shifted the axis on the divider 10° and caused a re-labelling of the now-tilted halves: the white was the Live, the black was the Dead. . . . God, who has a way of siding with the winners, took Life as His element. . . . (pp. 39-40)

The mention of Alicia's important role in re-shaping Marshfield's "circle" becomes more than humorous fancy when seen in Jungian terms. For Jung a male's psychic maturation takes place only after a series of encounters with his *anima* image, i.e. the unconscious feminine aspect of his own personality. For Jung the *anima* acts as a positive mediator between the conscious Ego and the Self and, just as the Self-mandala usually expresses itself as some kind of circular fourfold structure, so too does the *anima* image manifest four aspects or stages of development. Jung described these four stages:

> . . . Eve, Helen of Troy, the Virgin Mary, and Sophia. The nomenclature shows us we are dealing with the heterosexual Eros—or anima—figure, in four stages, and consequently with four stages of the Eros cult. The first stage—HAWWAH, Eve, earth—is purely biological: woman is equated only with mother and represents something to be fertilized. The second stage is still dominated by the sexual Eros but on an aesthetic and romantic level where woman has already acquired some value as an individual. The third stage raises Eros to the heights of religious devotion and thus spiritualizes him; Eros replaced by spiritual motherhood. Finally, the fourth stage illustrates something which unexpectedly goes beyond the almost unsurpassable third stage: Sapientia (or Sophia). . . . This stage represents the spiritualization of Helen and consequently of Eros as such. That is why Sapientia was regarded as parallel to the Shulamite in the Song of Solomon.[12]

The reason offered in the novel for Marshfield's diary-writing is that it has been prescribed as therapeutic with the result that the writing becomes itself a mode of healing. For Jung, the positive function of confronting one's *anima* in all its aspects occurs only when a man *fixes* the feelings, moods, expectations, and fantasies sent by his *anima* in some specific art-like form, such as writing, painting, or sculpture. While one works at this formative effort, other more deeply unconscious material will well up and connect with it. Throughout the process, however, the *anima*-form in its various stages must be continually re-evaluated ethically, intellectually, and emotionally before a psychic unity emerges.[13]

Marshfield's diary records in *the* Jungian order his erotic encounters with the four significant women in his life: Jane, his wife; Alicia, the church organist; Frankie Harlow, the devout believer; finally, the elusive Ms. Prynne.[14] Each corresponds with one of the four stages of the Jungian *anima*. In the novel, his wife Jane becomes merely an Eve, earth-mother figure, representing at best a biological relationship: "under my wife's good administration, sex had become a solemn, once-a-week business, ritualized and worrisomely hushed." (p. 34) Marshfield and Jane have begun to "look alike," are "mutual echoes," and yet she "does, by another light, appear *totaliter aliter*, an Other, a woman, and as such, marketable." (p. 58) While he appraises her in Barthian theological language, he recently has learned that she has become "allergic to the sun" and so he looks elsewhere.

His experience with Alicia, the organist, corresponds with Jung's second stage, i.e. one dominated still by Eros but on a more aesthetic and romantic level; here the *anima* becomes a Helen of Troy goddess. Marshfield tells us that "Alicia in bed was a revelation. At last I confronted as in an ecstatic mirror my own sexual demon." (p. 33) He describes himself with her in mythic language as a "lover as sky-god, cycling moisture from earth to cloud to earth," (p. 35) and says she eventually became "the soft center of my new world." (p. 67)

Marshfield's relationship with Frankie Harlow marks the third stage, that of the virginal *anima* who raises Eros to the heights of spiritual devotion. His first interview with her "in its shifting transparence and reflecting opacities seems an experience so gnostic I am blinding." (p. 111) Gnostic, in a sense, it remains. Frankie's virginal faith makes him sexually limp and, though never achieving true intercourse with her, each sexual encounter is described in devotional terms or pre-lapsarian language:

> Her forgiveness and pre-Adamic cave-woman fall of hair to her bare shoulders broke a capsule inside me. I dropped to my knees, a pro at that, and arranged her hands tangent as in prayer. . . . (p. 131)

Marshfield tells us that "we had everything; we were as astronauts; we were more than the world," that Frankie was a "creature of paradise" and possessed "a skein of glory," (pp. 152-53) and that "I would greet my impotence with her as the survivor within me of faith, a piece of purity within all the relativistic concupiscence, this plastic modernity, this adulterate industry, this animated death." (p. 139)

The enigmatic figure of Ms. Prynne thus becomes more than a literary in-joke on Updike's part or the chance for a somewhat silly sexual climax to the novel; she becomes the integrating symbol for the novel's whole movement on various levels. That Ms. Prynne corresponds with Jung's fourth stage of the *anima* as Sapientia is reflected in the language with which Marshfield addresses her *after* he has completed the accounts of the first three women. Descriptions of Jane were generally phrased in pragmatic language; Alicia summoned forth musical metaphors and Frankie Eden-esque ones; but Ms. Prynne is addressed in terms of exorcism, ultimacy, and survival.

> You ask, what of my case? A common fall, mine, into the abysmal complexity of the American female. I feel, however, not merely fallen, but possessed, and such is demonology that the case needs for cure another woman; and the only woman here, on this frontier, is, Ms., you. (p. 201)

> Have you been preparing me . . . for a return to this world and not a translation to a better? Is this the end of therapy, a reshouldering of ambiguity . . . ? One rite, one grail stands between me and renewed reality. You, Ms. Prynne. (p. 213)[15]

> Oh, I moved through you, understanding all this and more, and it came to me that love is not an e-motion, an assertive putting out, but a trans-motion, a compliant moving through.

> I saw through you, with you, Ms. Prynne. . . . As my end approaches everything grows vaporous, my future and my past are the same green cloud, and only you are solid, only you have substance; I fall toward you as a meteorite toward the earth, as a comet toward the sun. (p. 217)

So Ms. Prynne herself finally takes on an explicit mandala-like shape, for Marshfield falls toward her "as a meteorite toward the earth, as a comet toward the sun." Intercourse with her will signify his self's re-integration and re-birth, but it will also symbolize a good deal more. In Jungian psychology, the fourth anima-figure, Sapientia, is also "the soul of God," associated as she is with God's Wisdom in the Book of Proverbs. This is not surprising since, for Jung, the mandala-archetype for the Self is the same shape as the unconscious image of God. Jung stated:

> Strictly speaking, the God-image does not coincide with the unconscious as such, but with a special content of it, namely the archetype of the Self. It is this archetype from which we can no longer distinguish the God-image empirically. We can arbitrarily postulate a difference between these two entities, but that does not help at all. On the contrary, it only helps us to separate man from God. Faith is certainly right when it impresses on man's mind and heart how infinitely far away and inaccessible God is; but it also teaches His nearness, His presence. . . . The religious mind longs for wholeness, and therefore lays hold of the images of wholeness offered by the unconscious which, independently of the conscious mind, rise from the depths of our psychic nature.[16]

In *A Month of Sundays* this ambiguous tension between identification with and alienation from the Self and God archetype (since both are intuitively perceived and yet ultimately unknowable) are experienced by Marshfield the night before he writes that final sermon "that could be preached."

> . . . I stepped out of this omega-shaped shelter, testing my impending freedom, and looked up at the stars, so close and warmly blue in this atmosphere, yet so immutably fixed in their dome of night; and I felt, for an instant—as if for an instant the earth's evolution had become palpable—that particle or quantity within myself, beyond mind, that makes me a stranger here, in this universe. A quantity no greater than a degree's amount of arc, yet vivid and mine, my treasure. (p. 204)

Earlier Marshfield had realized that the desert he is in has another name: *La Palma de la Mano de Dios*, the Palm of God's Hand. In his diary entry on the night before final departure, Marshfield, by recording his last experience "under the dome of desert stars," recapitulates briefly most of the novel's thematic strands found on both the conscious and unconscious levels.

> The immanence of departure renders this bland room as strange as when I entered it. I leave no trace, no scar. Did I dream this? Meister Eckhardt, if I remember, talks of divinity as "the simple ground, the quiet desert" and of a process, so God can be born in the soul, of *entwerden*, the opposite of becoming, of travelling away from oneself. The day after tomorrow my month may seem a metaphor, a pause briefer than that rest of Alicia's I so reprehensibly interrupted.
>
> Last night after poker I went out under the dome of desert stars and was afraid, not afraid, afraid to be born again.
>
> Even so, come. (p. 226)

That final plea, "Even so, come," found as the last line of the Book of Revelation, is the Church's final plea for Christ's return that will inaugurate our final bodily resurrection. That these words are addressed here to Ms. Prynne is plurisignificant, for Marshfield's bodily "resurrection" is effected through intercourse with her. Her beauty and their congress are described in the baroque style of Preachers that began the book and was absent for a time, and reminds us of the elaborately ornate Song to the Shulammitess, the Jungian Sapientia figure found in the Song of Songs. Also, Ms. Prynne's "amazing breasts, so firm that they seemed small, the nipples erect upon little mounds of erectile tissue, so that a cupola upon a dome was evoked, an ascent in several stages, in architectural successiveness" (p. 228) recall the omega-shaped "dome" image of the two previous passages we quoted, and so she embodies here the "ascending stages" of the sexual, religious, and psychic.

In short, Marshfield's intercourse with Ms. Prynne, his unknown but Ideal Reader, dramatizes in a single symbolic act the psychic, erotic, religious, *and* artistic resolution of the novel. That Marshfield's "month may seem a metaphor" is true. His diary has become the verbal counterpart to the conjoined processes it describes; and, like metaphor, each process when referred to inevitably points to its opposing counterpart through its ironic similarity.

Marshfield's "month" records a man's psychic movement from his concerns with his *Ego*, that distillery of his conscious life, to his encounter with the unconscious symbol of his Self. The diary begins with the words "Forgive me," and its last entry starts with "Bless you" and ends with a communal "we" as it records their moment of meeting and union. In the interval, he has confronted not only the four stages of his *anima* but also his psychic "shadows" in the three clergymen with whom he makes a golf foursome throughout his stay until "these bankrupt clergymen have replaced the phantoms that chased me here." (p. 198)[17]

Finally, Marshfield's crisis of religious faith arises from his inability to reconcile the more rationalistic and objectivistic orthodoxy of Karl Barth's theology (to which his conscious *Ego* subscribes) with the more intuitive grasp of harmony and wholeness that his subjective, unconscious experience affords. Although he is capable of imagining himself as a "circle divided in half, half-white, half-black," because of his Barthian bias he cannot visualize God *theologically* in such imagery.

Psychologically, however, he can agree with "Freud's darkest truism: opposites are one. Light holds within it the possibility of dark. God is the devil, dreadfully enough. I, I am all, I am God enthroned on the only ego that exists for me; and I am dust, and like the taste." (p. 189) For Jung, the Self-archetype and corresponding God-image are more extensive than the Christian conceptualization of God precisely because that conceptualization excludes the darker, satanic aspects which the mandala usually includes. Consequently, Marshfield—despite his extensive "dialogue" with Christian theologians throughout—cannot resolve his faith-dilemma on a conceptual, theological level; it will be resolved only on the more existential and psychological level through the "agency" of Ms. Prynne. This association is made explicit when he tells her that "with the same unkillable intuition that leads me to laud the utterly *absconditus Deus*, I feel there is a place in you for me." And, by pursuing this un-killable intuition to its omega-point, Marshfield thus completes his three-fold exploration.

9: *The Coup*

The publication of *The Coup* in late 1978 was itself a *coup* for John Updike. Readers and critics who hitherto felt that they had a purchase on "Updike country" (a domain apparently abutting "Cheever country") and had pigeon-holed him as a dissector of suburban manners and morals were now peremptorily summoned into modern Africa, a turbulent never-never land, and were bade there by the perplexed voice of a slightly demented, deposed black dictator.

The Coup purports to be the memoir of Colonel Hakim Felix Ellellou, former President of Kush, written in exile on the Riviera. Its subject is the country of Kush, formerly a French colony called Noire, and the events and circumstances that brought about his decline and fall. Kush is a poverty-stricken African backwater, "a land of delicate, delectable emptiness," which Ellellou had hoped to transform into a nation governed by Islamic morality and Marxist ideology. Unfortunately, the reality of a severe drought impedes such idealistic goals, and so the action of the novel recounts Ellellou's many travels (each one in disguise, though accompanied by the Presidential Mercedes) to discover the cause of the accursed drought and to feel the pulse-beat of his Kushite people. Each travel encounter issues in either befuddlement or an impetuous gesture. Early on, at Ellellou's order, an American AID representative in a seersucker suit, symbolic of "Neo-capitalist harlotry," is burned alive atop a carton mountain of breakfast cereals, potato chips, and Carnation dried milk, all sent in sympathy by the "infidel" American government. The Colonel prefers instead the purity of poverty for his people which, in his confused imagination, he identifies with the Paradise passages he so loves to quote from the Koran. However, through his amiably dim, though dawning, awareness he comes to realize that not only his beloved capital city, Istiqlal, but even a regional outpost that bears his name, the city of Ellellou, have become hot-beds of consumerism, re-embodiments of

America in the 1950's and its rapacious materialism. Ellellou knew that 1950's America well and, it seems, despised it, for, while a student at McCarthy College in Franchise, Wisconsin, from 1954 to 1958, he originally embraced his Islamic faith in the militantly racist, eclectic version of it offered by the Black Muslim, Elijah Mohammed.

But Ellellou's actual ambivalence about America is betrayed by the text of his memoir. Not only does his narrative shift continually between first and third persons, but it seems to resist sequentiality. Each telling incident or odor on his African travels ushers in, willy-nilly fashion, a memory of some American experience. Like his country, Ellellou is a man without evident borders, and so is his memoir. Interwoven in the narrative are hilarious meetings with each of his four wives, made so by Ellellou's solemn density of mind; diplomatic exchanges with rather undiplomatic Soviet and American representatives; Byzantine manueverings regarding the disposal of the former king, Edumu IV, and the heading-off of the ambitious Ezana, his Minister of Interior and second in command. When the *coup* finally takes place—to Ellellou's surprise but not the reader's— it is both bloodless and casual, as inevitable as the heat and sun of Kush.

After twenty years of delicately creating his own legendary world of the middle America of Pennsylvania and New England, Updike seems to have thrown his critics a curve ball by creating this legendary Kush. But the curveball image is inexact; as Updike put it, *The Coup* is "a change of pace, taking something off the fast ball."[1] The pitches and the game are still the same; only the pace and the park have changed. For *The Coup* is not just a novel about Africa; true to Updike's previous fictional themes, it is also a novel about America, about the art of fiction-making, and about the human heart in conflict with itself.

The Coup is many things, as we shall see; but it is important to note first, in the light of this critical review of Updike's fiction, that this novel is also a summary work, a startling reminder of previous themes and characters. The creation of the mad Ellellou was a bold artistic stroke on Updike's part. A man of infinite variety, his many maunderings and meanderings have allowed Updike to exploit all at once, as it were, the full range of his stylistic gifts. Previous novels have demonstrated that Updike's quiver contains many stylistic arrows, but never in one novel has he been able to shoot them simultaneously and so accurately too.

In *The Coup* we re-encounter Updike's fastidious probing for metaphor, lush descriptive passages shaped like delicate filigree work, randy introspective realizations, the poetic eye and ear ever in evidence—all those features an Updike reader expects and welcomes. But in addition, other, often overlooked, stylistic traits are manifest in abundance: the remarkably accurate ear that can recapture the distinctive conversational sounds of Black Muslims, African technocrats, American bureaucrats, and domestic squabbles heightened by linguistic confusion; the artistic patience that can postpone the *mot juste* for the exactly apt location in a paragraph; the subtle interweaving of a particular image with a particular character so that both become subliminally identified in the reader's mind; the kinesthetically vivid rendering of precipitate action and disaster; the shaping of plot structure to evoke suspense and curiosity; the wide-ranging vocabulary that embraces both the familiar and the esoteric and yet is ever precise and unsloppy.

Furthermore, it is Ellellou's multi-faceted personality that makes him reminiscent of some central character trait possessed by each of Updike's previous fictional heroes: the quaint solemnity of Hook, the cultural conservatism of Rabbit, the cosmic befuddlement of George Caldwell, the fuzzy romanticism of Peter, the puzzled wariness with the opposite sex of Joey Robinson, the nostalgia of Piet, the sense of displacement of Bech, the messianism of Skeeter, the manic self-absorption of Marshfield, and the double-mindedness of Jerry Conant. Ellellou is Updike's Proteus, shape shifting and reincarnating the full gallery of Updike character inventions.

It is fitting, then, that throughout *The Coup* Ellellou is ever in disguise: as orange vendor, troubadour, magician, gum seller, insurance claims adjuster, beggar, and exile. He has an endless list of names: Hakim, Felix, Happy, Bini, Flapjack, and, most important, Ellellou which means "Freedom." He is also something of an Everyman: colonel, commoner, native and alien, exile, American, African. Consequently, his memoir will take on a legitimate Whitmanesque coloration; it becomes an extended "Song of Myself" in that he includes all within himself and, like Whitman, eludes all the varied identities proffered him by the world, by the past, by the conventional mind. Like Whitman, Ellellou will delight in cataloguing his world; his exuberant descriptions of Kush, piling detail upon detail, become objective correlatives for his all-embracing ego.

For Ellellou is the American Adam, African style. We are told that he was "born in a whirlwind," is an orphan, and remains a sexual naif ever untouched by repeated experience. Throughout he is an innocent outsider starting anew, spurred on by Edenesque visions of Kush here shaped by the Koran's descriptive visions of Paradise.[2] (pp. 12, 14, 21, 43, 114) Ironically, though, his memoir must recount his un-Whitmanesque Adamic Fall and expulsion instead. *He* is Whitmanesque, but his story is not. Thus the narrative structure of *The Coup*, like that of *Couples* and *Marry Me*, will reflect that structure proper to Hawthorne, Melville, and others who treated the myth of the American Adam in ironic, non-Whitmanesque fashion. R. W. B. Lewis' summary of that traditional structure reads like a plot outline of *The Coup*.

> The matter of Adam: the ritualistic trials of a young innocent, liberated from family and social history or bereft of them; advancing hopefully into a complex world he knows not of; radically affecting that world and radically affected by it; defeated, perhaps even destroyed—in various versions of the recurring anecdote hanged, beaten, shot, betrayed, abandoned—but leaving his mark upon the world, and a sign in which conquest may become possible for the survivors.[3]

Updike, of course, retains this traditional structure but up-ends it in comic fashion by having the tale shaped via the befuddled subjective voice of Ellellou himself. The only "mark" Ellellou will actually leave upon the world will be the marks of his memoir. Even this mark is suspect, though, for *The Coup* closes with these lines: "He is writing his memoirs. No, I should put it more precisely: Colonel Ellellou is rumored to be working on his memoirs." (p. 299)

Updike will also update the trial and fall structure by way of historical analogy. Updike has described *The Coup* as an allegory of America's Watergate crisis,[4] and Ellellou's drift into exile from 1973 on parallels Nixon's similar drift. His subsequent efforts to compose a memoir also recall Nixon, as do the results. Ellellou's memoir appears to be confessional at first, but soon becomes, in fact, something of a pompous *apologia* of a man still seemingly bewildered by what he sees as the machinations of subordinates and shadowy rivals. Earlier we noted that critics in the past have not been alert to the historical substratum present in each of Updike's novels, its rootedness in America's changing cultural and political history. Years ago, Updike protested this misappraisal of his work as unhistorically rooted by saying, "*The Centaur* is a distinctly Truman book, and *Rabbit, Run* an Eisenhower one. *Couples* could only have taken place under Kennedy."[5] We might also add that the Kennedy era is critically important to *Marry Me*, that the moon exploration is a central realistic and symbolic motif in *Rabbit Redux*, and that the unravelling of Watergate parallels Marshfield's unravelling in *A Month of Sundays*.

The Coup, however, makes comic capital of the historical moment. The former King Edumu is executed for "High Crimes and Misdemeanors." Ellellou's later plight begins to coincide with Nixon's when Ezana, the eventual usurper, ominously comments on Nixon that one should "reflect upon the purgative value of a leader who unravels before the nation's riveted eyes. If he falls, he will carry your nation's woes with him into the abyss." (p. 228) When Ellellou is finally deposed, the political reasoning has a familiar ring: "Now the honor of the *Presidency* must be safeguarded. We must show our friends the Americans that we too value the office above the man." (p. 289) Nixon, though, is not the only Presidential comic target. Kush's dependence on peanut production also inspires Ellellou's mind with indirect allusions to America's President in 1978. For example, he recalls that in "battle he found himself possessed of a dead calm that to his superiors appeared commendable. In truth it was peanut behavior. . . . Ellellou had faith that the pull of fate would rescue him if he be numb enough, and submit to being shelled." (p. 9)

But in *The Coup* historical allusions are not the only vehicles for comic effect. Literary allusions also serve. Kush is an Eliot-like *Waste Land*, not only in the literal sense of its being in fact mostly desert, but in that the Kushites' craving for materialistic satisfactions and the spiritual emptiness such craving brings recall Eliot's symbol for the modern industrial world. As in the Fisher-King myth on which *The Waste Land* is based, Ellellou sees himself as a knight errant replacing the former maimed king and as one who, via travels and travails, will magically restore his land to pristine purity. Ezana's words late in the novel remind us of the comic twisting of this Eliot motif and slyly recall Eliot's famous critical dictum when Ezana observes: "Our President also . . . rules by a mystical dissociation of sensibility, if I understand the phrase . . . he explores the wider land for omens, to discover the religious source of the drought." (p. 230)

Aligned with this *Waste Land* motif is Updike's comic transformation of the Oedipus story. Ellellou is a vest-pocket Oedipus who, as leader of his land, seeks out the reason for the curse upon his beloved Kush only to discover finally that "*I* was the curse upon the land." (p. 261) Like Oedipus, Ellellou is a killer of his king and surrogate father, Edumu IV, while Edumu also doubles as Teresias, for like him he is a blind seer given to oracularly pertinent utterances. At their first meeting Edumu tells Ellellou that "You have cursed this land with your hatred of the world." (p. 9) In his speech right before his execution Edumu states: "I say Kush is a fiction, an evil dream the white man had, and those who profess to govern her are twisted and bent double. There are in truth white men,

though their faces wear black masks." (p. 69) Later the disembodied head
of Edumu, now tricked up by wires and a loudspeaker, returns to these
twin themes: "This man [Ellellou], while proclaiming hatred of the
Americans, is in fact an American at heart. . . . He has projected upon
the artificial nation of Kush his own furious though ambivalent will; the
citizens of this poor nation are prisoners of his imagination, and the barren
landscape, where children and cattle starve, mirrors his exhausted spirit."
(pp. 212-13)

This latter theme—that Kush is but a figment of Ellellou's imagination—is of special importance for appreciating *The Coup* and is reminiscent of Nabokov's greatest works. In addition to the ornately fastidious
language, the crazed memoir structure of this novel is Updike's bow to the
master—as was *A Month of Sundays*. Kush is Ellellou's Lolita and, when we
meet him composing his memoir, he is much like Humbert Humbert, a
character now *in extremis*, suspected of mental aberration. The memoir
itself, of course, also recalls the crazed coloration of Kinbote's voice in *Pale
Fire* and that mad king's recreation of distant Zembla. Nabokov-like,
the comic conflict in *The Coup* is between the real Kush (if there is such
a place), that "land of delicate, delectable emptiness," and Ellellou's romantic distortion of it, a passionately excessive investment that will go
unrequited. The suggestion that Kush is identical with the inside of Ellellou's "head" is offered early when he interrupts his politico-geological account of Kush and remarks, "But even memory thins in this land, which
suggests, on a map, an angular skull whose cranium is an empty desert."
(p. 6)

Throughout, the actual borders of Kush are ever vague, to say the
least; in fact, in the northeast it is "nine tenth's imaginary." (p. 33) When
Ellellou takes the scimitar in order to behead Edumu—the previous embodiment of Kush—we hear: "In this life woven of illusions and unsub-
stantial impressions it is gratifying to encounter heft, to touch the leaden
center of things, the *is* at the center of *be*, the rock in Plato's cave. I
thought of an orange. I lifted the sword high. . . ." (p. 72) This orange
image will thereafter continue to be associated with the human head and
with the power of imagination. For, immediately after, Ellellou in the
disguise of a singing orange peddler will offer his starving citizenry images
of oranges in song. "People would attempt to bribe him to sing of bananas,
or couscous, or spring lamb turned on a spit with peppers and onions, but
he would say No, he was a seller of oranges, and could conjure up only
their image amply enough to banish the reality of hunger." (p. 78) Kush
resides within his skull, not so much an orange as an image of one.

At times this reality-imagination polarity is made explicit. Ellellou recalls a political conversation in his college days when he asked, "the crucial question isn't Can you prove it? but Does it give a handle on the reality that otherwise would overwhelm us?" And the memoir continues with this reflection: "Of course he had in mind not the parochial concerns of these Americans . . . but the dim idea stirring, of distant Kush." (p. 141) Soon after, upon hearing Black Muslim rhetoric, Ellellou remembers that "I perceived this then: government is mythological in nature. These step-children of Islam were seeking to concoct a counter-myth." (p. 160) More Black Muslim Temple meetings prompt the realization that "I was to imagine myself in absolutist form. Crystals of dreaming were erected within me, and the nation of Kush as it exists is the residue of those crystals." (p. 162)

Once Ellellou actually becomes President, however, the saving cynicism of such a political viewpoint departs, and he himself becomes possessed by his own self-created myth of Kush. He too will eventually be deposed by a counter-myth, that of "the Canada of Africa" proposed by Ezana. The composition of the memoir, then, marks Ellellou's efforts (reminiscent of Joey Robinson in *Of the Farm* and Marshfield in *A Month of Sundays*) to confront the Kush of illusion and so recover the reality of his "self" by sorting out the facts from the fanciful. Unfortunately, he and Kush have been so identified in and by his imagination that the tone and content of the memoir—continually admixing memory and imagination—mirror his own confusion about the very nature of reality itself. Just as Nabokov, by making Humbert Humbert the controlling voice of the "reality" of *Lolita*, succeeded in unsettling readers in such a way that they were forced to scrutinize their own notions of "reality," so too does Updike through the manic instrumentality of Ellellou. Ellellou's account is that of a man who cannot possibly separate what seems from what is, whether the subject be his sexual relationships, his own recollections, his own self.

Consequently, his memoir records a Bunyan-like pilgrimage of one fleeing the City of Destruction (the Americanized Istiqlal) and in search of the Celestial City, but here the pilgrimage is transposed into a love-quest, a search for the delectable Kush of his dreams, a Paradise wherein Eros dwells. Since he is now a frustrated pilgrim in fact, for Ellellou the very act of writing must be the vehicle and substitute for recapturing his dream. Through this memoir motif Updike taps that American novelistic tradition described so well by Richard Poirier in *A World Elsewhere*.[6] Poirier, by emphasizing the stylistic aspect of the American Adam tradition, notes that in American writers there is "ever a resurgence of the Emersonian dream of possibly 'building' a world out of the self in a style that is the self. The effort in *Lolita* to preserve an 'intangible island of entranced time' succeeds no more than did the efforts in Cooper's *The Crater*, over a hundred years before, to preserve an island paradise from the contamination of modern democratic America."[7]

So the fall is ever the American-African Adam's fate, and harsh reality greets the heroes of its fiction-making. In Ellellou's case, the confusion of styles manifest in his memoir is a linguistic counterpoint to this. On the dramatic level, at the end of *The Coup* Ellellou's vision of Kush, the country of his dreams, must confront the city of his Fate, the jerry-built town of Ellellou that bears his name and is a throwback to 1950's America—in short, in the city of Ellellou he reluctantly confronts his very self, his past and present.

Ellellou is the very character Updike has been in quest of for some time. Updike chose this quotation from Kierkegaard's Journals as the first epigraph to his play, *Buchanan Dying*.

> I wanted to write a novel in which the chief character was to have been a man who had a pair of spectacles with one lens that reduced as powerfully as oxy-gas-miscroscope and the other that magnified equally powerfully; in his interpretation everything was very relative.[8]

In his Afterword to the play, Updike commented on this Kierkegaard quote and admitted that early in his career he attempted to write just such a novel as the journal of a wicked high school principal but then abandoned the project.[9] In Ellellou he has finally succeeded, whether intentionally or not. Ellellou needs no such spectacles, though; he is man cursed with double-vision and eyes ever fighting for focus.

Like the man himself, Ellellou's memoir is always slightly cock-eyed. This circumstance allows Updike to evince his considerable comic gifts. First of all, Ellellou finds it impossible to keep his narrative voices straight and his account keeps shifting from past to present tense and from third to first person and back. Early on, he offers us an earnest explanation for this confusion.

> Yet a soldier's disciplined self-effacement, my Cartesian schooling, and the African's traditional abjuration of ego all constrain this account to keep to the third person. There are two selves: the one who acts, and the "I" who experiences. The latter is passive even in a

whirlwind of the former's making, passive and guiltless and astonished. The historical performer bearing the name of Ellellou was no less mysterious to me than to the American press. . . . Ellellou's body and career carried me here, there, and I never knew why, but submitted. (p. 7)

We readers begin to know better: poor Ellellou cannot keep his own myths straight, much less his "hes" and "Is." Like that of Kierkegaard's character, one eye in his memoir—to recall Allen Tate's distinction— will reflect the vision of the "angelic" imagination while the other reflects that of the "symbolic imagination."[10] Here their unfocussed relationship will issue in comedy. Tate's phrase "angelic imagination" refers to that artistic conviction that humans, like angels, can directly perceive timeless essences. As Ellellou's rhapsodic descriptions and repeated quotes from the Koran (so misapplied to Kush's status) reflect, the angelic imagination denies the sensible world and tries to create its own abstract one, the Kush of essence, as it were. By contrast, it is the business of the "symbolic imagination," true of Ellellou's other eye, "to return to the order of temporal sequence—to *action*."[11]

It is this contrast, so manifest in the memoir, that creates and controls the novel's comic richness. Updike's previous novels do contain sprightly comic moments, most notably in *The Centaur*, *Bech* and *A Month of Sundays*, but it is this ever-present double-focus and blurring overlay of the angelic and symbolic perspective that makes *The Coup* more comically integral. Ellellou's essentialistic angelic imagination is present everywhere, not only in the inappropriate use of the Koran quotes that punctuate even the goriest or most dire events; but also in his self-absorbed, abstracted rendering of dramatic situations that, let us say, a more perceptive man might have found insulting. Throughout, deflating events evoke inflated language (the eyes have it!), and the solemn dignified tone often contradicts the indignity related in the temporal action.

> I live. Perhaps the white devil's offer of free beer saved my life, for the crowd was in too much of a thirsty hurry to halt and pummel me with the annihilatory zeal my address had attempted to instill. One cracked rib, a fat lip, the removal of my shoes, the bestowal of a quantity of derisive spittle, and they were through with my body. The life of a charismatic national leader cannot be all roses. (p. 257)

As this passage demonstrates, a resourceful range of comic styles is at work in *The Coup*. Throughout there will be an inter-animation of the formal word and the fastidiously precious description with the slangy, the trite, and the vague. Like Ellellou, the style itself is ever in double focus. American colloquialisms will interact with snippets of French and native African in the same paragraph. When Ellellou desires to be most formal, i.e. on those occasions when he and Kush aparently share their abstract symbiosis, he will consistently use French (as in the many hilarious episodes where the revelation "*Je suis Ellellou*" is meant to inspire awe but issues in consternation). His native African, though, will be his instrument for linguistic precision and moral resonance and will often be employed with a pedant's exactitude. For example, when his successor and usurper Ezana assumes the name *Dorfu* on becoming President because it means "solidarity," we are told that *dorfu* actually means "crocodile-torpid-on-the-riverbank-but-far-from-dead," as distinguished from *durfo*, "crocodile-thrashing-around-with-prey." (p. 265) Such a definition suggests a sly assessment of Ezana's character and exposes Ellellou's addled pedantry simultaneously.

These comic linguistic contrasts are most evident in those episodes where Ellellou meets each of his four wives. Each of these dialogues will be characterized by Ellellou's own stilted formality of expression, that appropriate to presidential pronouncements, with that of his wives' blunt candor or mimicry of him. For Ellellou there might be two selves, the one who acts and the I who experiences, but these women address only the one they know: Bini, Happy, and so on; none of his disguises ever fools them, especially the disguise of Ellellou. Each of the four wives speaks with a distinctive voice—itself a clever artistic feat for Updike—and each voice accurately captures those dramatic cultural transitions in Ellellou's life. Ellellou might despise change and even deny it, but each of these women and their voices represent its inevitability.

Another comic thread that parallels Ellellou's misguided assessment of Kush is his obliviousness regarding his own sexual sterility vis-a-vis these women; those interludes of conscious impotence he will excuse by reason of the distracting concerns with matters of state. His women, however, know otherwise; and like Kush seeking after the strange gods of materialism, each of them has sought out other more virile men.

Furthermore, like the Jungian quaternity of *anima* figures that we found in A Month of Sundays, these four wives will reveal a like configuration; but, in addition, each will represent some aspect of Ellellou's central *anima* of fascination, the land of Kush. His first wife, Kadongolimi, represents "earth-strength," the Kush of memory. Candace, his second wife, was once an Eve-like temptress; now transported to Africa, she represents the blandishments of American materialism that seduce all Kushites. His third wife, Sittina, takes on in Ellellou's imagination features of Jung's third, virginal *anima*, for "the reality of her was more mixed than the thought, the inner image of her." (p. 59) Sittina is both the daughter of a Tutsi chief and a former sprint champion at an Alabama college, and so she embodies the inevitable wedding of Africa and America taking place in Kush. Since Ellellou himself unwittingly embodies such a wedding, it is fitting that she accompany him into exile. Ellellou's fourth wife, Sheba, is the improbable embodiment of his Jungian *Sophia* or *Sapientia anima*. His descriptions of Sheba are always inappropriately ethereal since she is perpetually stoned on kola nuts, Ethiopian khat, and Iranian bang. Sheba is Kush's future but Ellellou is blind to it. Instead he will see her with the lyrical eyes of Humbert Humbert. For example, when she is stoned beyond all responsiveness, we hear the explanation that "Her gentle spirit rarely descended to earth." (p. 145)

> I loved in her what the others, the cruel illiterates of the desert, scented—her vacancy. Where other women had an interior, a political space that sent its emissaries out to bargain for her body and her honor, Sheba had a space that asked no tending, that supported a nomadic traffic of music and drugs. Such a woman is an orphan of Allah, a sacred object. Sheba never questioned, never reflected. (p. 148)

Sheba is a marvelous comic creation, and creation is the appropriate word. Ellellou's etherealized vision that transforms her patent emptiness into spirit coincides with his demented vision of the vacant land of Kush (and the geo-political imagery of that quoted passage reflects this admixture). It is unsurprising, then, that once Sheba vanishes—appropriately sold into slavery in Yemen—Ellellou begins his downfall. Kush-Sheba is now lost to him. One consolation, though, comically sustains the sterile Ellellou, namely: the "fantasy that he had impregnated the *disparue* Sheba." (p. 222) A similar fantasy that he is the father of his country and has impregnated Kush with new life is the occasion for his memoir.

One remarkable outcome in *The Coup*, however, is that Ellellou, despite his evident folly, manages to retain our sympathy. The reason is that, although Updike brilliantly satirizes solemn and silly targets in America and Africa, he consistently avoids the tone of facile cynicism so popular in fiction since the early 1960's. Tone here is all. Strict satire demands an objective tone and the perspective of an outsider, but in *The*

Coup we only hear Ellellou's honestly perplexed, highly subjective voice. This makes the novel an African novel with a difference, something like Waugh's *Black Mischief* with a heart, Conrad's *Heart of Darkness* with a smile, Bellow's *Henderson the Rain King* turned inside out. As in *Lolita*, the satire here is mainly a matter of filling out the comic texture; it enters more as an aside than directly, for the basic parody is that of a jilted lover of Kush, straining mightily to re-create in language his ecstasies and agonies. Memory, of course, is always a blend of recollective effort and imaginative restructuring, a compound whose elements are often indistinguishable. Every memoir thus partakes of artistic techniques and the inspirations of fancy; the very metaphoric nature of language further compounds the process since words have other symbolic resonances beyond the designation of facts or happenings. All memoirs are at once recovery and discovery. Updike exploits all of these paradoxical truths and compounds them by making Ellellou both a perversely distracted memorialist, fascinated with the possibilities of language, and an unwittingly honest narrator, anxious to sort out the "facts."

The Coup's structure, then, is similar to that of *Of the Farm* and *A Month of Sundays* in that through the act of writing itself Ellellou is attempting to discover his "self" and recover his dream of Kush. This effort to define his own character and his fate, though, points up the ever-possible, in fact likely, conversion of reality and imagination, fact and legend, into each other that make up all endeavors to define one's "self." Consequently, once the reader engages Ellellou's pursuit of his self in the light of all its historical permutations and identity-shifts, he soon realizes that Ellellou is Man writ large—or, better, Man writ comically crooked—but it is this factor that makes him a universal character beyond the comical, and so he engages our smiling sympathy. Ellellou is Everyman and Everyman is, after all, us.

Epilogue

I write this epilogue ten months after completion of the text. In the interim Updike has published two short story collections: the first, a compilation of his stories about the Maple family which was also nicely adapted in a television production, entitled *Too Far To Go*; and the second, a selection of his post-1972 stories, entitled *Problems and Other Stories*. Both ventures have met with exceptional critical success. At present he is working on a new novel as well as more stories; and so, as he moves forward, I unfortunately must look back.

A backward look reveals to me all those efforts that I wish I had made, such as an examination of Updike's distinctive and eminently resourceful style. I did explore his elaborate probing of the potentialities of metaphor a notable feature of his style—but those subtleties of tonal variation, of shifts in rhythm and cadence, of the accurate "mix" of voices throughout his prose escaped my close attention. In contemporary fiction Updike's voice is as recognizable as that of a Bellow or a Cheever or a Mailer or a Roth, but it eludes any fixing in our usual stylistic categories and, unlike theirs, it is not so obviously either musical or rhetorical. To call him a prose-poet, as some do, is too easy a shorthand, for it merely points up the precise area of our critical difficulty without clarifying it. Where other writers worry about sound, Updike seems to worry about shape. Therefore, a prose-painter or prose-sculptor might be closer to the mark but only that. As a youngster he wanted to be a cartoonist; after college he attended the Ruskin School of Drawing in Oxford. In his comments on his writing efforts he continually returns to analogies with drawing, to the odd shapes like zigzags, sandwiches, and such that inspired his novels, to concern with how the words "look" on a page, to the importance of the impression the dust-jacket cover of a novel makes. Perhaps here lies a clue that I never followed.

In conjunction with such a discussion of style, I also wish that I had investigated Updike's personal debt to those writers whom he repeatedly praises as inspirations: Marcel Proust, Henry Green, and Vladimir Nabokov. His early fiction with its emphasis on nostalgia, on the recovery of apparently meaningless sensations—not so different from Proust's recollection of the taste of a madeleine dipped into tea, of a metallic sound, of the feel of uneven steps—manifests a Proustian passion for accuracy of remembered detail that Updike praised in his acceptance speech for his National Book Award in 1964.

His debt to Henry Green, although made explicit in his introduction to the new 1977 edition of *The Poorhouse Fair*, is more difficult to pinpoint. Mimetic honesty, similar and yet quite different from Proust's, is perhaps the key here. At any rate, Updike does give us a hint and possibly an avenue to follow in his eloquent tribute to Green that ends a lengthy critical appreciation he wrote in 1977. That Green tribute summarizes, in almost ironic fashion, precisely those specific virtues one so often finds in Updike's own fiction.

> Green's human qualities—his love of work and laughter; his absolute empathy; his sense of splendor amid loss, of vitality within weakness— make him a precious witness to any age. No stranger to the macabre and the vicious, he glorifies the petty virtues bred of human interdependence. . . . His novels, as Horace prescribed, give pleasure and instruct; moreover, they give that impression, of an irreducible density and self-possessed rhythm, that belongs to reality and its most ardent imitations in art. They live, in short, and like all living things feed on air, on the invisible; the spaces between the words are warm, and the strangeness is mysteriously exact, the strangeness of the vital.

The Nabokovian connection I alluded to in the chapters on *A Month of Sundays* and *The Coup*. Nabokov's influence becomes a pronounced replacement for Proust's in the diaries of the distracted Marshfield and the memoir of the mad Ellellou. Proust was a nostalgist; Nabokov, as he expressed it in *Pale Fire*, is more a "preterist," that is, an artist who commands the past as past but never confuses it with the present, even though his characters often do so. The preterist, unlike the nostalgist, therefore has access to richer and more wide-ranging material, tapping but transcending the necessarily finite resources of memory. Such a transition from nostalgist to preterist appears to characterize Updike's present stage in his writerly pilgrim's progress. Furthermore, Nabokov's inspiration also appears to have liberated Updike's genuine comic gifts (note his recent delight in parodying what was once considered his own baroque style) and energized his own philosophical and speculative talents.

Another regret is that I was not clearer and more consistent in my interpretive methodology. In several chapters my reading of a particular novel or story was close in an exacting way. I prefer to think of the process as like that of uncovering by way of patient scraping the hitherto undisclosed configurations beneath a palimpsest rather than as pedantry. Those particular chapters betray a bias borrowed from the New Critics. Unfortunately, other chapters are decidedly archetypal in perspective, and so my efforts to "stand close" here and "stand back" there no doubt struck the reader as somewhat schizophrenic. Northrop Frye described my diverse approaches well in an extended simile, evoked in language that is perhaps appropriate for a prose-painter like Updike.

> In looking at a picture we may stand close to it and analyze the details of brush-work and palette knife. This corresponds roughly to the rhetorical analysis of the New Critics in literature. At a little distance back, the design comes into clearer view, and we study rather the content represented; this is the best distance for realistic Dutch paintings, for example, where we are in a sense reading the picture. At a great distance from, say, a Madonna, we can see nothing but the archetype of the Madonna. . . . In the criticism of literature, too, we often have to "stand back" from the poem to see its archetypal organization.

I might argue in defense that I am a champion of critical pluralism or that Updike's work is far too complex for a single frame of reference. I do, in fact, support these assertions, but in all honesty they were not my specific intentions at the time. Instead, I had hoped that, by varying the stand-close, stand-back procedures, the reader would begin to assume that the absent alternative perpective might serve almost as well in the appreciation of a particular novel. I see now that I was not wholly successfully in this blithe endeavor, for where I had hoped to broaden the discussion, I often unwittingly narrowed it.

An inevitable narrowing was, of course, implicit in that my argument was essentially thematic in design. I remain convinced that the Three Great Secret Things continually emerge conjointly as a configuration in Updike's work. They provide not only a consistent thematic pattern, but also avenues or differing modes of entry into his fiction. As Updike's later fiction becomes—as it has—more speculative and philosophical in tone,

I foresee that, as I indicated in the Introduction, certain Ur-questions will necessarily come to the forefront of critical attention.

As for the Three Great Secrets of Sex, Religion, and Art, each is interrelated in that each involves myth-making exercises that reflect man's encounter with Nature within and outside himself (creation, generation, mutability) and with Nature's finality in death. In the face of that finality each secret spurs efforts to transcend Nature through its own instinctively specialized instruments: procreation or its simulation, worship and guilt, and mimetic or eisemplastic re-making.

Unfortunately, I did not emphasize enough the fact that a novelist imbued with concern for these three great secrets must of necessity concentrate on the one Great Secret that is Sex. The obvious reason is that it is the one secret of which *all* his readers are aware, and so it becomes the most intelligible vehicle for his further exploration of those other two secrets to which readers are less sensitive. In this connection it is worth noting an important comment Updike made in his essay "The Future of the Novel":

> I wish to describe merely the Novel as a product of private enterprise, for which a market is created when the state, the tribe, or church, withdraws itself from the emotional sector of an individual's life. Erotic love then becomes a symbol, a kind of code for all the nebulous, perishable sensations which we persist in thinking of as *living*.

This is a point worth re-stressing, for it is crucial to my thematic argument. In Updike's work the great secret of sex is pursued seriously in and for itself. As Updike himself put it, "About sex in general, by all means let's have it in fiction, as detailed as needs be, but real, real in its social and psychological connections. Let's take coitus out of the closet and off the altar and put it on the continuum of human behavior. . . . In the macrocosm of the individual consciousness, sexual events are huge but not all-eclipsing; let's try to give them their size." Besides its realistic depiction, then, one must emphasize that sex functions as a symbol, as "a kind of code" for the myriad of complex signals we associate with the word "life," a word more sizeable than "sex."

With the exception of Jung, I found other psychological interpretations inadequate for understanding the life-size questions that the three secrets conjointly elicit. For example, Freud's disdain for religion, his identification of it with unresolved Oedipal feelings were denied by Jung who saw in the religious impulse an important stage in psychological maturation, as well as a recovery of a nebulous range of significant psychic energies welling up from the unconscious. Furthermore, Freud had little enthusiasm for the great secret of Art. He thought it to be a kind of day-dreaming, a form of wishful thinking that compensates for some lack in the dreamer's waking life. Thus for Freud and those who follow him, the consolations of Art, like those of Religion, are at best illusory. Life's secrets are evidently elsewhere.

By contrast, Jung felt that the images an artist produces are drawn from the collective unconscious of the race and possess a power to assist us in the complex adjustments to reality on which life and psychic growth depend. Hence, the artistic endeavor is similar to that of the religious in that the function of both is to restore psychic balance. Living as we do in a rationalistic, non-image oriented, secular age, the artistic and the religious thinkers correct our one-sidedness and do so by evoking those very psychic image- and spiritual-laden energies we have not developed, in order that man might achieve a balanced wholeness.

In this connection, then, I must also emphasize, as I did not, that my Jungian readings of some of Updike's work were not meant to imply that Updike is a conscious Jungian or that a particular novel was shaped by Jungian insights. Rather, they were meant to be a demonstration that Updike's concern for the Three Great Secret Things and their inter-relationship in his fiction enjoys a more universal psychological legitimacy than a particular novel's narrative mode might evince, and also that there is a more profound fictional unity among these three diverse themes than a more reductionist or exclusivistic approach would disclose.

I am sure that my own sympathies regarding the importance of the three great secrets have not gone undetected. However, I am also aware that some readers might object that my analyses of particular novels and of the *corpus* itself have not been sufficiently evaluative. Questions like "How good is Updike?," "How does he *rate* among his contemporaries or with the giants in the American tradition?," or "Is his religious perspective good, bad, or in between?" have not been answered in an explicit way.

Deliberately so. E. D. Hirsch in his excellent *Validity in Interpretation* offers an important distinction to which I subscribe. Hirsch distinguishes between "interpretation" and "criticism," a difference that itself rests upon the distinction between the words "meaning" and "significance." Meaning, for Hirsch, is "that which is represented by the text; it is what the author meant by his use of this particular sign sequence; it is what the signs represent." Interpretation is related to meaning; it is an attempt to discover what the author intended and to bring that meaning to words other than the author's own. Of course, an author's meaning might be complex and carry a host of implications, but it is determinate—not only because some authors tell us their intentions but because we can share and understand the language of their sign systems as readers.

Criticism, though, involves another step beyond interpretation in that it addresses the question of significance, and the word "significance" implies a relationship to some value-standard. Consequently, significance refers to what *we* make of the meaning, how we relate it to our scheme of values. When we interpret, we try to recover the author's meaning; when we criticize, we make some statement about the *value* of the author's meaning. Interpretive agreement about meaning is possible or at least is potentially delimited by the text despite difficulties; but critical agreement is well-nigh impossible as long as different readers hold different values— as they so evidently do.

This study of Updike, then, has tried to be interpretive rather than critical in Hirsch's definition. This is the reason why I devoted so much attention to Updike's own remarks about his intentions as a propaedeutic to the analyses, and why I attempted, when it seemed appropriate, to consider each novel or story as a separate text—though admittedly with different approaches. In this instance I feel that I chose not only the safer but the wiser course. No two readers of Updike with differing values (sexual, religious, aesthetic, or whatever—three secrets compound the problem) will agree with my own evaluation—merely that of a third reader, after all—of Updike's significance. What is more, to complicate matters, Updike himself has said that "what (a writer) makes is ideally as ambiguous and opaque as life itself." In a recent letter to me he admitted that "my work is annoying, jesterish, by the way—some things [others] haven't grasped." Given such expressed intentions plus the added facts, it is small wonder that reader response to Updike will vary.

However, if the reader is genuinely curious about my own critical estimate, let me say simply that I believe that Updike is a most significant writer, a "precious witness to any age," as he said of Henry Green, and let that be an end on't. Updike himself observed that the true acid test would be whether his novel(s) "float after twenty years." They seem to float very well indeed; in fact some even do so swimmingly. But my main concern has been with interpreting Updike and his individual works. If I have succeeded, then at best I have prompted the reader to be a better critic by providing another basis for evaluation.

But evaluation and value are different concepts, the one an activity, the other an ideal or cherished, though elusive, object. This study has taken evident pains to show that Updike is a writer very much concerned with value, one whose artistic instincts are positive and never negative. In the early chapters I placed my emphasis on Updike's grappling with the dark issues of Nothingness and found him opting for the opposite side. If Wayne Booth in his *Modern Dogma and the Rhetoric of Assent* is right— and I believe he is—Updike has simply made more explicit and dramatic the radical choice all artists make implicitly. Booth claims that "the great original choice between being and nothingness was, and eternally is, a fantastic, uncomprehensible act of assent rather than denial; the universe is, nothingness is not." And it is in art that we experience a vivid kind of communion, a sharing in what the expression human "being" means and, by doing so, implicitly say Yes to Being itself. Booth describes this artistic sharing in words appropriate to Updike's own stated efforts.

> [F]rom birth our primary movement is toward the world, to grasp it, assenting to and taking on other selves, new truths, the whole world. Our withdrawals and rejections come always in the light of some affirmation that has been denied or is being threatened. If man is essentially a rhetorical animal, his essential human act is that of making himself a self, in the symbolic communion with his fellows: that is, each of us makes himself or herself by assenting to and incorporating whoever and whatever represents life at its most immediate and persuasive.

Furthermore, if, as we have suggested, a writer like Updike also betrays a keen religious and specifically Christian sensibility, then the mode of his "assent" will take on a Biblical and implicitly theological coloration. W. H. Auden in his essay "The Virgin and the Dynamo" describes the quasi-theological effect of a beautiful poem. If one allows the substitution of "story" or "novel" for poem, I think Auden's words are an appropriate summary for my own ineloquent attempts to characterize both Updike's recognition of human ambiguity and his efforts to achieve at least a muted reconciliation of the contending impulses manifest or hidden in the three great secrets.

> Every beautiful poem presents an analogy to the forgiveness of sins; an analogy, not an imitation, because it is not evil intentions which are repented of and pardoned but contradictory feelings which the poet surrenders to the poem in which they are reconciled.

The effect of beauty, therefore, is good to the degree that, through its analogies, the goodness of created existence, the historical fall into unfreedom and disorder, and the possibility of regaining paradise through repentance and forgiveness are recognized.

In closing, then, with apologies to Booth, let us call Updike a "rhetorician of assent" and, with apologies to Auden, an "analogist of fall and possible redemption"—and let us allow him the last word. In an interview over ten years ago, Updike—as usual—described his own writing efforts best by saying:

I have from the start been wary of the fake, the automatic. I tried not to force my sense of life as many-layered and ambiguous, while keeping in mind some sense of transaction, of a bargain struck, between me and the ideal reader. Domestic fierceness within the middle class, sex and death as riddles for the thinking animal, social existence as sacrifice, unexpected pleasures and rewards, corruption as a kind of evolution—these are some of the themes I have tried to objectify in the form of narrative. . . . I think of my books not as sermons or directives in a war of ideas but as objects, with different shapes and textures and the mysteriousness of anything that exists. My first thought about art, as a child, was that the artist brings something into the world that didn't exist before, and that he does it without destroying something else. A kind of refutation of the conservation of matter. That still seems to me its central magic, its core of joy.

Notes

1: *The Poorhouse Fair* and *Rabbit, Run*

1. John Updike, *Verse* (Greenwich: Fawcett, 1965), p. 161. This volume contains those poems published in his two previous volumes of poetry: *The Carpentered Hen and Other Tame Creatures* (New York: Harper & Row, 1958) and *Telephone Poles and Other Poems* (New York: Knopf, 1963).

2. John Updike, *Midpoint* (Greenwich: Fawcett-Crest, 1969), p. 58. Hereafter references to this paperback edition will be included in the text.

3. Frank Gado, ed., *First Person: Conversations on Writers and Writing* (Schenectady: Union College Press, 1973), pp. 88-89.

4. Ronald Gregor Smith, ed. and trans., *The Last Years: Journals, 1853-55* (London: Fontana, 1965). Updike's review, entitled "The Fork," is reprinted in Josiah Thompson's *Kierkegaard: A Collection of Critical Essays* (Garden City: Doubleday Anchor, 1972), pp. 164-82. This review demonstrates not only Updike's expertise but also his familiarity with Kierkegaard's writings. He begins the review by noting the discrepancies, three of which he quotes, between Smith's selection of quotations and those of Alexander Dru. See Alexander Dru, *The Journals of Kierkegaard* (New York: Harper, 1966).

5. Charles Samuels, "The Art of Fiction, XLIII: John Updike," *The Paris Review*, vol. 12, no. 45 (1968-69), p. 97. In a private letter to me, dated May 7, 1976, Updike reiterated that remark, saying "I am still a Barthian so far as I am theological. A *Month of Sundays* was to some extent a critique of the antinomianism latent (or even explicit) in Barth."

6. *Time* Magazine cover story, "The Adulterous Society" (April 26, 1968), p. 68.

7. John Updike, *Assorted Prose* (Greenwich: Fawcett, 1962), p. viii. The review of Barth is found on pp. 212-19.

8. *Time* cover story, p. 74. That the Christian message is a scandal is a tradition that is found as far back as the Gospels and St. Paul. Updike no doubt assumes that traditional meaning, but the reference to Kierkegaard indicates a further Kierkegaardian accent.

For Kierkegaard Christianity is "not less than a scandal" because the object of Christian faith is Jesus Christ Who is revealed as the God Man. But God and man, as he stressed, are absolutely unalike ("qualitatively distinctive" as he puts it); therefore, the would-be Christian believer necessarily confronts the unthinkable, i.e. mutually exclusive intellectual categories united in one assertion, and so he is called upon to believe in an "Absolute Paradox." Consequently, for Kierkegaard, human thought and the absolute paradox of faith cannot meet without arousing the possibility of scandal; even after a faith-commitment is made, that possibility of scandal necessarily remains— otherwise, one has not in fact reached the Paradox, that point where genuine faith begins. Christ is an "Offense" (Kierkegaard's term), then, because he claimed to be the God-Man and demanded belief; since such faith involves self-surrender, such a potential surrender "scandalizes" not only the intellect but the entire moral person. The best sources in Kierkegaard's writings for the development of these notions are *Philosophic Fragments* (Princeton: Princeton Univ., 1962), pp. 46-67; and *Training in Christianity* (Princeton: Princeton U., 1941), pp. 79ff. The most explicit example of the early Barth's "borrowing" this emphasis on the scandal of Christianity is found in his *Epistle to the Romans* (London: Oxford, 1965 ed.), pp. 279-80.

Updike's second conviction that "our life is a scandal" is puzzling at first and suggests more than sinfulness; it is best understood in the light of Kierkegaard. For him human existence itself was "scandalous" in that it also continually confronted paradox, the paradox of human living, namely: the conflict between the necessities of logic and the imperatives of human existence wherein choices must oftentimes be made when reason itself cannot adjudicate.

9. For those interested, a remarkably pellucid summary of the historical circumstances that prompted Barth's theology and his appropriation of Kierkegaard is found in my own memorial article on Barth. See George W. Hunt, "Karl Barth: Ten Years Later," *America*, vol. 139, no. 14 (November 4, 1978), pp. 301-304.

10. The *Life* interview, p. 80.

11. John Updike, "Soren Kierkegaard," in *Atlantic Brief Lives: A Biographical Companion to the Arts* (Boston: Little, Brown, 1972), p. 429.

12. *Paris Review*, p. 85.

13. The *Life* interview, p. 74.

14. *Paris Review*, p. 101.

15. Howard and Edna Hong, *Soren Kierkegaard's Journals and Papers* (Bloomington: Indiana Univ. Press, 1970), p. 753.

16. Karl Barth, *The Word of God and the Word of Man* (New York: Harper Torchbook, 1957), p. 206.

17. *Paris Review*, p. 100.

18. *Atlantic Brief Lives*, p. 430.

19. In a private letter to me Updike stated that he had read *Philosophic Fragments*, *Sickness Unto Death*, *The Concept of Dread*, and parts of *Concluding Unscientific Postcript*—Kierkegaard's major and most difficult works—as well as a good number of the *Edifying Discourses*.

20. Only one of the six book-length studies devoted to Updike even considers Kierkegaard at all. This exception is that of Alice and Kenneth Hamilton, *The Elements of John Updike* (Grand Rapids: Eerdmans, 1970). The Hamiltons, however, only trace Kierkegaard's influence in a *specific* way in their analysis of "Lifeguard" (pp. 88-91); otherwise, Kierkegaard is referred to only in a most general way with the emphasis on the three stages of existence.

21. This is especially true of the following "existentialist" readings of Updike: David Galloway, "The Absurd Man as Saint," in *The Absurd Hero in American Fiction: Updike, Styron, Bellow, Salinger* (Austin: University of Texas, 1970), pp. 21-50, 184-208; and Howard Harper, "John Updike: The Intrinsic Problems of Human Existence," in *Desperate Faith: A Study of Bellow, Salinger, Mailer, Baldwin and Updike* (Chapel Hill: University of North Carolina Press, 1967), pp. 162-90. See also Sidney Finklestein, "Acceptance of Alienation: John Updike and James Purdy," in *Existentialism and Alienation in American Literature* (New York: International, 1965).

22. I do not wish to imply that this was the universal assessment here in America of Kierkegaard's thought, even in the 1940's and 1950's. Kierkegaard has always enjoyed

exceptional commentators who have appreciated the extensive range of his thought beyond the more narrow "existentialist" approach. For a taste of these, see David F. Swenson, *Something About Kierkegaard* (Minneapolis: Augsburg Publishing House, 1941); Stanley Romaine Hopper, *The Crisis of Faith* (New York: Abingdon-Cokesbury, 1944); Paul Holmer, "On Understanding Kierkegaard," in *A Kierkegaard Critique*, ed. Howard A. Johnson and Niels Thulstrup (New York: Harper, 1962).

23. Gregor Malantschuk, *Kierkegaard's Thought*, ed. and trans. Howard V. and Edna H. Hong (Princeton: Princeton University Press, 1971).

24. Louis Mackey, *Kierkegaard: A Kind of Poet* (Philadelphia: University of Pennsylvania Press, 1971); Edith Kern, *Existential Thought and Fictional Technique: Kierkegaard, Sartre, and Beckett* (New Haven: Yale University, 1970). For a view opposite to the above authors, see Josiah Thompson, *Kierkegaard* (New York: Knopf, 1973).

25. Ralph Henry Johnson, *The Concept of Existence in the Concluding Unscientific Postscript* (Martinus Nijhoff: The Hague, 1972).

26. A study which traced just the following "Kierkegaardian sensations" as they relate to Updike would be most rewarding. 1) Kierkegaardian "Nature" imagery (flowers, birds, water), familial analogies, journey imagery; 2) his technique of irony and humor; 3) his discussion of sexuality and its relationship to anxiety; 4) his emphasis on a "low" Christology, i.e. greater concern with the suffering "human" aspect of Christ rather than the Christ of exaltation; 5) the over-all structure of SK's authorship, i.e. its deliberately shaped dialectical framework; 6) the suggestiveness of the sacrament of the Eucharist. Each of these (and no doubt more) has its counterpart in one or more of Updike's works.

27. John Updike, *Pigeon Feathers and Other Stories* (Greenwich: Fawcett-Crest, 1962), 125-29. Hereafter, references to this edition will be incorporated into the text.

28. The sole exception is Robert Detweiler, *John Updike* (Twayne's United States Authors Series) (New York: Twayne, 1972), p. 74.

29. Kierkegaard's influence on Auden's thought is well known and is especially evident in *The New Year Letter* and *The Sea and the Mirror*. Less well known is Percy's expressed debt to Kierkegaard as a major influence on his four novels. See Bradley Dewey, "Walker Percy Talks About Kierkegaard: An Annotated Interview," *Journal of Religion*, 54 (July 1974), pp. 273-99.

30. Søren Kierkegaard, *Philosophical Fragments*. Translated with an introduction by David F. Swenson. New Introduction and Commentary by Niels Thulstrup. Translation revised and Commentary translated by Howard V. Hong (Princeton: Princeton University Press, 1962).

31. Throughout his writings Kierkegaard's favorite analogy for faith is that of the confidence one needs for learning to swim. He says in *Stages on Life's Way* that "the believer lies constantly out upon the deep, with 70,000 fathoms of water under him," and in *Concluding Unscientific Postscript* "to sit placidly on board the ship in fair weather is not a picture of what it means to believe, but when the ship has sprung a leak, then to keep it afloat by working the pump, that is the picture of it." Updike makes conscious use of this analogy in "The Lifeguard," in *Pigeon Feathers*, p. 147.

32. Søren Kierkegaard, *Concluding Unscientific Postscript*, tr. David F. Swenson and Walter Lowrie (Princeton: Princeton University Press, 1941). For Kierkegaard's discussion of humor, see especially pp. 447-48, 453-55, 489-93.

33. I cited above Ralph Henry Johnson's recent study of *The Concept of Existence in Concluding Unscientific Postscript*. Updike's story reads like a dramatic presentation of Johnson's analysis. Johnson concentrates on Kierkegaard's stated objective: "to remind men who had forgotten what it means to exist," and applies it to the situation of the

modern scientist, like Bela here. According to his interpretation, scientists often "forget what it means to exist" because they assume the perspective of the scientific community and speak with its voice; as a result, they "forget" the human, existential problems they as *individuals* are heir to. Also, since scientists tend to see life's evolution in cosmic, collective terms, they often "forget" that any one "moment" can have decisive significance for them and actually change their personal lives. Kierkegaard felt that such men must be "exorcised" back into existence, back into subjective concerns. In this story Bela will be so "reminded" by his experience of dread. For this discussion, see Johnson, pp. 150ff, 182ff.

34. Søren Kierkegaard, *The Concept of Dread*, tr. Walter Lowrie (Princeton: Princeton University Press, 1967 ed.), esp. 73ff. The word "Moment" translates the Danish *Øjeblikket* which literally means "a glance of the eye"; another familiar translation of the word is "Instant."

35. Gregor Malantschuk, *Kierkegaard's Thought*, pp. 244ff.

36. I suspect that failure to realize the dialectical character of these two works, as Malantschuk implies, has had the most crucial repercussions for both theology and philosophy in this century, at least that influenced by Kierkegaard. Karl Barth, who in his early theology was so influenced by Kierkegaard, concentrated on the argument "from above" present in *Philosophical Fragments* to the exclusion of the more subjective, human-centered issues found in its dialectical twin, *The Concept of Dread*. On the other hand, "existentialist" philosophers have tended to ignore the theistic-centered *Philosophical Fragments* and concentrated instead on the analysis of the self in *The Concept of Dread*. Kierkegaard, however, was a dialectician and never intended that they be read separately.

37. Louis Mackey, *Kierkegaard: A Kind of Poet*, esp. pp. 241ff.

38. Søren Kierkegaard, *The Point of View for My Work as an Author*, tr. Walter Lowrie, ed. Ralph Nelson (New York: Harper Torchbook, 1962), pp. 22ff.

39. Charles Thomas Samuels, "The Art of Fiction, XLIII: John Updike," *The Paris Review*, XII (Winter, 1968), pp. 85, 117, 101.

40. John Updike, *Picked-Up Pieces* (New York: Knopf, 1975), p. 502.

41. John Updike, *Assorted Prose* (Greenwich: Fawcett, 1965), p. 142.

42. Updike's introduction is found in Frank Sheed, ed., *Soundings in Satanism* (New York: Sheed and Ward, 1972). It is reprinted in Updike's collection, *Picked-Up Pieces*. All page references will be to this second edition.

43. Karl Barth, *Church Dogmatics: A Selection* (New York: Harper and Row, 1962). Updike's citations are drawn from the third chapter, pp. 134ff.

44. Barth's idea of *das Nichtige* is discussed at length only in his *Church Dogmatics*, III, 3, pp. 289ff. See Karl Barth, *Church Dogmatics* I, 1 to IV, 4 (Edinburgh: T. & T. Clark, 1936-69).

45. *Church Dogmatics*, III, 3, pp. 297-99. For even stronger evidence of Barth's enthusiasm for Mozart in this connection, see Barth's article, "Wolfgang Amadeus Mozart," in *Religion and Culture: Essays in Honor of Paul Tillich* (Freeport: Books for Libraries, 1972); see also a less substantial but delightful radio interview with Barth entitled "Music for a Guest" (*Final Testimonies*; Grand Rapids: Eerdmans, 1977).

46. Wilfred Sheed, *The Morning After* (New York: Bantam, 1970), p. 62. This is a reprint of Sheed's review of *Couples* that appeared in the *New York Times Sunday Book Review* in 1968.

47. Books on Barth are extensive. On this subject, see David Ray Griffin, *God, Power, and Evil* (Philadelphia: Westminster, 1976), pp. 150ff.; Hans Urs von Balthasar, *The Theology of Karl Barth* (New York: Holt, Rinehart, Winston, 1971 ed.); Colin Brown,

Karl Barth (Chicago: Inter-Varsity Press, 1967); Geoffrey W. Bromiley, An Introduction to the Theology of Karl Barth (Grand Rapids: Eerdmans, 1979). See also Eberhard Busch, Karl Barth: His Life from Letters and Autobiographical Texts (Philadelphia: Fortress, 1976).

48. Picked-Up Pieces, pp. 473-517.

49. Karl Barth, Church Dogmatics, III, 3, pp. 349ff. See also Griffin, God, Power, and Evil, p. 299.

50. Joseph Waldmeir, "It's the Going that's Important, Not the Getting There: Rabbit's Questing Non-Quest," Modern Fiction Studies, 20 (Spring 1974), pp. 13-28.

51. John Updike, The Poorhouse Fair (New York: Knopf, 1977), p. xvii.

52. For some very fine readings of The Poorhouse Fair, see Detweiler, John Updike, pp. 31-44; the Hamiltons, The Elements of John Updike, pp. 119-36; Joyce Markle, Fighters and Lovers: Themes in the Novels of John Updike (New York: New York University Press, 1973), pp. 13-36; Edward P. Vargo, Rainstorms and Fire (Port Washington: Kennikat, 1973), pp. 28-50.

53. John Updike, The Poorhouse Fair (New York: Fawcett-Crest, 1958). References in the text will be to this paperback edition.

54. Picked-Up Pieces, p. 502.

55. John Bunyan, The Pilgrim's Progress (New York: Oxford, 1945), p. 9.

56. David Galloway, The Absurd Hero in American Fiction: Updike, Styron, Bellow, Salinger (Austin: U. of Texas, 1966), pp. 27-40.

57. Larry Taylor, Pastoral and Anti-Pastoral Patterns in John Updike's Fiction (Carbondale: Southern Illinois, 1971), pp. 70-85.

58. Richard Gilman, "A Distinguished Image of Precarious Life," Commonweal, LXIII (October 28, 1960), p. 129.

59. Private letter from John Updike (May 8, 1976).

60. Karl Barth, The Word of God and the Word of Man (New York: Harper and Row, 1957), pp. 183-217. John Updike, Assorted Prose, p. 212.

61. Church Dogmatics IV, 1, pp. 79, 436, 410.

62. Church Dogmatics, III, 3, pp. 527-28.

63. Barth, The Word of God and the Word of Man, pp. 287ff.

64. Fred Standley, "Rabbit, Run: An Image of Life," Midwest Quarterly, VIII (July 1967), p. 375.

2: The Centaur

1. John Updike, Picked-Up Pieces (New York: Knopf, 1975), p. 17.

2. John Updike, The Centaur (New York: Knopf, 1963). Henceforth references to this, the hard-bound version, will be included in the text.

3. Robert Detweiler, John Updike (New York: Twayne, 1972), p. 82.

4. Detweiler, p. 84.

5. Larry Taylor, Pastoral and Anti-Pastoral Patterns in John Updike (Carbondale: Southern Illinois, 1971), pp. 86f.

6. Suzanne Uphaus, "The Centaur: Updike's Mock Epic," The Journal of Narrative Technique, vol. 7, no. 1 (Winter 1977), pp. 25f.

7. Joyce Markle, Fighters and Lovers: Themes in the Novels of John Updike (New York:

N.Y.U., 1973), pp. 61f.; Alice and Kenneth Hamilton, *The Elements of John Updike* (Grand Rapids: Eerdmans, 1970), pp. 156f.

8. Alice and Kenneth Hamilton, pp. 156-57.

9. W. B. Yeats, *The Collected Poems of W. B. Yeats* (New York: Macmillan, 1961), p. 247.

10. *Picked-Up Pieces*, p. 16.

11. David Morrell, *John Barth: An Introduction* (University Park: Penn State, 1972), p. 141.

12. Northrop Frye, *The Secular Scripture* (Cambridge: Harvard, 1976), pp. 185f.

13. Northrop Frye's essay appears in *An Honoured Guest*, ed. Denis Donoghue and J. R. Mulryne (London: Edward Arnold, 1965).

14. *The Secular Scripture*, pp. 9f.

15. *The Secular Scripture*, p. 14.

16. *The Secular Scripture*, pp. 60f.

17. *Picked-Up Pieces*, p. 499.

18. *Picked-Up Pieces*, p. 499.

19. Charles Samuels, "The Art of Fiction, XLIII: John Updike," *The Paris Review*, no. 45 (1968), p. 103.

20. *Paris Review*, p. 104.

21. Updike's choice here seems quite deliberate. As the Hamiltons point out, Updike relies far more on H. J. Rose's *A Handbook of Greek Mythology* than he does on Miss Peabody's book. (I would add Robert Graves' *The Greek Myths: 1 & 2* as well.) In addition to these secondary scources, he made use of Hesiod's *Works and Days* and *Theogony* as well as Pliny's *Natural History*. See the Hamiltons, p. 163.

22. For example, John B. Vickery sees another dimension beyond the religious reference in the epigraph, namely that connected with myth and the story-teller. For Vickery the operative words are not heaven and earth but "conceivable" and "inconceivable" in relation to the artist's imagination. "Man's ultimate and basic position on the boundary between the inconceivable and the conceivable is identical with his power to narrate what Aristotle called probable impossibilities, to tell stories that breach the constructions of what mankind conceives to be the case." See John B. Vickery, "The Centaur: Myth, History, and Narrative," *Modern Fiction Studies*, 20 (Spring 1974), pp. 29-44.

23. Karl Barth, *Dogmatics in Outline* (New York: Harper, 1959). Hereafter references to this work will be included in the text.

24. Robert Graves, *The Greek Myths: 1* (London: Penguin, 1962), p. 30.

25. *The Greek Myths: 1*, p. 32.

26. Northrop Frye, *Anatomy of Criticism* (Princeton: Princeton U., 1957), p. 306. In his glossary (p. 367), Frye defines the Romantic as: 1) A fictional mode in which the chief characters live in a world of marvels (naive romance), or in which the mood is elegiac or idyllic and hence less subject to social criticism than in mimetic modes; 2) the general tendency to present myth and metaphor in an idealized human form, midway between undisplaced "myth" and realism.

27. Philip Wheelwright, "Notes on Mythopoeia," in *Myth and Literature*, ed. John B. Vickery (Lincoln: U. of Nebraska, 1966), p. 65.

28. *The Secular Scripture*, p. 122.

29. Northrop Frye, "New Directions from Old," in *Myth and Mythmaking*, ed. Henry A. Murray (Boston: Beacon, 1961), pp. 127-28.

30. *The Secular Scripture*, p. 157.

31. Frye, "New Directions from Old," pp. 128-29.

32. Joseph Campbell, *The Hero with a Thousand Faces* (Princeton: Princeton U., 1949), pp. 245-46.

33. *Anatomy of Criticism*, pp. 141-45.

34. Although I differ with his interpretation of *The Centaur* as Christian allegory, I am indebted to David Myers for many salient points, oblique references, *obiter dicta* that have greatly aided my own scrutiny of the text. Do see David Myers, "The Questing Fear: Christian Allegory in John Updike's *The Centaur*," *Twentieth Century Literature*, vol. 17 (January-October 1971), pp. 73f.

35. Mircea Eliade, *Images and Symbols* (New York: Sheed and Ward, 1961), pp. 44f.

36. *Images and Symbols*, p. 161.

37. *The Jerusalem Bible* (Garden City: Doubleday, 1966), pp. 339-40.

3: *Of the Farm*

1. John Updike, *Olinger Stories* (New York: Vintage, 1964), p. vi.

2. Charles Thomas Samuels, "The Art of Fiction, XLIII: John Updike," *The Paris Review*, XII (Winter 1968), pp. 90-91.

3. John Updike, *Picked-Up Pieces* (New York: Knopf, 1975), p. 83.

4. *Picked-Up Pieces*, pp. 82-83.

5. Personal letter to me, October 18, 1975.

6. John Updike, *Of the Farm* (New York: Knopf, 1965), pp. 46-47. Henceforth all references to this hard-backed volume will be included in the text.

7. Robert Detweiler, *John Updike* (New York: Twayne, 1972), p. 100.

8. Larry Taylor, *Pastoral and Anti-Pastoral Patterns in John Updike's Fiction* (Carbondale: Southern Ill., 1971), pp. 102ff.

9. John L'Heureux, "Of the Farm," *The Critic*, vol. XXIV, no. 4 (Feb.-Mar. 1966), p. 62.

10. Joyce Markle, *Fighters and Lovers: Themes in the Novels of John Updike* (New York N.Y.U. Press, 1973), pp. 84ff.

11. Alice and Kenneth Hamilton, *The Elements of John Updike* (Grand Rapids: Eerdmans, 1970), pp. 181ff.

12. Norman Mailer, *Cannibals and Christians* (New York: Dell, 1966), p. 107.

13. *Picked-Up Pieces*, p. 82.

14. Mark Schorer, "The Necessity of Myth," in Henry A. Murray, ed., *Myth and Mythmaking* (Boston: Beacon, 1960), p. 355.

15. C. G. Jung, *Psyche and Symbol* (Garden City: Doubleday Anchor, 1958), p. XXIX.

16. Joseph Campbell, *The Hero with a Thousand Faces* (Princeton: Princeton U., 1949), p. 116.

17. *The Hero with a Thousand Faces*, pp. 110ff.

18. *Psyche and Symbol*, p. XXXI.

19. *Psyche and Symbol*, pp. 113ff.

20. *Psyche and Symbol*, p. 127.

21. *Psyche and Symbol*, pp. 132-33.

22. *Psyche and Symbol*, p. 133.

23. C. G. Jung, *The Development of Personality*, Bollingen Series, vol. 17 (Princeton: Princeton U., 1950), p. 198.

24. *Psyche and Symbol*, p. 10.

25. *Psyche and Symbol*, p. 11.

26. *Psyche and Symbol*, p. 19.

27. Karl Barth, *Church Dogmatics: A Selection* (New York: Harper & Row, 1962), pp. 194ff.

28. For a critical overview of this aspect of Barth's theology, see Hans Urs von Balthasar, *The Theology of Karl Barth* (New York: Holt, Rinehart, 1971), pp. 197ff. and David L. Mueller, *Karl Barth* (Waco, Texas: Word Books, 1972), pp. 150ff.

29. *Church Dogmatics: A Selection*, pp. 216-17.

30. *Church Dogmatics: A Selection*, p. 212.

31. *Church Dogmatics: A Selection*, p. 212.

4: The Music School

1. "The Art of Fiction, XLIII: John Updike," *The Paris Review*, 12 (Winter 1968), p. 94.

2. John Updike, *Picked-Up Pieces* (New York: Knopf, 1975), pp. 38-39.

3. *The Paris Review*, pp. 90-91.

4. Robert Detweiler is the only critic who has given concentrated attention to *The Music School* collection as a unit. For a most perceptive reading, see Robert Detweiler, *John Updike* (New York: Twayne, 1973), pp. 111-29. For other less concentrated and more random readings, see Rachel Burchard, *John Updike: Yea Sayings* (Carbondale: Southern Illinois Press, 1971), pp. 152-59; Alice and Kenneth Hamilton, *The Elements of John Updike* (Grand Rapids: Eerdmans, 1970), *passim*.

5. Frank Gado, ed., "A Conversation with John Updike," *First Person* (Schenectady: Union College Press, 1973), p. 83.

6. These lines comprise the second stanza of "To the One of Fictive Music"; Wallace Stevens, *The Collected Poems of Wallace Stevens* (New York: Knopf, 1967), p. 87.

7. This interpretation of the stanza agrees with those explications offered by the most reputable exegetes of Stevens. See Edward Kessler, *Images of Wallace Stevens* (New Brunswick: Rutgers, 1972), pp. 111-13; Eugene Paul Nasser, *Wallace Stevens: An Anatomy of Configuration* (Philadelphia: University of Pennsylvania, 1965), pp. 64-67, 127-28; Frank Doggett, *Stevens: Poetry of Thought* (Baltimore: Johns Hopkins, 1966), p. 192; also, *Letters of Wallace Stevens*, ed. Holly Stevens (New York: Knopf, 1966), pp. 251-52.

8. An excellent analysis of this three-fold process in Stevens' poetry is found in J. Hillis Miller, *Poets of Reality* (Cambridge: Harvard U. Press, 1965), pp. 217-84.

9. *Poets of Reality*, pp. 258ff. Miller reminds us that "dialectical" in reference to Stevens' technique means the continual presentation of contradictories and *not* the argumentative process of the dialectician whereby the mind moves from thesis to antithesis via elimination or unification and on to synthesis; rather, his "dialectic" is a mode of discovery in a different sense.

10. Wallace Stevens, *Opus Posthumous*, ed. Samuel French Morse (New York: Knopf, 1966), p. 159.

11. Wallace Stevens, *The Necessary Angel: Essays on Reality and Imagination* (New York: Vintage, 1951), pp. 117-18.

12. For an excellent analysis of this in Stevens, see J. Hillis Miller, *Poets of Reality*, pp. 217-84.

13. *Picked-Up Pieces*, p. 518. "The Sea's Green Sameness," originally published in 1960, is in *Museums and Women and Other Stories* (New York: Knopf, 1972).

14. For an analysis of the complex metaphoric interaction in this novel, see my own analysis in my chapter on *A Month of Sundays* following.

15. Richard Gilman, *The Confusion of Realms* (New York: Random House, 1969), p. 67.

16. J. Hillis Miller, p. 237.

17. For an appreciation of this aspect of Stevens' work, see not only Miller but also Stanley Romaine Hooper, "Wallace Stevens: The Sundry Comforts of the Sun," *Four Ways of Modern Poetry*, ed. Nathan Scott, Jr. (Richmond: John Knox, 1965); and Todd Lieber, "Robert Frost and Wallace Stevens: 'What to Make of a Diminished Thing,' " *American Literature*, 47 (March 1975), pp. 64-83.

18. Rust Hills, ed., *Writer's Choice* (New York: McKay, 1974), pp. 391-92.

19. John Updike, *The Music School* (Greenwich: Fawcett, 1966), pp. 44-47. Hereafter all page numbers within the text enclosed by parentheses will refer to this edition.

20. John Updike, *Of the Farm* (Greenwich: Fawcett, 1965), pp. 39, 47-48, *passim*. For a close analysis of this association in this novel, see Larry Taylor, *Pastoral and Anti-Pastoral Patterns in John Updike's Fiction* (Carbondale: Southern Illinois Press, 1971), pp. 102-11.

21. John Updike, "More Love in the Western World," *Assorted Prose* (Greenwich: Fawcett, 1965), pp. 220-21. Similar sentiments are expressed in *The Paris Review*, p. 102 and are found in Updike's *Couples* (New York: Knopf, 1968), p. 429.

22. Todd Lieber, "Robert Frost and Wallace Stevens: 'What to Make of a Diminished Thing,' " *American Literature*, 47 (March 1975), pp. 66-70.

5. Couples and Marry Me

1. John Updike, *Picked-Up Pieces* (New York: Knopf, 1975), p. 505.

2. Howard V. and Edna H. Hong, *Soren Kierkegaard's Journals and Papers*, vol. 2, F-K (Bloomington: Indiana University Press, 1970), p. 196.

3. *Journals and Papers*, vol. 2, p. 195.

4. Søren Kierkegaard, *The Concept of Dread*, tr. Walter Lowrie (Princeton: Princeton U., 1944). Those sections which I attempt to summarize are on pp. 32-46, 56-66. There are many excellent studies explicating Kierkegaard's argument that, over the years, have become indistinguishable from my gestures at explication. For the most memorable clarifications on the subject of dread, see Gregor Malantschuk, *Kierkegaard's Thought* (Princeton: Princeton U., 1971), pp. 257-72; Walter W. Sikes, *On Becoming the Truth* (St. Louis: Bethany Press, 1968), pp. 127ff; Vernard Eller, *Kierkegaard and Radical Discipleship* (Princeton: Princeton U., 1968), pp. 235ff.

5. *The Concept of Dread*, p. 38.

6. Søren Kierkegaard, *Sickness Unto Death* (Princeton: Princeton U., 1954).

7. Interview on the Dick Cavett show, WNET–New York, December 15, 1978.

8. Charles Thomas Samuels, "The Art of Fiction, XLIII: John Updike," *The Paris Review*, XII (Winter 1968), p. 101.

9. For example, see L. Hartman, *Catholic Biblical Quarterly*, 20 (1958), pp. 26-40.

10. *The Concept of Dread*, p. 55.

11. *The Concept of Dread*, p. 61.

12. *The Concept of Dread*, pp. 63-64.

13. John Updike, *Bech: A Book* (New York: Knopf, 1970), p. 130.

14. John Updike, *Couples* (New York: Knopf, 1968), p. 14. Hereafter references to this, the hardback edition, will be included in the text.

15. Robert Detweiler, *John Updike* (New York: Twayne, 1972), pp. 138-42; Joyce Markle, *Fighters and Lovers: Themes in the Novels of John Updike* (New York: N.Y.U. Press, 1973), pp. 137-45; Edward A. Vargo, *Rainstorms and Fire* (Port Washington: Kennikat, 1973), pp. 142-43; Linda A. Plagman, "Eros and Agape: the Opposition in Updike's *Couples*," *Renascence*, vol. XXVIII, no. 2 (Winter 1976), pp. 83-93.

16. John Updike, *Assorted Prose* (Greenwich: Fawcett, 1965), pp. 220-33.

17. *Paris Review*, p. 102.

18. For an interesting analysis of this and the other games in *Couples*, see Alden T. McKenzie, " 'A Craftsman's Intimate Satisfactions': The Parlor Games in *Couples*," *Modern Fiction Studies*, vol. 20, no. 1 (Spring 1974), pp. 53-58.

19. *Paris Review*, p. 104.

20. *New York Times Book Review*, August 29, 1976, p. 7.

21. Northrop Frye, *Anatomy of Criticism* (Princeton: Princeton U., 1957), pp. 304ff. See also F. O. Matthiessen, "The Crucial Definition of Romance" and Richard Chase, "Novel vs. Romance" in *Pastoral and Romance: Modern Essays in Criticism*, ed. Eleanor Terry Lincoln (Englewood: Prentice-Hall, 1969), pp. 268-74, 282-88; Perry Miller's chapter, "Romance and the Novel," in his *Nature's Nation* (Cambridge: Harvard U., 1967), pp. 241-78.

22. John Updike, *Marry Me* (New York: Knopf, 1976), p. 140. Henceforth references to this edition will be included in the text.

23. At the risk of being overly precious, I must admit to a strong suspicion that van Huyten's name is symbolic. The Dutch is close to the German *Hüten* which, as a verb, means to "tend" or "care for." As a warning it means to "beware." In the light of Eden allusions in this episode, both these meanings are pertinent to those who, like Ruth, find themselves either fortunately or unfortunately on van Huyten's land.

24. *Marry Me* was rather unusual in that it was greeted by almost diametrically opposite reactions. Peter Prescott in *Newsweek* (November 8, 1976) said, "It is, quite simply, Updike's best novel yet." Timothy Foote in *Time* (November 15, 1976) was less kind, saying "Readers in search of another adult serial may be forgiven if they switch to *Mary Hartman, Mary Hartman*. . . ." So too was Maureen Howard less enthusiastic in *The New York Times Book Review* (October 31, 1976); she closed by recommending to readers that they take down *Madame Bovary* or *Anna Karenina* from their shelves instead of reading *Marry Me*. The most outrageous, in fact vicious, criticism was offered, if that is the proper word, by Brigid Brophy in *Harper's* (December 1976), but then again Ms. Brophy is always outrageous in all the multiple senses of that word. I feel that the most temperate, balanced, and insightful review was, of course, my own in *America* (January 8, 1977).

25. George W. Hunt, "John Updike's 'Sunday Sort of Book,' " *America*, vol. 132, no. 4 (June 21, 1975), p. 478.

26. R. W. B. Lewis, *The American Adam* (Chicago: U. of Chicago, 1955), p. 7. See also Judith Fryer, *The Faces of Eve: Women in the Nineteenth Century American Novel* (Oxford: Oxford U., 1978).

27. *The American Adam*, p. 111.

28. *The American Adam*, p. 113.

29. For evidence of this mixture of sympathies in relation to nineteenth-century American Literature, see Updike's excellent article, "Walt Whitman: Ego and Art," in *The New York Review of Books,* vol. xxv, no. 1 (February 9, 1978), pp. 33f.

30. Hyatt H. Waggoner, "Nathaniel Hawthorne," in *Six American Novelists of the Nineteenth Century,* ed. Richard Foster (Minneapolis: U. of Minnesota, 1968), p. 76. See also F. O. Matthiessen, *American Renaissance* (London: Oxford, 1941), pp. 345-51; Richard H. Fogle, *Hawthorne's Fiction: the Light and the Dark* (Norman: U. of Oklahoma, 1952), pp. 4-14.

31. See A. N. Kaul, "The Blithedale Romance," in *Hawthorne: A Collection of Critical Essays,* ed. A. N. Kaul (Englewood: Prentice-Hall, 1966), pp. 153-63.

32. More's Essay is reprinted in *The Recognition of Nathaniel Hawthorne*, ed. B. Bernard Cohen (Ann Arbor: U. of Michigan, 1969), pp. 142-43.

6: *Bech: A Book*

1. R. W. B. Lewis, *The American Adam* (Chicago: U. of Chicago, 1955), pp. 118-19.
2. *The American Adam*, p. 118.
3. John Updike, *Picked-Up Pieces* (New York: Knopf, 1975), pp. 505-6.
4. Frank Gado, ed., *First Person* (Schenectady: Union College Press, 1973), p. 83.
5. *Picked-Up Pieces*, p. 507.
6. John Updike, *Bech: A Book* (New York: Knopf, 1970). Hereafter references to this edition will be included in the text.
7. *Picked-Up Pieces*, p. 507.
8. *First Person*, pp. 84-85.
9. *First Person*, p. 85.
10. This speech "The Plight of the American Writer" is reprinted in *Change,* December 1977, pp. 37-41.
11. *Change,* p. 38.
12. *Change,* p. 38.
13. *Change,* pp. 40-41.

7: *Rabbit Redux*

1. John Updike, *Picked-Up Pieces* (New York: Knopf, 1975), p. 510.
2. John Updike, *Rabbit Redux* (New York: Knopf, 1971), p. 13. Hereafter references to this, the hardbound edition, will be included in the text.
3. Richard Locke, *The New York Times Book Review,* November 17, 1971, p. 24.
4. Paul Theroux review, *Book World,* November 14, 1971.
5. Norman Mailer, *Cannibals and Christians* (New York: Dell, 1966), p. 120.
6. *Picked-Up Pieces*, p. 509.
7. Gene Lyons, "John Updike: The Beginning and the End," *Critique,* vol. 14,

no. 2 (1974), p. 50. Although I do not share the vehemence of Lyons' negative criticism of *Redux*, his article does point up well some of the novel's defects, and certain insights that Lyons offers have been most helpful to me in organizing my own critique.

8. Charles Samuels, "The Art of Fiction, XLIII: John Updike," *Paris Review*, vol. 12, no. 45 (1968-69), p. 112.

9. Private letter to Samuel Beckoff, 1974.

10. To my mind Robert Detweiler has offered the finest analysis of *Rabbit Redux* thus far. Given Detweiler's particular approach to his investigation of Updike's fiction—namely his "secular baroque" style—he concentrates on the novel's major tropes and their orchestration. See Robert Detweiler, *John Updike* (New York: Twayne, 1972), pp. 152-66. Although I disagree with several critical points in his argument, another interesting interpretation is offered by Wayne Falke in "*Rabbit Redux*: Time/Order/God," *Modern Fiction Studies*, vol. 20, no. 1 (Spring 1974), pp. 59-76.

11. Ronald Knox, *Enthusiasm* (New York: Oxford U. Press, 1961), p. 4.

12. *Enthusiasm*, Chapter VI: "The Pattern of Medieval Heresy," pp. 92-116.

13. *Picked-Up Pieces*, p. 510.

8: *A Month of Sundays*

1. This is not to deny, of course, that each Updike book since *Couples* has been reviewed widely, but to emphasize the obvious difference between a reviewer's appraisal and a close scholarly reading. Recent Updike scholarship generally ignores his post-*Couples* achievement although there have been two very commendable articles on *Rabbit Redux*. See Robert Detweiler, *John Updike* (New York: Twayne, 1972), pp. 152-66; and Wayne Falke, "*Rabbit Redux*: Time/Order/God," *Modern Fiction Studies*, vol. 20, no. 1 (Spring 1974), pp. 59-76. For a different interpretation of *A Month of Sundays*, see Suzanne Henning Uphaus, "The Unified Vision of *A Month of Sundays*," *The Univ. of Windsor Review*, XII, 2 (Spring 1977), pp. 5ff.; and also Thomas LeClaire, "Updike's Anti-Metafiction," *Fiction International*, 4/5 (1975), pp. 130-32.

2. Gerald J. Galgan, "After Christianity, What?," *Commonweal*, vol. CIII, no. 23 (November 5, 1976), pp. 723-25. Galgan's reading of the novel, like that of many of its original reviewers, is more sociological than literary in emphasis, and such an approach tends to see the book as an updated version of *Couples*. No doubt such a sociological (or philosophico-cultural) interpretation has its merits; here, however, I offer a more positive, *intra-literary* reading.

3. John Updike, *A Month of Sundays* (New York: Knopf, 1975). Subsequent references will be indicated in the text.

4. Robert Alter, *Partial Magic: the Novel as a Self-Conscious Genre* (Berkeley: Univ. of California, 1975), pp. x-xi. Alter's "self-conscious genre" is his lucid definition of what other critics such as Robert Scholes and Frederic Jameson would offer under their rubric of "Metafiction." For example, see Robert Scholes, "Metafiction," *Iowa Review*, vol. 1, no. 4 (1970), pp. 100-15; Frederic Jameson, "Metacommentary," *PMLA*, 86 (1971), pp. 9-18.

5. Both John Barth and Robert Coover in separate interviews recorded in Frank Gado, ed., *First Person* (Schenectady: Union College, 1973), pp. 110-59, discuss Updike as a novelist with fictive concerns opposite to theirs. However, I find adumbrations of

the techniques found here early on in Updike's short story collection, *The Music School* (New York: Knopf, 1966). See especially the stories "Leaves," "Harv is Plowing Now," and "The Hermit."

6. John Updike, *Assorted Prose* (New York: Fawcett, 1965), pp. 142ff.

7. In an interview Updike said of his books that they "all are meant to be moral debates with the reader. . . . The question is usually, 'What is a good man?' or 'What is goodness?' and in each an issue is examined." John Updike, *Picked-Up Pieces* (New York: Knopf, 1975), p. 502. In this novel the issue of "goodness" is examined both humorously and seriously in its wide variety of colloquial meaning.

8. *Picked-Up Pieces*, pp. 499-500. Robert Detweiler, *John Updike*, 100-103, has explicated in brilliant fashion the X-shaped design he finds in *Of the Farm*.

9. No doubt the title itself, since "a month of Sundays" is the cliché-equivalent for "an indefinite time" or "never"—in addition to the "o" for zero or nothing—is meant to arouse our imaginative suspicions.

10. For example, see John Updike, *Pigeon Feathers* (New York: Fawcett, 1962), p. 79.

11. C. G. Jung, "Definitions" in *Psychological Types, Collected Works*, vol. 6 (Princeton: Princeton U., 1956); on *Mandala Symbolism, Collected Works*, vol. 9, Part I (Princeton: Princeton U., 1959); *Man and His Symbols* (New York: Dell, 1964).

The only other Jungian reading of Updike's work is found in Robert Alton Regan, "Updike's Symbol of the Center," *Modern Fiction Studies*, vol. 20, no. 1 (Spring 1974), pp. 77-96.

12. C. G. Jung, "From the Psychology of Transference," *Basic Writings of C. G. Jung* (New York: Random House, 1959), pp. 403-4.

13. C. G. Jung, *Man and His Symbols*, pp. 186ff.

14. Updike once said of *The Centaur* that the "mythology answers to my sensation that the people we meet are *guises*, do conceal something mythic, perhaps prototypes or longings in our minds. We love some women more than others by predetermination, it seems to me." See *Picked-Up Pieces*, p. 500.

15. In Jungian psychology the tale of a Knight's pursuit of the Holy Grail was an archetypal narrative symbolizing the quest for the Self. Jung's further contention that the Grail's own intrinsic symbolism as the sacramental receptacle for the Corporeal Son of God, plus its significance as the rite for the communicant's own "life-renewal" through the Blood, illuminates greatly the many other multiple allusions made to Ms. Prynne elsewhere. See Edward F. Edinger, *Ego and Archetype* (Baltimore: Pelican, 1973), pp. 225-59.

16. C. G. Jung, *Psychology and Religion: East and West*, Bollingen Series XX, vol. II (Princeton: Princeton U.), pp. 468-69.

17. The golf matches themselves are replete with Jungian symbolism, for, as Marshfield observes, "we men are spirits naked to one another; on a golf course we move through one another like fish a-swim in one another's veins." (p. 190) Besides, since a golf swing is omega-shaped, "the way a golf swing reveals more of a man than decades of conversation" (p. 190) fits in nicely with the swing's goal, the hole which is the apt symbol for the self's journey.

9: *The Coup*

1. Interview with Dick Cavett, WNET–New York, December 15, 1978.

2. John Updike, *The Coup* (New York: Knopf, 1978). Hereafter references to the novel will be included in the text.

3. R. W. B. Lewis, *The American Adam* (Chicago: U. of Chicago, 1955), pp. 127-28. pp. 127-8.

4. Cavett interview, December 15, 1978.

5. Charles Thomas Samuels, "The Art of Fiction, XLIII: John Updike," *The Paris Review*, XII (Winter 1968), p. 105.

6. Richard Poirier, *A World Elsewhere: the Place of Style in American Literature* (New York: Oxford, 1966).

7. Poirier, p. 140.

8. John Updike, *Buchanan Dying* (New York: Knopf, 1974), p. vi.

9. *Buchanan Dying*, pp. 251-52.

10. Allen Tate, *The Man of Letters in the Modern World* (New York: Meridian, 1955), pp. 92-131.

11. Allen Tate, p. 96.

Index

Adam and Eve (see also American Adam Myth and Mythology), in Genesis 97-98; as theological basis 98-101; on dust jackets 119-20; Kierkegaard and original sin 122-30; in American Adam tradition 147-52; in *Bech* 161-62; African American Adam in *The Coup* 197-202.

Alter, Robert, quoted 183.

American Adam Myth 119; in *Couples* 147-52; in *Bech* 153-63; and Jewish writers 156-58; in *Redux* 165; Africa-style in *The Coup* 197-202.

Anima (see also Jung and Sexuality), in *Of the Farm* 95-96; in *Month of Sundays* 189-94; shadows 193, 227; in *The Coup* 204-5.

Apostles' Creed (see also Creation) 32-37.

Aquinas, Thomas, and *The Poorhouse Fair* 38-39; transcendentals 49-50.

Art (see also Museums, Three Great Secrets), and vacillation in *Centaur* 52-59; in *Of the Farm* 86-87; of writing 103-4; concerns in *Music School* 105-16; artists 153; and contemporary fiction writer 154-63; self-consciousness or metafiction 183-86, 198-206; and psychic wholeness 211.

"Astronomer, The," analyzed 21-30.

Auden, W. H., quoted 2, 116, 149-50, 213-14.

Barth, John, and *Chimera* 58; quoted 183.

Barth, Karl (see also Nothingness, Creation, Sexuality), praised by Updike 13-15; connection with Kierkegaard and orthodoxy 16-17; the Power of Nothingness 30-38; and Kruppenbach 42-44;

and epigraph to *Centaur* 63-64; and final scene in *Centaur* 77-79; theology of creation and sexuality 98-101; and Marshfield 182, 188-94; and Kierkegaard 218; and Mozart 219.

Bech: A Book, analyzed 153-63.

Bible, quotes from
    Colossians 1:13-20   75
    Psalm 22   76
    Philippians 2:5-11   79
    Genesis 2:18-23   97
    Psalm 45   182
    Psalm 22:19   182
    Matthew 12:39   185
    Revelation 22:20   187, 192.

Booth, Wayne, quoted 213.

Brooks, Cleanth, quoted 6.

"Bulgarian Poetess, The" 159, 161-62.

Calvinism, versus Barth 35-36; in *Couples* 127, 134-35, 148-51.

Campbell, Joseph, quoted 73, 88.

Centaur, The, analyzed 49-80; connection with *Of the Farm* 82.

Cheever, John, quoted 7.

Children, and Dread 123.

Chiron (see also Prometheus and Mythology), myth explained 61-63; and Philyra 74.

Christ (Jesus) (see also Karl Barth, Creation and Covenant), Barth's Christocentrism 35-36; the volvox 65; tree images 74-75; and Caldwell 74-79; in *Of the Farm* sermon 98-101; and Skeeter 177-79.

Coup, The, analyzed 195-206.

Couples, analyzed 131-38.

Covenant (see also Barth, Christ, Creation, Sexuality) 33-36; 63-66; 98-101.

Creation (see also Barth, Covenant, Nature, Nothingness), versus Nothingness 32-38; in *The Poorhouse Fair* 39-41; and Covenant 33-36; 63-66; 98-101; versus science and Eros myth 65-66; and end of *Centaur* 77-79; Sexuality and Covenant 98-101, 116; artistic re-creation in *Music School* 106-9; in *Bech* 159-61; generation and rebirth in *Month of Sundays* 185-86.

Dante 69-71.

Death, in *Rabbit, Run* 46-47; in *Centaur* 68-69, 72; and ascension 78-79; and sexuality 129-30; and potency 159-61; and renewal 192-94.

de Rougemont, Denis (see also Tristan) 8, 132, 142, 162.

Detweiler, Robert, critique of *The Centaur* 50-51; of *Of the Farm* 84-85.

Devil or Satan (see also Evil, Nothingness) 34-35; 43-45; Freddy Thorne 135-38; demonic in *Marry Me* 144-47.

Dialectic, in Kierkegaard and Barth 18-21; in Stevens 222.

"Dogwood Tree, The: A Boyhood" 2-3, 32.

Donoghue, Denis, quoted 55.

Dread, in Kierkegaard and "The Astronomer" 24, 27-30; and Adam and Sexuality 120-30; and children 123, 146; in *Bech* 159-61.

Dream(s), in *Centaur* 75; in *Of the Farm* 93-94; in "Leaves" 114-15; and Dread 122-27; in *Rabbit, Run* 173.

Earth (see also Nature) 32-38, 53-55; in *Of the Farm* 86-87; in "Leaves" 109-16; ambivalent in *Bech* 159-62.

Earth-Mother (see also Mythology, Nature, Woman), and Sky-Father 66; in *Of the Farm* 88-91, 95-96.

Eden or Paradise (see also Adam), and Fall in *Centaur* 66, 71-72; in *Bech* 160-63; in *The Coup* 195-201.

Eliade, Mircea, and the Cosmic Tree, quoted 74.

Eliot, T. S., and "The Waste Land" 199-200.

Eros (see also Mythology), in *Centaur* 65-66, 71; in *Of the Farm* 91-92; in *The Coup* 201.

Eve (see Adam, Nature, Woman)

Evil (see also Goodness, Nothingness, Sin) 31-32; Barth and 32-38; Conner in *Poorhouse Fair* 39-40; and Rabbit 44-48; Knowledge of Good and Evil 122-30, 142-43, 146-47; Marshfield's image 188.

Farm and the Self 86-87, 89-90, 92-93, 101.

Freedom, Sartre's epigraph 85; Barth's idea 99-101.

Freud, Sigmund 89, 120, 128, 193; versus Jung 210-11.

Frye, Northrop, on Yeats 59; on Sacred and Secular Scripture 59-66; on Romance 67-69; on descent/ascent themes 68-69; on Christian topocasm 71-72; critical approaches 209; distinction between novel and Romance 220.

Games, "Wonderful" 136-37.

Gilman, Richard, quoted 42, 77, 108.

Goodness (see also Evil, Nothingness, Sin), versus Nothingness 31-37, 44-48; and Joy 77-79; Knowledge of Good and Evil 122-30, 142-43, 146-47; and Fidelity in *Month of Sundays* 186-88.

Guilt (see also Sin), and Peter/Prometheus 55-56; in "Leaves" 109-16; and Sin 120-21.

Hamilton, Alice and Kenneth, critique of *Centaur* 51-52; of *Of the Farm* 85.

Hawthorne, Nathaniel (see also American Adam) 147-52, 153-59; and Ms. Prynne 185-94.

Herrick, Robert 139-40.

Hirsch, E. D., quoted 211-12.

Humor, in Kierkegaard 25-26; absent in *Redux* 170; comic in *Month of Sundays* 181-82 and *The Coup* 196-200.

Imagination (see Metaphor and Style)

Johnson, Ralph Henry, Kierkegaard and the scientific mentality 217-18.

Jung, Carl G. (see also Anima and Mythology) 87, 89; individuation 92; libido 93; child archetype 93-94; anima 95-96;

mother image 96; mandala image of the Self and God 187-94; anima and shadow 189-94, 227; writing as recovery of the self 86-87, 201-6; anima images in *The Coup* 204-5; versus Freud 210-11; Grail symbolism 227; shadows in *Month of Sundays* 227.

Kant, Immanuel 49-50.
Kennedy, John, era 131, 140-41, 149-50; and Nixon era 182, 198-99.
Kierkegaard, Søren (see also Barth, Dialectic, Dread, Sexuality), praised by Updike 13-15; connection with Barth 16-17; and dialectic 18-21; as "existentialist" 21-22; influence on "The Astronomer" 22-30; explication of *Philosophic Fragments* and *The Concept of Dread*, of "truth" and the "moment" 24-25, 27-28, 218; "humorist" 25-26; indirect communication 29-30; on dread and sexuality 120-30; in *Bech* 160-61; and double-focus in *The Coup* 202-4; and scandal 215-16; and scientific mind 217-18; swimming analogy 217; dialectic authorship 218.
Knowledge of Good and Evil (see Adam, Evil, Goodness)

"Leaves" 10, analyzed 109-16.
Lewis, R. W. B., and the American Adam, quoted 147-48, 153-54, 198.
Locke, Richard, quoted 167.
Lyons, Gene, quoted 167.

Mackey, Louis, quoted 29.
Mailer, Norman, quoted 86, 169.
Malantschuk, Gregor, 28.
Markle, Joyce, critique of *Centaur* 51; of *Of the Farm* 85.
Marry Me, analyzed 139-47.
Metaphor (see also Mythology and Stevens) 6; Stevens-like probing 106-9; in *Couples* 117-18; moon in *Redux* 172-77; and history 173-74; in *Month of Sundays* 185-88; in *The Coup* 200-1.
Middleness 5-6; as dialectic 18-21.
Midpoint and Other Poems 17-18.
Miller, J. Hillis, quoted 108-9.
Milton, John, and *Paradise Lost* 127, 138-40.

Month of Sundays, A, analyzed 181-94.
More, Paul Elmer, quoted 152.
Museums, Vermeer memory 56-57; topocasm in *Centaur* 71-73.
Music School, The, analyzed 103-16.
Mythology (see also Adam, Frye, Jung), the Prometheus myth 55-58; Frye's Sacred and Secular Scripture 59-66; Chiron-Prometheus myth 61-63; versus Scriptural saga 63-66; Eros myth 65-66; Sky-Father and Earth-Mother 66; ascent/descent themes 68-70; Campbell's hero 73, 88; Eliade and the Cosmic Tree 74; apocalypse-apotheosis 73-79; in *Of the Farm* 87-88; Earth-Mother 89-91, 96; Adam and Eve 98-101, 119-47; American Adam 147-63; Moon 175-76; Jung and *Month of Sundays* 187-94; American Adam in *The Coup* 197-202; Waste Land and Oedipus 199-200; and women 200.

Nabokov, Vladimir 183; and *The Coup* 200-6; 208-9.
Nature (see also Woman), relation to Nothingness 32-38; and Religion in *Centaur* 53-55; in Stevens' epigraph 105-7; in "Leaves" 109-16; ambivalent in *Bech* 159-62, 209-10.
New York, as symbol of Paradise 52, 56, 70.
Nixon and Watergate 182, 198-99.
Nothingness (see also Barth and Evil), Barth's concept 32-38; in *Poorhouse Fair* 39-41; in *Rabbit, Run* 11-18, and creation in *Centaur* 77-79, 116, 175.
Novel, The (see also Romance) 67-73, 140-41, 220.

O'Connor, Flannery, quoted 4, 9.
Of the Farm, analyzed 81-101.
Olinger Stories 50, 81-82, 104.
Orwell, George 38-39.

Paradise (see Eden)
Pascal, Blaise 25; epigraph 42-43.
Peabody, Josephine Preston, Chiron myth epigraph 62-63.
Pennsylvania 81-82.
Pilgrim's Progress (John Bunyan) 30-31, 38; and *Rabbit, Run* 41, 45; and *The Coup* 201.

Plato, sexual parable 97, 99.
Poirier, Richard, quoted 202.
Poorhouse Fair, The, analyzed 38-41.
Prometheus, legend 54-59; Chiron-Pro-
metheus myth 61-63.
Proust, Marcel 208.

Rabbit, Run, analyzed 41-48; compared with
Redux 170-71.
Rabbit Redux, analyzed 165-79; compared
with Rabbit, Run 170-71.
Religion (see specific references)
Romance (see also Frye and the novel), in
Centaur 67-73; in Marry Me 140-41, 220;
Blithedale Romance 150-51.

Saga, versus Myth 63-66.
Satan (see Devil)
Schorer, Mark, quoted 87.
Scripture (see also Bible), Secular versus
Sacred 59-66.
Self-consciousness (or Metafiction, Fabu-
lation), in Centaur 57-58; in Month of
Sundays 183-85; in The Coup 198-206.
Sexuality (see also Adam, Barth, Kierkegaard, Three Great Secrets, Woman)
7-9; and Nothingness in Rabbit, Run
46-47; in Centaur 52, 55, 71-73; theol-
ogy of sexuality in Of the Farm 98-101;
mystery of woman's 106-16; in Couples
117-18; and relation to Dread 120-30;
in Tarbox 131-38; in Greenwood 141-47;
in Bech 159-62; in Redux 175-78; in
Month of Sundays 184-94; in The Coup
204-5; in Epilogue 210.
Sheed, Wilfred, quoted 35.
Sky-Father Myth (see also Earth-Mother
and Mythology) 66.
Sin (see also Adam, Evil, Guilt), and guilt
120; original sin and Dread 122-30.
Stages in Kierkegaard 25-26, 101.
Standley, Fred, quoted 46.
Stevens, Wallace (see also Art, Metaphor)
105-10, 115-16; and the dialectical 222.
Style (see also Metaphor), in Centaur
49-51; in Music School 181-85; and Mil-

ton and Herrick 139-41; in Month of
Sundays 181-85; in The Coup 196-97,
203-5; in Epilogue 207-8.

Tate, Allen, quoted 203.
Taylor, Larry, critique of The Centaur 51;
of Of the Farm 85.
Three Great Secret Things (see also Art,
specific religious references, and Sexuality) 2-3; in Centaur 50, 52-59; in Of
the Farm 86-87; in Couples 117-18; in
Bech 161-63; in Redux passim; in Month
of Sundays 185-94; in Epilogue 209-10.
Tillich, Paul 15; criticized 16, 29; quoted
187.
Time/Eternity (see also Creation, Nothingness), in Centaur 52-53; and Kierkegaardian Dread 120-30.
Tree image, in Centaur 54, 74-75.
Tristan and Iseult (see also de Rougemont)
8, 132, 142, 162.

Updike, John (see specific references
throughout the Index)
Uphaus, Suzanne, critique of Centaur 51.

Venus 72-73, 91-95.
Vickery, John, on The Centaur epigraph
220.

Waldmeir, Joseph, quoted 38.
Warren, Austin, quoted 10-11.
Wheelright, Philip, quoted 68.
Wimsatt, W. K., quoted 5-6.
Woman (see also Adam, Anima, Mythology, Nature, Sexuality) 8-9; in essay
83-84; in Of the Farm 88-89; Barth on
the Creation of Woman 98-101; mystery
of Woman in Music School 106-16; in
Bech 160-62; in Month of Sundays 184-94;
in The Coup 204-5; private mythology
and women 227.

Yeats, William Butler, and vacillation
53-54, 59.